Zapatista!

Reinventing Revolution in Mexico

Edited by
John Holloway and Eloína Peláez

Pluto Press
LONDON • STERLING, VA

First published 1998 by Pluto Press
345 Archway Road, London N6 5AA
and 22883 Quicksilver Drive, Sterling, VA 21066–2012, USA

British Library Cataloguing in Publication Data
A catalogue record for this book is available from the British Library

ISBN 0 7453 1178 4 hbk

Library of Congress Cataloging in Publication Data
Zapatista!: reinventing revolution in Mexico/edited by John Holloway
and Eloína Peláez.
    p. cm.
    Contents: History and symbolism in the Zapatista movement/
Enrique Rajchenberg and Catherine Héau-Lambert — Chiapas and the
global restructuring of capital/Ana Esther Ceceña and Andrés
Barreda — Zapatista indigenous women/Márgara Millán — The
Zapatistas and the electronic fabric of struggle/Harry Cleaver —
Breaking the blockade: the move from jungle to city/Patricia King
and Francisco Javier Villanueva – Zapatismo: recomposition of
labour, radical democracy, and revolutionary project/Luis
Lorenzano — Dignity's revolt/John Holloway.
    ISBN 0–7453–1178–4 (hc.)
    1. Chiapas (Mexico)—History—Peasant Uprising, 1994– —Influence.
2. Mexico—Politics and government—1988– 3. Ejército Zapatista de
Liberación Nacional (Mexico)—History. 4. Social movements—Mexico
—History—20th century. 5. Marcos, subcomandante. I. Holloway,
John, fl. 1978– . II. Peláez, Eloína.
F1256.Z27   1998
972'.750836—dc21   98–15897
                                                   CIP

Designed and produced for Pluto Press by
Chase Production Services, Chadlington, OX7 3LN
Typeset by Stanford DTP Services, Northampton
Printed in the EC by Athenaeum Press Ltd, Gateshead

Contents

Notes on Contributors

Andrés Barreda is a Professor in the Faculty of Economics of the Universidad Nacional Autonóma de Mexico. Member of the editorial committee of the journal *Chiapas*. He specialises in questions related to the role of strategic resources in contemporary capitalism.

Ana Esther Ceceña is a Researcher in the Institute of Economic Research in the Universidad Nacional Autónoma de Mexico. She specialises in questions related to the spatial organisation of production, strategic resources and technology. Director of the journal *Chiapas* and coordinator of a research project on 'Maya paradise: International competition and strategic resources'.

Harry Cleaver is an Associate Professor of Economics at the University of Texas at Austin. He is a member of the group Acción Zapatista and also the creator/moderator of the Chiapas95 Internet lists and web page. His research and writing has long been concerned with Marxist theory and recently, with the international circulation on the Internet, of struggle against neoliberalism.

Catherine Héau-Lambert is a Sociologist and historian. Professor in the Escuela Nacional de Antropología e Historia, Mexico City. Her present research is on Zapatista culture during the Mexican revolution.

John Holloway is a professor/researcher at the Insitute of Social Sciences and Humanities of the Universidad Autónoma de Puebla and lecturer in Politics at the University of Edinburgh. He has written widely on Marxist theory and the critique of political economy.

Patricia King and **Javier Villanueva** were professors in the Faculty of Science in the Universidad Nacional Autónoma de Mexico (UNAM) between 1971 and 1984. Since then, they have been doing research on problems linked to social practice, especially on the relation between class and group and between practice and knowledge. They have taken postgraduate courses in the philosophy of science in the Institute of Philosophical Research of the UNAM and in the Universidad Autónoma Metropolitana – Iztapalapa. They have been involved in working for the formation of the Zapatista National Liberation Front since the idea was proposed in the Fourth Declaration of the Lacandon Jungle on 1 January 1996.

Luis Lorenzano Since being exiled from Argentina after the military coup of 1976, he has been living in Mexico, where he is now professor/researcher in the Division of Social Sciences and Humanities of the Universidad Autónoma Metropolitana – Xochimilco. He is co-author of *Argentina: The Malvinas and the End of Military Rule*, published by Verso in 1984, and of numerous essays on social and political topics.

Márgara Millán is a Sociologist/Researcher in the Centre for Latin American Studies in the Universidad Nacional Autónoma de Mexico. Her current research project is on indigenous women in Chiapas.

Eloína Peláez has worked in the University of Edinburgh and the Universidad Nacional Autónoma de Mexico on the history and sociology of computing and the development of new forms of social resistance.

Enrique Rajchenberg is a sociologist and historian. Professor in the Faculties of Economics and of Philosophy and Literature in the Universidad Nacional Autónoma de Mexico. His present research is on social movements during the Mexican revolution and the contemporary historiography of the revolution.

Preface

This book is one of the many outcomes of the Zapatista uprising which began on the first day of January 1994. The uprising has brought not only political upheaval but also an enormous renaissance of oppositional culture in Mexico and beyond, an outpouring of articles, books, journals, videos, songs, poems, paintings, plays and other things in between.

There are two things about the uprising that have inspired this creative high. The first is that rebellion has seized the initiative. For possibly the first time since the early 1970s, radical dissent is setting the agenda, forcing the authorities into clumsy reaction and exposing their brute incomprehension. After years of being pushed on to the defensive by the tide of reaction, in Mexico as elsewhere, after years of listening to the seductive, deadening tones of 'there is no alternative', the voice of those 'without voice' is again being heard: it has again become palpably obvious that there is an alternative, that there are other ways of organising society and that radical change is both possible and desperately urgent. The surge of oppositional self-confidence which the uprising has brought immediately carries the rebellion far beyond the confines of the state of Chiapas to which it is seemingly confined by the Mexican army.

The second factor which has inspired such creativity is that the uprising itself is enormously creative. The Zapatista Army of National Liberation (EZLN) has overflowed with new political ideas and new ways of doing politics. The uprising does not fit into any of the previously established moulds of what a revolution should look like. The received ideas of both left and right have been challenged over and over again: the right, because the worn old tags that they have tried to apply (subversives, guerrillas, terrorists) have convinced nobody, not even themselves; and the left, because all the attempts to define the EZLN into the pre-set moulds of Trotskyist, social democratic or anarchist thought have failed. Even after four years of the uprising, it is difficult to avoid the questions, 'What is the EZLN? What is Zapatismo?'

This book has grown out of the uprising in both of those senses. It hopes to convey both the renewed self-confidence of the revolutionary question and the creative stimulus of the Zapatistas. Above all, it has grown out of the question 'what is Zapatismo?' It is an attempt by various authors to come to terms with the uprising, to explore and to explain. There is no attempt to impose a unified approach, although clearly all the articles grow out of an undisguised enthusiasm for the rebellion. There is also no attempt to provide a definitive answer to the question: indeed it is argued that what distinguishes Zapatismo as a political movement is the fact that it has resisted definition.

Most of the literature on the Zapatista uprising provides an implicit definition of the movement by focusing on its relation to its immediate context. In most cases, the contextualisation that is given to the uprising is the state of Chiapas, with its notoriously bad social conditions and its history of social conflict: this is so much the case that, for many, reference to Chiapas is immediately reference to the uprising and vice versa. In other cases, the movement is seen in the context of the struggles and living conditions of the indigenous people of Mexico as a whole. Still other studies focus on the close interrelation between the Zapatista uprising and the prolonged crisis of the Mexican political system. Yet other studies locate the uprising in the context of the Latin American revolutionary movements of this century. All of these approaches are important, but they have the disadvantage of implicitly limiting the movement to the context in question.

The emphasis that we have chosen for this book is different. Although all the contexts mentioned above are explored in the different chapters of the book, what interests us most is the question of the newness of the Zapatista movement. What is this new thing called 'Zapatismo'? What is new about it, and in what way is this newness important not just for Chiapas, the indigenous movement, Mexican politics or revolution in Latin America, but for the whole way that we (in any part of the world) think about politics, life and the possibility of revolutionary change? In other words, we take the Zapatistas seriously when they claim not just to be an indigenous or Mexican movement, but to be truly 'intergalactic', to be struggling for humanity.

The book consists of contributions from several authors on different aspects of the Zapatista uprising. The introduction, by the editors, presents the themes of the book and of the different chapters, and gives a brief account of the uprising itself. The first chapter, by Enrique Rajchenberg and Catherine Héau-Lambert, explores the use of symbolism by the EZLN and explains its relation to the original

Zapatistas of the Mexican revolution (the one at the start of the century). The second chapter, by Ana Esther Ceceña and Andrés Barreda, explains the connection between the uprising, the social and economic conditions in Chiapas and the development of world capitalism. The role played by women in the rebellion, both as members of the EZLN and in the many related struggles in the state of Chiapas, is the theme of Chapter 3, by Márgara Millán. The fourth chapter, by Harry Cleaver, places the uprising firmly in a global setting by examining the role of electronic communications in weaving a world wide web of Zapatismo. Patricia King and Francisco Javier Villanueva look at the particular difficulties of the developing relation between the Zapatista movement and the world's biggest city (Mexico City) in Chapter 5, while Chapter 6, by Luis Lorenzano, moves from a detailed examination of the origins of the Zapatista uprising to discussing its place in the global restructuring of the relation between labour and capital. The final chapter, by John Holloway, develops the question of the global relevance of the movement and its contribution to revolutionary thought by focusing on the concept of dignity and its importance for the Zapatista movement.

We would like to thank many people. First of all, each other, of course, for our unfailing support and inspiration, and also the contributors, for their hard work to meet the deadlines that we, the editors, imposed but did not always respect, as well as for the stimulus of so many discussions on the Zapatista uprising. Our thanks too to Alfonso and Roberto Vélez Pliego, for providing in the Instituto de Ciencias Sociales y Humanidades of the Universidad Autónoma de Puebla, a utopian space within which much of the work for this book has been done, as well as for the Instituto's support in covering part of the costs of translation of the chapters which were written in Spanish; and to the Department of Politics of the University of Edinburgh for granting the leave that has made the book possible. To the translators themselves we owe a particular debt for their hard work and patience: all members of the Tlatolli Ollin translating collective, they are Elaine Burns (Chapters 1 and 6), Elaine Levine (Chapter 2), Heather Dashner (Chapter 3) and Emily Ryan (Chapter 5). Thanks too to Dolores Peláez Valdez, for keeping us always supplied with copies of *La Jornada*, stimulus and information even when we were away from Mexico. Most of all, thanks to the women, men and children of the EZLN for changing the world. This book is dedicated to them.

John Holloway and Eloína Peláez

The book has been produced with the support of the Instituto de Ciencias Sociales y Humanidades of the Universidad Autónoma de Puebla.

Map 1 The Zapatista Uprising & the Chiapas Region of Mexico

Map 2 The Economic Regions of Chiapas (showing some of the towns mentioned in the text)

Introduction: Reinventing Revolution

John Holloway and Eloína Peláez

Opening the World

The Zapatista uprising opens a world that appeared to be closed, gives life to a hope that seemed to be dead.

The uprising took Mexico and the world by surprise. When the Zapatista Army of National Liberation (EZLN)[1] occupied the city of San Cristóbal de las Casas and six other towns in the early hours of 1 January 1994, they burst upon a world that denied their existence. It was not just that their existence was unknown, that nobody had ever heard of this organisation that revealed itself for the first time when thousands of armed indigenous men and women marched into San Cristóbal. It was more than that: the reaction was rather that they should not be there, that they could not be there. And yet they were there, saying loudly and clearly 'Here we are!' Soon it became clear that their 'here we are!' was not just a particular cry but the 'here we are!' of all of us who, in whole or in part, have been painted out of the world's picture of itself, all of us who have been told, in a million subtle or unsubtle ways, that we do not, or should not, exist. That is why the importance of the uprising stretches far, far beyond the state of Chiapas where it originated, far beyond Mexico, far beyond Latin America or the so-called 'Third World'.

There was no subtlety about the way in which the indigenous people of the Lacandon Jungle, a huge, forested area in the southeast of Mexico, had been told that they had no place in the postmodern world. They, and their forebears, had been driven out ever since the Spanish conquest of Mexico in the sixteenth century. But, by the beginning of 1994, they were facing extermination as a community. Their land was wanted by cattle ranchers, by oil companies, by paper producers eager to replant the jungle with fast-growing eucalyptus trees, and by capitalist planners eager to exploit the unique biodiversity of the jungle as a resource for future developments in genetic engineering. If all that wasn't enough, the grinding daily poverty, the deaths from curable diseases, the lack of schools and hospitals, and the gradual suppression of their languages

1

all told them clearly and with no subtlety that they were redundant in the new world of neoliberalism (see Chapter 2).

Neither the indigenous peoples of the countryside nor the poor of the city had any place at all, except perhaps as tourist attractions, in the image portrayed by the Mexican government. Mexico was the golden child of neoliberalism. After precipitating the 'debt crisis' of the 1980s, with its announcement in August 1982 that it would not be able to keep up with its debt repayments, Mexico had risen through the application of draconian austerity policies to become the darling of the world's financial press, the fastest emerging of all the emerging markets. Mexico's was one of the success stories of the neoliberal market-oriented policies that had gained such a hold throughout the world in the 1980s. The government had opened the economy to the world market, and privatised a large part of the state-owned sector, including the banks which had been nationalised in 1982. Capital was flowing in; the economy was growing. The economic success was crowned by Mexico's acceptance in 1993 into the Organization for Economic Cooperation and Development (OECD), which groups the world's richest states, and by the conclusion of the North American Free Trade Agreement (NAFTA) between Mexico, Canada and the United States, which came into force on that first day of January 1994. The Mexican president, Carlos Salinas de Gortari, was favourite to become the first head of the World Trade Organization when he stepped down from office at the beginning of December 1994. In this successful, modern Mexico, and in the economic statistics that underscored its success, there was no mention of the growing number of poor who beg, clean windscreens or sell their wares at every set of traffic lights in the major cities, nor of the peasants who struggle to produce or earn enough to eat. (For a discussion of the 'two Mexicos', see Chapter 1.)

In all this, Mexico is not so very different from the rest of the world. Neoliberalism is not peculiar to Mexico: it has left its mark everywhere. The imposition on the world of policies which promote the market and cut back on those activities of the state which do not immediately favour business has brought prosperity to some and poverty to many. The gap between rich and poor has grown, both within and between individual countries. The dynamic of capitalism has let very many people know that they are redundant, that a market-driven world would function better if they simply did not exist. For the miners of Britain the message was reinforced with police truncheons to help them to understand. In other cases the message has often been much more violent. For over a thousand million people, the message is received through extreme poverty, the daily struggle just to get enough food to be undernourished, with all the illness and degradation that that involves. Such people are no longer even the 'industrial reserve army' that capital requires for its economy to function: they are simply redundant, superfluous to an economy which is driven not by people's needs but by profit. In the dominant images of society, the economic statistics, the politicians' speeches, the Hollywood films, these people have already been painted out of existence.

Neoliberalism, however, does not just increase the gap between rich and poor, between the included and the excluded. The subjection of life to the market cripples us all. Those who have jobs, even 'good' jobs, are increasingly insecure and increasingly exploited. The stress and the long hours of work entailed trying to gain security leave little scope for activities that might point to another type of life. The pressures and the growing individualisation of working conditions bring increasing isolation (see Chapter 5). There is a narrowing of life, a closure. Fantasies, dreams, ideas, emotions, projects for different forms of living, collective enjoyment: all get squeezed, suppressed, excluded. Nowhere is this more obvious than in universities and other places of education. Funding drives both research and teaching to become more managerial, more oriented towards the success of the students on the market, more concerned with the management of society. For the voices that say 'no!', for the dreams of a human society, there is no place. Neoliberalism attacks humanity, not only in the sense that it kills millions by starvation and disease, but also in the equally devastating sense that it kills humanity as a project.

The failure of so many revolutions in this century and the dying-out of revolutionary movements in the last 15 years or so is, then, something that strikes deeply at all of us, whether or not we ever thought of ourselves as 'revolutionaries'. The failure of revolutions becomes part of the neoliberal chorus telling us constantly that, in Margaret Thatcher's famous phrase, 'there is no alternative'. There is no alternative, we are told, to a market-driven society, whatever its costs may be. Humanity as a project is dead.

But if humanity as a project is dead, protest is not, and cannot be. There is, however, a great danger that the response of those whose existence is threatened or denied, in whole or in part, by neoliberal capitalism will become increasingly particularistic, a mere assertion of identity. Threatened by capitalist development ('globalisation'), groups have easy recourse to a romanticised identity which separates them from others rather than uniting them with others. The world of protest becomes so easily a world of so many identities, counterposed one to another, each claiming exclusive right: blacks, women, Muslims, gays, Basques, Irish. In so far as protest asserts mere identity, and in so far as neoliberalism's denial of the project of humanity is extended into the struggles against it, these struggles can easily take on a brutal and absolutely destructive form.

This is where the Zapatistas' importance lies. Their 'here we are!' is not the defensive, romantic 'here we are!' of a threatened identity. They are not saying: 'We are Tzeltals[2] and we want to defend our glorious traditions,' but rather: 'We want a world in which there are many worlds, a world in which our world, and the worlds of others, will fit: a world in which we are heard, but as one of many voices.' Their 'here we are!' simultaneously asserts identity and transcends it (see Chapter 7). Their project is summed up in the title of the Inter-continental Meeting which the Zapatistas organised in their territory in July 1996: 'For Humanity against Neoliberalism'. Such a world, they argue, can be constructed only on the basis of freedom, justice, democracy. This is the struggle, not of a past to be defended, but of a world to be constructed.

This understanding of their struggle means that, unlike almost all previous revolutions, the Zapatista revolution does not aim to take power – neither through the ballot box nor through any form of seizure of power. The project of humanity cannot be achieved through the winning of power. This marks a radical break with the traditions of the revolutionary and the non-revolutionary left. This is what has been so difficult for politicians both of left and right to understand. As the Zapatistas put it in a recent communiqué:

> The 'centre' asks us, demands of us, that we should sign a peace agreement quickly and convert ourselves into an 'institutional' political force, that is to say, convert ourselves into yet another part of the machinery of power. To them we answer 'NO' and they do not understand it. They do not understand that we are not in agreement with those ideas. They do not understand that we do not want offices or posts in the government. They do not understand that we are struggling not for the stairs to be swept clean from the top to the bottom, but for there to be no stairs, for there to be no kingdom at all.[3]

They do not understand because there is no room in the mind of the politician, nor in the mind of the political scientist, for the simplest, most ordinary statement of all: 'We do not want to struggle for power, because the struggle for power is central to the world we reject; it does not form part of the world we want.' This is the most ordinary of statements simply because it is a statement evident in the practice of most people every day. Whereas the discourse of politicians and political scientists revolves around an assumption that people pursue power, such a pursuit is not central to the daily activities of most people. The fact that a revolutionary organisation such as the EZLN say that they are struggling not to take power but to abolish power makes them very ordinary and thereby very extraordinary.

Breaking the Blockade

Zapatismo is a struggle, not for power, but against it. A struggle for power implies adopting methods similar to those of the powerful. A struggle against power implies that the methods adopted cannot be those of the powerful. But then how?

When the EZLN took their dramatic action on 1 January 1994, they started a political movement which involved a reinvention of revolution. How can one fight against the powerful without adopting the methods of the powerful? How can one even survive without adopting the methods of the powerful? That tension has been at the centre of the Zapatista uprising since that day. The Zapatistas speak of themselves as being 'armed with truth and fire': their main weapon is truth, the truth of their humanity. But in a world in which the powerful constantly seek to impose their dictate through armed force, it is necessary for the Zapatistas too to be armed with fire.

The thousands of women and men who occupied San Cristóbal and the other towns at the beginning of 1994 did so peacefully. (On the role of women in the Zapatista movement, see Chapter 3.) They appeared to have come from nowhere. Very few people knew of the existence of the EZLN before the occupation of San Cristóbal. Of course, they had not come from nowhere. Almost all were indigenous, members of different ethnic groups who lived in the Lacandon Jungle. They had come from a long history of indigenous resistance to exploitation and domination, from '500 years of struggle', as they put it in the 'Declaration of the Lacandon Jungle' which they issued to explain their action. They had come too from the work of a small group of revolutionaries who had been active in the jungle for more than ten years and who had had the wisdom to submerge their ideas of revolution in the accumulated experience of the people of the region. (On the origins of the EZLN see Chapter 6.) They had come, perhaps most directly, from their own particular experience of a world-wide phenomenon. Neoliberalism, the capitalism of the 1980s and 1990s with its emphasis on the destruction of obstacles to the free market and the free movement of money, had meant for most of the people of Chiapas, as for millions of others throughout the world, a drastic deterioration in living conditions. Like so many other people in the world, they learnt through poverty and violence that they, the way they lived, the way they worked, the way they celebrated, the dreams they had and the land they occupied, were obstacles to capitalist development. When an amendment in 1992 to Article 27 of the Mexican constitution threatened the survival of their communities by opening the ownership of the land to the free market, more and more of the inhabitants of the jungle said 'Enough!' (*¡Ya Basta!*) and joined the EZLN. If they were threatened with extinction anyway, they would rather die with dignity.

Although the occupation of the towns themselves was, with few exceptions, peaceful, since the Zapatistas had taken the authorities by surprise,[4] the first ten days of the uprising became very violent when the Mexican army attacked and the air force started to bomb the Zapatistas and their villages. The reaction in Mexico, in nearly all sectors of the population, was one of revulsion at the violence and sympathy for the cause, if not necessarily for the methods, of the Zapatistas. A massive demonstration in Mexico City led to a declaration of cease-fire by the government on 10 January, which was accepted by the rebels. The cease-fire did not establish peace, but a situation in which the Zapatistas remained within the jungle, surrounded by a military cordon. It was after the smoke had cleared that it became clear that this was not just another guerrilla movement but an enormously innovative and articulate popular uprising, trying to invent revolution in a world in which there were no models to follow.

The path of armed but peaceful revolution has been a tortuous one. The declaration of cease-fire placed the EZLN army in a situation for which they were not prepared. They had expected a prolonged armed conflict in which either the people would rise up and join them to overthrow the government or they would be isolated and under open military attack. The popular response had been not to join the Zapatistas but to call for an end to violence. This reaction was almost certainly influenced by images of Bosnia, Rwanda, and Northern Ireland, as well as by memories of the violent destruction of the guerrilla movement in Mexico in the 1970s and what people had seen of the revolutionary movements in neighbouring Guatemala and El Salvador, where many years of bloody civil war had brought enormous misery, but no social revolution. No one wanted to see Mexico embroiled in such a cycle of destruction. The popular reaction, and the cease-fire which followed, placed the EZLN, an army with weapons, in a situation where they had to find different ways of pursuing their struggle.

That the struggle would continue became clear almost immediately. To the government's offer of a pardon to the rebels, the Zapatistas replied, in a communiqué dated 17 January:

What are we supposed to ask pardon for? What are they going to pardon us for? For not dying of hunger? For not being silent in our misery? For not having accepted humbly the giant historical burden of contempt and neglect? For having risen up in arms when we found all other roads blocked? ... Who should ask for pardon and who should grant it? Those who, for years and years, sat at a laden table and ate their fill while death sat with us, death, so everyday, so ours that we stopped being afraid of it? Those who filled our pockets and our souls with declarations and promises? Or the dead, our dead, so mortally dead of 'natural' death, of measles, whooping cough, cholera, typhoid, tetanus, pneumonia, paludism and other gastrointestinal and pulmonary delights? Our dead, so equally dead, so democratically dead of pain because nobody was doing anything, because all the dead, our dead, just went off like that, without anybody keeping the count, without anyone saying at last the 'Enough!' that would restore meaning to those deaths, without anyone asking those dead of always, our dead, to come back and die again, but now in order to live ... Who should ask for pardon and who should grant it?[5]

From that moment, it was clear both that the Zapatista acceptance of a cease-fire did not mean a capitulation, and that in the communiqué they had found a new and powerful weapon. They might be encircled by a military cordon, but the communiqués gave them an effective way of overcoming the blockade (see Chapter 5). The communiqués were published in full in some of the national newspapers and attracted a large readership. It was not long before they began to be translated into other languages and put out on the Internet by Zapatista supporters – hence the description of the uprising as the 'first revolution of the electronic age' (see Chapter 4). The communiqués are filled with humour, stories, poetry. They project a new type of revolutionary movement: one which does not aim to take power, but simply to create a world in which people can live with dignity.

The language of the communiqués is not that of other revolutionary movements of the twentieth century. Much of the traditional vocabulary of revolution is left aside, made barren by the experience of the past ('proletariat', 'socialism', 'vanguard'). The communiqués take up the battle in other categories previously dismissed as being irrevocably compromised by their liberal use ('freedom', 'democracy', 'justice', for example). They give new life to categories and symbols that seemed empty or insignificant (see Chapter 1). Their central category is dignity, 'that which made us live, that which made our step rise above plants and animals, that which made the stone be beneath our feet' (see Chapter 7).

Through the communiqués, interviews with the press and media and the newspaper reports from the Zapatista territory in the jungle, and through videos, a picture emerged not of a revolutionary group, but of a community in rebellion: a community of men, women and children, with all the traditions and practices of cooperation that the word 'community' implies (see Chapter 5), and with all the transformation of those often patriarchical and oppressive traditions and practices that 'rebellion' implies (see Chapter 6). Their aim, they said, was to make a revolution, but not a Revolution.

But how could they make a revolution (with a small 'r'), without armed struggle, without trying to take power? How might it be possible to pursue a non-violent revolution that eschewed the traditional goal of both social democratic and Leninist parties: the winning of power? How could they change the world when they were encircled in the jungle?

The Mexican government offered to negotiate. The EZLN replied that they would not negotiate but that they would take part in a dialogue with the government, principally as a way of establishing a dialogue with 'civil society', that is, with all those who were struggling, in whatever way, to transform the political regime, the 'party-state'. The dialogue took place in the Cathedral of San Cristóbal between the end of February and beginning of March 1994. The Zapatistas used the occasion to further circumvent the government's blockade. They gave daily press conferences and established informal contacts with sympathisers from all over the country who had come to express their support. At the end of the dialogue, they insisted that they would have to submit the terms offered by the government during the dialogue to the democratic decision of all their communities. Just as the war had been started after a process of discussion by all the men, women and children over twelve years of age in their communities, so the settlement of their demands would have to go through the same process.

After nearly three months of consultation and discussion,[6] the Zapatistas rejected the terms offered them by the government. The principal reason was that the government was offering concessions only in relation to the state of Chiapas, whereas the Zapatistas had made it clear from the beginning that their struggle was a national one, not just for material concessions, but for freedom, justice and democracy. That did not mean, however, that they would return to armed action. Instead, they called a meeting of all those who shared their aims, to be held in the Lacandon Jungle at the beginning of August, just a few weeks before the Mexican presidential elections.

More than 6,000 people from all over Mexico went to Chiapas for the meeting, the National Democratic Convention (Convención Nacional Democrática – CND). The Zapatistas had cleared a space in the jungle and used the tree trunks to construct an auditorium large enough to hold all the participants, a meeting place they named Aguascalientes, after a convention held in 1914 during the Mexican Revolution. The Convention did not align itself with any political party for the presidential elections, although a considerable number of the participants were members of the principal centre-left party, the PRD (*Partido Revolucionario Democratico*– Revolutionary Democratic Party). The general conclusion of the meeting was that it was time to give priority to the struggle of civil society. The EZLN would remain armed, but if the civil struggle for freedom, democracy and justice was successful, then they would simply return to the mountains from whence they had come.

The Convention had been a great success in bringing civil struggle into close contact with the EZLN, but it did not, and did not seek to, define a clear way forward. The months which followed were a time of difficulty, disillusionment and tension. The party which had been in power for more than 60 years, the PRI (*Partido Revolucionario Institucional*) won the presidential elections comfortably, with the PRD coming in third place. The PRI's victory was probably due not so much to direct electoral fraud as to the encrusted position in networks of patronage, corruption and self-interest that it had acquired after being in office for so many years. In an election held on the same day, the PRI also retained the governorship of Chiapas, and in this case there was considerable evidence of fraud. In Chiapas itself, tension between the army and the EZLN increased as the army increased its low-intensity warfare against the Zapatistas, with the increased use of surveillance flights, increased harassment of people at military checkpoints and attacks on peasants in other parts of the state. The situation further deteriorated at the beginning of December when the newly inaugurated president, Ernesto Zedillo, showed his support for the new governor of Chiapas by participating in his inauguration.

The EZLN responded to the military pressures with a military action, but a military action very different from the violence of the state. On 19 December, the EZLN called a press conference in the jungle to announce that they had broken through the military cordon and undertaken actions in 38 municipalities of Chiapas, without a shot being fired. They had effectively surrounded the army surrounding them, without being seen, without violence, without suffering violence – a brilliant and mischievous display of their strength.

On the following day, the government responded to a massive outflow of capital by devaluing the peso, and blaming the Zapatistas for the devaluation. In the days that followed, the continuing outflow of capital forced the government to allow the peso to float, and within a few days it had lost 40 per cent of its value. The devaluation sparked off a financial crisis throughout the world and led to a period of severe economic crisis in Mexico itself. In the financial negotiations that followed, the Mexican government came under pressure from at least some of the US banks to break the cease-fire and intervene militarily against the Zapatistas.

On 9 February 1995, the army moved into the Zapatista territory in pursuit of the EZLN leaders. The EZLN refused to be drawn into a confrontation of violence against violence and fled into the mountains together with the people of the region. The army occupied villages and destroyed crops, but did not succeed in capturing any members of the EZLN. There were enormous demonstrations in Mexico City and other cities, and protests throughout the world. Under pressure, the government called off the military pursuit, although the army continued to occupy the territory. The cease-fire was restored and the orders for the arrest of the Zapatistas were suspended, under condition that the EZLN agreed to begin a new dialogue.

The extent to which the Zapatistas had succeeded in breaking the blockade over the previous year was shown by the fact that the principal cry of the demonstration in Mexico City was no longer just a call to stop the violence, but 'We are all Zapatistas!' and 'We are all Marcos!' (a reference to the spokesman of the EZLN, Subcomandante Marcos). This mirrored a statement by Marcos in one of the communiqués:

> Marcos is gay in San Francisco, a black in South Africa, Asian in Europe, a Chicano in San Isidro, an anarchist in Spain, a Palestinian in Israel, an indigenous person in the streets of San Cristóbal, a gang member in Neza, a rocker on campus, a Jew in Germany, an ombudsman in the Department of Defence, a feminist in a political party, a communist in the post-Cold War period, a prisoner in Cintalapa, a pacifist in Bosnia, a Mapuche in the Andes, a teacher in the National Confederation of Educational Workers,[7] an artist without a gallery or a portfolio, a housewife in any neighbourhood

in any city in any part of Mexico on a Saturday night, a guerrilla in Mexico at the end of the twentieth century, a striker in the CTM,[8] a sexist in the feminist movement, a woman alone in a Metro station at 10 p.m., a retired person standing around in the Zocalo, a peasant without land, an underground editor, an unemployed worker, a doctor with no office, a non-conformist student, a dissident against neoliberalism, a writer without books or readers, and a Zapatista in the Mexican southeast. In other words, Marcos is a human being in this world. Marcos is every untolerated, oppressed, exploited minority that is resisting and saying 'Enough!'[9]

Breaking the blockade, in other words, meant making real the unity of the Zapatistas with all those 'without face, without voice, without future' who stand against neoliberalism. Revolution involves establishing the unity of a heterogeneous subject, recognising and simultaneously transcending identities in a process that can be seen as the recomposition of class struggle (see Chapter 6).

The new dialogue began a couple of months later in San Andrés Larráinzar, a small town in Chiapas, in which there is very strong Zapatista influence. The initial meetings between the representatives of the Zapatistas and of the government, in the presence of two groups of intermediaries, one parliamentary (the Cocopa)[10] and the other non-parliamentary (the Conai),[11] agreed on an agenda for further talks. The first theme chosen was indigenous rights and culture. It was agreed that each side could invite a number of assessors and guests to take part in the sessions. The EZLN published a list of several hundred assessors, including representatives of the most important indigenous organisations in Mexico, most of the leading academics in the field and a number of people being held in prison for their supposed involvement with the Zapatista uprising. The government invited a much smaller number of functionaries and academics. In the discussions that followed, held in San Cristóbal and San Andrés, the Zapatista side was of course by far the stronger, in terms of the strength of their cause, their ideas and their intellectual force. The two sessions of discussions were followed by a Forum on Indigenous Rights and Culture, held in January 1996 in San Cristóbal and attended by hundreds of people actively involved in indigenous struggle from all over the country. The Forum was followed by a meeting a month later between the government representatives and the representatives of the EZLN, at which a number of agreements were signed on indigenous rights and culture, the Agreements of San Andrés. The Agreements included a number of measures to improve the position of the indigenous peoples of Mexico and to give them a certain degree of autonomous self-government. The government promised to introduce legislation and constitutional reforms to implement the Agreements.

The theme of the second phase of the dialogue was the reform of the state. Again the Zapatistas chose hundreds of assessors, including both those involved in all sorts of social and political struggles and left-wing and liberal academics. The government took a more obstructive line this time, to indicate their reluctance to accept that the Zapatistas should discuss anything beyond the local and the ethnic: they did not appoint assessors and their representatives did not take any active part in the discussions. The two sessions were again followed by a week-long Forum, held in San Cristóbal with the participation of over a thousand representatives from all over the country, from all sorts of different backgrounds, but united by a common enthusiasm and a sense of being part of the Zapatista struggle for a different society. Support for the Zapatistas was no longer thought of in terms of solidarity, but primarily in terms of being a Zapatista, of participating in the struggle for a new politics. The Forum discussed such questions as alternative forms of economic organisation, experiences of social struggle in the city and the countryside, the formation of a constituent assembly to frame a new constitution, the meaning of neoliberalism and the political future of the Zapatista movement.

The Forum was followed, some weeks later, at the end of July 1996, by the 'Intergalactic', the first Intercontinental Meeting for Humanity and against Neoliberalism, attended by more than 3,000 representatives from 43 different countries. The Intergalactic demonstrated clearly that the Zapatistas' struggle was not just a local one, nor an ethnic, nor a national one, but a struggle understood as the struggle of humanity for humanity. The meeting was held at different sites within the Lacandon Jungle, in five different meeting places or 'Aguascalientes' constructed by the Zapatistas and taking the place of the first Aguascalientes (constructed for the National Democratic Convention), which had been destroyed by the army when it attacked in February 1995. The meeting, which had been proposed by the Zapatistas in January and prepared in five continents for months, was a week of mud, dancing and discussion and, above all, participation in the attempt to construct a different politics. The meeting ended with a call for the construction of an international network of opposition to neoliberalism, and for a second intercontinental meeting to be held in Europe a year later. (The second meeting was held in Spain in July 1997.)

The year and a half leading up to the Intergalactic had seen a fertile and imaginative development of peaceful revolutionary politics – not just the dialogue, the Forums and the Intergalactic itself, but also the national consultation in July 1995 on the future of the EZLN, in which over a million people participated, the formation of civil committees throughout the country to support the Zapatistas and develop Zapatista politics and the formation of the National Indigenous Congress to coordinate indigenous struggle throughout the country.

In the summer of 1996, however, there were indications of the limits to what such a politics might achieve. The struggle against power is constantly encroached upon and threatened by the struggle for power. The violence, both by the authorities and by right-wing paramilitary groups backed and often established by the authorities as part of the strategy of low-intensity warfare, continued. Then, the end of June saw the appearance in the south-western state of Guerrero, of a new guerrilla group, the EPR (*Ejército Popular Revolucionario* – Popular Revolutionary Army), which started to undertake direct military action against the army. The EPR projected itself as a much more traditional type of hard-line guerrilla group, and undoubtedly appealed to those who were growing impatient with the lack of tangible progress in the realisation of the EZLN's demands. At the same time, it became more and more clear that the government intended to do nothing to implement the Agreements of San Andrés.

In these circumstances, and given the arrogance with which the government had treated particularly the second phase of the dialogue, the EZLN suspended the dialogue with the government: there seemed little point in carrying on when the government did not take even take seriously the agreement it had alredy signed, and when the militarisation of Chiapas was continuing apace. The principal condition which the EZLN set for the resumption of the dialogue was the fulfilment of the government's commitments under the San Andrés agreements. A renewal of talks, not with the government, but with the parliamentary and non-parliamentary intermediaries, the Cocopa and the Conai, failed to solve the stalemate when a proposal for legislation made by the Cocopa was accepted by the EZLN but rejected by the government at the beginning of 1997. The EZLN fell into a prolonged period of 'struggle by silence' in the first half of 1997. By the middle of 1997 however, the political situation seemed to be changing again. In the mid-term elections of July the PRI lost its absolute majority in the Congress for the first time and, equally important, the PRD won the first elections ever for the mayor of Mexico City. After its long silence, the EZLN announced a march of 1,111 Zapatistas (corresponding to the number of Zapatista communities) to Mexico City, to demand the implementation of the Agreements of San Andrés and to be present at the inauguration of the civil *Frente Zapatista de Liberación Nacional* (FZLN – Zapatista Front of National Liberation), a political organisation set up to coordinate the struggle for democracy, freedom and justice. The march, joined by many other organisations on its way from Chiapas, received a tumultuous welcome when it entered the central square of Mexico City on 12 September. After a few days, the Zapatistas returned to Chiapas, where the situation remains unresolved and the aggression of the authorities and the paramilitary groups increases.

The massacre of 45 people in the community of Acteal by right-wing paramilitaries on 22 December 1997, a direct or indirect consequence of the government's strategy of low-intensity warfare against the Zapatistas, has aroused a wave of revulsion in Mexico and around the world. The pressures on the government to implement the San Andrés Agreements have grown enormously, but the government continues to prevaricate, making conciliatory noises while increasing military activity.

Reinventing Revolution

Four years have passed since the first appearance of the EZLN. In Chiapas, the violence and the oppression continues. In Mexico there has been no revolutionary transformation, although the presence of the Zapatistas has undoubtedly accelerated the decomposition of the old regime. In the world, the unbridled capitalism of neoliberalism still rules. However, any appreciation of the Zapatistas' achievements has to be seen not only in terms of what exists but in the strengthening of that which does not (yet) exist.

In what way does the Zapatista uprising strengthen the project of revolution, the project of creating a human society (what might be called 'communism', even though the word has been so brutally degraded)?

First, by keeping this project alive, when it appeared to be almost dead. In spite of the obvious horrors of neoliberalism, the idea of revolution has fallen into discredit in recent years. This discredit has much to do with the experience and fate of the Soviet Union, China and other countries: the result of the revolutions of this century has often been oppressive – bureaucratic, macho, anti-creative – and far removed from the dreams of most revolutionaries. The discredit also has much to do with the difficulty of imagining a revolution in today's conditions, however desirable it might be considered. How can one even think of a successful revolution when states are so heavily armed, have such sophisticated means of establishing consensus (parliamentary democracy, mass media, education), and are tightly integrated into a global economic/political capitalist system? Even for those horrified by the violence of neoliberalism against ourselves and others, it very often seems that there is no alternative, no hope. The world, it seems, is closed.

Against this, the message of the Zapatistas has been one of hope. They prise open the lid of closure. They turn 'there is no alternative' on its head. In a world in which we are all crippled by neoliberalism, in a world in which millions of people are condemned by the functioning of the market to degradation, hunger, illness, redundancy and isolation, there is no alternative: we must rebel. Humanity is the struggle against dehumanisation. We start not from a means-end logic – will our rebellion lead to the desired results; do the objective conditions make the construction of a human society possible? – but from the much simpler realisation that there is no alternative to struggling against dehumanisation, in whatever way we can. Hope is central to the Zapatista uprising, but it is not a hope that springs from the certainty of the end result, but from confidence in the necessity of the project. Hope is dignity, the struggle to walk upright in a world which pushes us down.

Talk of hope, rebellion and revolution cannot, however, simply be a revival of the revolutionary ideals of earlier years. The project of creating a society based on human dignity cannot be based on the authoritarian discipline which has characterised so many revolutionary movements of the past. Revolution itself now presupposes a reinventing of itself. This has inevitably brought the Zapatistas repeatedly into conflict with the received ideas of the revolutionary left. As Subcomandante Marcos commented at the end of the first year of the uprising:

> Something was broken in this year, not just the false image of modernity which neoliberalism was selling to us, not just the falsity of governmental projects, of institutional alms, not just the unjust neglect by the country of its original inhabitants, but also the rigid schemes of a left dedicated to living from and of the past. In the midst of this navigating from pain to hope, the political struggle finds itself bereft of the worn-out clothes bequeathed to it by pain; it is hope which obliges it to seek new forms of struggle, new ways of being political, of doing politics. A new politics, a new political ethic is not just a wish, it is the only way to advance, to jump to the other side.[12]

Developing a new revolutionary politics is not an easy task. As Comandante Tacho puts it, it is like trying to learn lessons in a school that has not yet been built.[13] There is no model to follow. The old conception of bringing about revolution through winning state power at least has the merit of defining a clear goal: the drawback, of course, is that the goal is a mirage, that the state does not have power, that the state itself is just one form of the capitalist social relations which the revolution aims to destroy. But, mirage or not, the aim at least provides a clear framework for revolutionary action. When the aim is to change the world without taking power, not to conquer the world, but to make it different,[14] then the way forward is far from linear. It can only be understood as the attempt to bring together and make effective the struggle for humanity which already exists in all our lives, in a million different ways.

The Zapatistas have made clear that any such attempt must go far beyond the confines of what is usually understood as politics, whether bourgeois or revolutionary. An (anti-)politics directed against power cannot be understood in the same way as a politics of power. It involves an (anti-)politics of the non-political: humour, stories, dance, openness to new ideas and a willingness to admit mistakes, and, perhaps above all, ever renewed experimentation to find ways of channelling the struggle for humanity.

Inevitably, any such project also involves problems and uncertainties. The idea of a revolutionary path that is made in the process of making it, of a revolution that 'walks asking', as the Zapatistas put it, implies that the revolution may get lost on the way, that it may either be destroyed physically in confrontation with the army, or (worse, according to the Zapatistas themselves) that it may gradually become integrated into the political system. So far, the EZLN has managed to avoid both of these dangers, but there are considerable pressures (from the left as much as from the right) on the EZLN to convert itself into an institutional force which would function as part of the political system.

In the Zapatista project, there is no room for a concept of the 'correct line'. But does this mean a total relativism, that all forms of rebellion are equally valid, even fascist or racist ones? Clearly not. The central notion of dignity, so much emphasised by the Zapatistas, implies not only a recognition of one's own dignity but also of the dignity of others: it thus implies an aversion to violence and precludes the denial of dignity to others on the basis of race, gender, nationality or any other supposed identity. Beyond that, the crucial issue is not which form of struggle is correct, but how the different forms of struggle are articulated or brought into relation with one another. That is why all the political initiatives of the EZLN point towards experimenting with political forms with the aim of making effective the principle of 'commanding obeying', the principle that those who lead should be effectively subjected to the rule of those whom they claim to lead.

To sing the praises of the Zapatista uprising is not to deny that there are a whole host of ambiguities and unresolved problems. Conversely, however, to recognise these ambiguities is no reason to stop singing their praises. The Zapatista uprising has provided an enormous stimulus to oppositional thought, both in Mexico and beyond. In a world in which we appear to be cornered on all sides, they offer a way forward. Neoliberal capitalism becomes daily more obscene and unstable, in the extremes of wealth and poverty it engenders, in the intensity of its exploitation and in its unrelenting subjection of all life to the dictates of the market. Experience has made it clear time and time again that the state offers no possibility of bringing about radical change. Armed struggle to bring about change through the seizure of state power reproduces the structures of the very power it is trying to combat and has had little success in bringing about radical social change. So what is left? The only possibility is to reinvent revolution. That is what the Zapatistas are doing.

That is why this book is not a neutral one. Although not uncritical of the Zapatista movement, our attempt to understand it is a partisan attempt. When the Zapatistas occupied San Cristóbal and the other towns of Chiapas they sent flares of hope, dignity and revolutionary enthusiasm into the sombre night sky of the world. If this book succeeds in contributing to and deepening that hope, dignity and enthusiasm, then it will have succeeded in its aim.

Notes

1. *Ejército Zapatista de Liberación Nacional.*
2. The members of the EZLN are indigenous inhabitants of the Lacandon Jungle, drawn from different ethnic groups, of which the most important are the Tzeltal, Tzotzil, Tojolabal and Chol.
3. Communiqué of 8 August 1997, *La Jornada*, 11–13 August 1997. See also Ana Esther Ceceña, 'De cómo se construye la esperanza', *Cahiers Marxistes*, Winter 1997.
4. The most notable exception was the occupation of Ocosingo, where the authorities were prepared for some sort of action.
5. EZLN, *La Palabra de los Armados de Verdad y Fuego* (Mexico City: Editorial Fuenteovejuna, 1994/ 1995) Vol. 1, p. 121.

6. During this period the candidate of the ruling party for the presidential election was assassinated on 23 March. On the enormous impact of this, see Chapter 5.

7. The teachers' union, dominated by the PRI.

8. The confederation of trade unions, dominated by the PRI.

9. *Zapatistas! Documents of the New Mexican Revolution* (New York: Autonomedia, 1995) pp. 310–311.

10. *La Comisión de Concordia y Pacificación* (the Commission of Concord and Pacification), an all-party committee established after the army intervention of 9 February 1995.

11. *La Comisión Nacional de Intermediación* (the National Commission of Intermediation), an unofficial mediating body chaired by the Bishop of San Cristóbal, Samuel Ruiz.

12. Subcomandante Marcos, quoted by Rosario Ibarra, *La Jornada*, 2 May 1995.

13. Yvon Le Bot, *El Sueño Zapatista* [The Zapatista Dream] (Mexico City: Plaza & Janes, 1997) p. 191.

14. See the First Declaration of La Realidad, January 1996, *La Jornada*, 30 January 1996.

1

History and Symbolism in the Zapatista Movement

Enrique Rajchenberg and Catherine Héau-Lambert

> The struggles of our ancestors come to life once again through us.
> The proud cry of Vicente Guerrero, 'Live for Our Country or Die
> for Liberty', resounds within our throats anew.
>
> Second Declaration of the Lacandon Jungle

History and the collective imagination

Marcos surprised everyone when he appeared on horseback, his
chest crossed with cartridge belts. For Mexicans, his appearance
provoked not only amazement, but an awakening and recovery of
a collective memory which had been pushed into a corner, numbed
by neoliberalism, and on the brink of being forgotten altogether. It
also immediately evoked another, distant, image: that of Emiliano
Zapata on horseback, dressed in traditional *charro* style, with his broad
hat and his chest crossed with bands of bullets. This unforgettable
photographic image has served as a model for Mexican filmmakers,
and had become the archetype of the good revolutionary. Since
Marcos's individual identity was hidden behind his balaclava, what
remained was the symbolic identity of an agrarian guerrilla hero. This
astonishing appearance from a remote past was more eloquent even
than his speeches. He represented the re-emergence of the emblematic
defender of peasants who had died for his ideals.

Mexican history is a long chain of remembrances of popular
heroes: Marcos is reminiscent of General Zapata, who in turn recalls
the memory of the victorious rebellion of General Morelos,[1] whose
roots reach back into biblical memory. Real time operates over a
backdrop of mythical time – an eternal path towards liberation.

According to the testimonies left us by the popular songs of the
Revolution (the *corridas*), the public image of Zapata evolved and grew
during the course of his struggle, to take on its own dimensions in
the popular imagination after his death. The need to provide the 1991
Zapatista mobilisation with historical legitimacy made Zapata the

19

natural heir first of Hidalgo, Morelos and Juárez,[2] then of Cuauhtémoc[3] and the indigenous race, and then finally, at his death, gave him a mythic-religious lineage which associated him with the greatest liberators of any people, Moses and Jesus.[4]

As heir of Hidalgo and Morelos, Zapata represents the liberation of Mexicans from the Spanish, from the owners of the land. The memory of the victorious war for independence makes it possible to foresee a similar destiny for the Zapatista movement. The land and the power of political decision making must be recovered for the people. The siege of Cuautla in May 1911 (the first great Zapatista victory) is associated in popular memory with the siege of Cuautla in May 1812.[5] The social discourse of the peasants in 1911 incorporates the people's ethnic memory into the religious discourse, the hegemonic discourse which provided a hierarchical reordering for all else. In effect, they consider themselves to be the worthy heirs of Cuauhtémoc. The Zapatistas of 1911 see themselves as a people of oppressed Indians, who through a mythical metamorphosis become the chosen people of God, led by a liberator who is also a new Messiah: Zapata.[6] The ideological vicissitudes of the Zapatista cause admirably illustrate how popular movements appropriate a preexisting collective memory, together with the available ideologies and myths contained within this memory, and thus legitimate their present struggles.

According to the popular tale, on certain days the proud silhouette of Emiliano Zapata can be clearly discerned on the hilltops, and at times he can be seen galloping just above the crest of the sugar cane fields. As long as the struggle for land continues, Zapata will remain alive. His heirs visually evoke this glorious ancestry when they ride up on horseback, their chests crossed with cartridge belts.

This is the living memory of the old Zapatismo, but in Mexico another memory has also existed since the Revolution: the graphic memory to be found in the giant frescos which freely and didactically teach national history from the walls of public buildings. This is socially committed art in which the heroes and anti-heroes are symbolised: 'Less discursive than text or word, the visual world has its own place: it can ensure the permanence of a historical memory, it can permeate even everyday people, those who are passive or indifferent.'[7]

One of these didactic 'symbols' of national history, strange as it may seem, has been the horse. In Mexico the sign of a hero is not a gun but a horse, and the Mexican popular imagination has woven a series of representations around the horse, which have changed according to historical circumstance. It is a very interesting case of an anti-heroic symbol (the horse was introduced by the Spanish) whose meaning has been turned around by the people. The horse has been appropriated as a symbol of victorious strength at the service of the popular hero. One myth which crosses the American continents is that of the centaur, the man-on-horseback. [8] From the cowboy to the *gaucho*, from Paul Revere to Martin Fierro, the American hero rides tirelessly across the two continents. The horse in its warrior role is part of the myth of the hero. Even Don Quixote had to procure a Rosinante in order to fulfil his mission of justice. Mexican heroes prance their bronze horses in city parks, silent witnesses of a historical epoch. Siqueiros painted fiery horses as a symbol of popular strength: the horse as a symbol of a heroic people and not just of one hero. In his mural at the Palace of Cortés in Cuernavaca, Diego Rivera painted a white horse as the stand-in for Emiliano Zapata; the mythical white horse of all great generals. Furthermore, there is not a single film about the Mexican Revolution which does not include spectacular cavalry charges. Villistas and Zapatistas were exceptional horsemen. French historian Maurice Agulhon, ever sensitive to the workings of the historic imagination, writes:

> Without a doubt, the history of political images merits study, not just because of the adage that there is nothing which does not merit study, but because this theme is not necessarily situated at the margins of 'great' history. It has at times played a central role and at times a marginal one, always with the possibility of once again playing a fundamental role. [9]

Now if on the one hand the EZLN manages to recover certain visual symbols, it also manages to convert certain historical experiences into symbols. This is particularly true in the case of the Sovereign Revolutionary Convention which took place between October and November of 1914 in the city of Aguascalientes. This event served as the historical reference for the call in June 1994 for a meeting of civil society 'somewhere in Chiapas', a place they baptised Aguascalientes. That particular event had represented the most democratic moment in the course of the Mexican Revolution and perhaps for that reason, the one which had been most overlooked by historians. The Convention of 1914 signified the first experiment in true citizenship. It was a public discussion, an attempt to contain violence through dialogue among armed citizens, not between soldiers. Through their repeated insistence on the Convention as a meeting of armed citizens, the participants distanced themselves from the nineteenth century and its series of military coups. This insistence also contained the demand for social rights over and against a military asphyxiation of the newly emerging civil society.

Having ventured along the rugged paths of popular memory, let us now return to the present to observe how the memory of Zapata has transcended regional borders to become a national symbol.

The uses of national history

'Zapata vive, la lucha sigue' ('Zapata lives, the struggle continues') is one of the favourite slogans of the demonstrators who have marched time and again in Mexico City since the first day of January 1994. In the collective imagination, the popular heroes continue their earthly existence long after their bodily death.

Immortality constitutes an intrinsic characteristic of heroes, but it is necessary to explain why certain individuals are awarded the character of national heroes and, thus, of patriotic symbols, unquestionable by definition. In the case of Zapata, it is a question of explaining the apparent paradox of how a figure from early twentieth-century rural Mexico who struggled for 'land and liberty', continues at the end of this century to be a symbol of struggle for those who, in the best of cases, consider the countryside to be that which begins where buildings and asphalt end.

Zapata: the birth of a disputed myth

Historian Friedrich Katz noted that, of all the revolutionary leaders of the twentieth century, the only ones who continue to serve as heroic figures are Zapata and Villa. Lenin, Mao and Tito have all been knocked off their symbolic pedestals in recent years. In contrast, Zapata and Villa not only still hold their places, but the power of their example continues to multiply. They endure, along with Che Guevara, partly because they remained out of power. In other words, it is not enough to embrace popular causes, one must keep one's distance from that which dirties whoever touches it: power and its symbols.[10] There is nothing more illustrative of this than the photograph of Zapata and Villa seated in the presidential chair in 1914 after the peasant armies had taken Mexico City. On one side is a Villa mocking the circumstance and perhaps a little smug; on the other is Zapata, who is obviously ill at ease and wishing for an end to this part of the carnival in which the poor occupy the place of secular power. Maybe this, together with his horse and cartridge belts, explains why Marcos is identified with Zapata: a poet, he once said, would make a terrible head of government. Thus he took distance from that which some have attributed to him, an ambition for power. But there is more: Zapata and Villa were assassinated by the government. Zapata through an act of betrayal; Villa in his car, after the Revolution, while he lived in an hacienda in the north surrounded by his former soldiers turned farmers. Zapata was killed on horseback, cornered, in the midst of the starving communities of his origin. This is the symbol of someone who never compromised in the defence of the principles and values which had sustained his rebellion.

However, Zapata is not exclusively the symbolic patrimony of the popular sectors of Mexican society. If in the course of the Mexican Revolution, the peasants had been not only defeated but also conquered, wiped out as a social and political force, then today they would have a monopoly on Zapata, and he would not constitute a symbolic figure disputed by the state. However, the defeat of the peasant armies between 1915 and 1916 did not mark the end of their rebellion nor of peasant discontent.[11] They remained armed for many years more and constituted a threat, although dispersed, to that entity which called itself the 'Mexican State', but which, in reality, did not have a monopoly of violence, competing rather for the legitimacy of its use with *caciques*, *caudillos* and armed bands of peasants scattered throughout the territory – in short a mere project of state power which wished and proclaimed itself to be sovereign without truly being so. Ideologically, the state resolved the deficit of social and political cohesion through a post-mortem assemblage of figures who, while alive, had been rivals and bearers of irreconcilable social projects. In the 'official' imagination, Venustiano Carranza, who ordered the assassination of Zapata, appears alongside Zapata, while Zapata himself, the '*Caudillo del Sur*', stands next to Francisco Madero, the man who sent in the federal army to 'settle' the peasant rebellion. Similarly, ex-president Carlos Salinas announced the reform of Article 27 of the Constitution, which in practice promotes the legalisation of the *latifundio* (the large estates) and the elimination of the *ejido*,[12] with a portrait of Zapata as his background. His aeroplane was called *Emiliano Zapata*, his son was named Emiliano and his doctoral advisor was John Womack, the author of the leading history of Zapatismo. In this way, the most radical of the protagonists of the 1910 Revolution is given a sugar coating in an official gallery of heroes which makes it impossible to discern different political alternatives and at the same time converts heroes into the property of the State, or, to be more precise, of the victorious faction of the Revolution. Zapata is made into the co-founder and consecrator of the political regime, giving it his blessing and providing legitimacy to a project which is contrary to his own, especially since an end was declared to agrarian reform.

In the days following 1 January 1994, this symbol was reappropriated. Zapata was no longer to be shared with those in power, but rather was to become the symbol of the Chiapan rebels and all the social groups which were formed or reactivated. Demonstrators shouted: '*Si Zapata viviera, en la lucha estuviera*' ('If Zapata were alive, he were to be [sic] in the struggle'), in an obvious lack of concern for proper conjugation, since in the symbolic struggle all linguistic weapons are legitimate. And this battle appears to be won. From now on, the invocation of Zapata by the state will involve risks, and will surely be avoided. As has been observed by many analysts, after 1 January 1994 Salinas de Gortari changed the backdrop for his televised declarations, choosing instead a portrait which conveyed a precise meaning – that of Venustiano Carranza, the man who ordered Zapata's assassination.

But let us return to the initial question: why use the image of Zapata to champion a struggle at the close of the second millennium? Here, anthropologist Guillermo Bonfil's emphasis on Mexico's cultural duality is of particular use.[13] According to Bonfil, on the one hand there exists the 'deep Mexico' ('*México profundo*'), rooted in the pre-hispanic, and thus indigenous, past. On the other is the 'imaginary Mexico',[14] that of the myth of modernity, of the undefined progress which obliges us to follow the socio-technological path of the West, and thus leads to a homogenisation of cultural values and of the peoples who produce and re-create them. According to the perspective of this 'other' Mexico, the Indians should be converted to Western faith, if not eliminated. The attempt to annihilate this substratum of ancient civilisation has been taking place for a little more than half a millennium, without complete success, although 'de-Indianisation' (Bonfil's description) and the stigmatisation of indigenous identity have permeated the social fabric and the collective consciousness. The scheme of the two Mexicos, one deep and the other imaginary should not be understood in an essentialist or fundamentalist sense. The meaning of 'indigenous' in the twentieth century is not the same as before the Conquest, but resistance to subjugation by the imaginary Mexico wears an indigenous face. This will remain present within the realm of the oneiric as long as deep Mexico persists.

This brief digression helps us understand the meaning of the earth and the struggle for land.[15] Certainly, it is the earth which feeds us and for that reason appears as the mother of all who inhabit her. Life itself is organised around the land, and cultural production expresses this in many ways. The defence of the land is thus simultaneously the defence of the means which guarantee existence and of the cultural universe which the people control. The commercialisation of land implies the loss of both. However, as always occurs with symbols, the signified acquires autonomy in relationship to the signifier. The struggle for land acquires the value of a symbol of community resistance to being deprived of the capacity for self-determination, while simultaneously constituting the foundation for community sentiment, that which connects people.

Indigenous and peasant Mexico still fights for the land and against invasion by the large landowners in a continuous line of struggle which began with movements 500 years ago. The adoption of an indigenous face does not imply, therefore, the idealisation of the pre-hispanic past. We are not dealing with a glorification of the 'pure' Indian, but rather of the rebellious Indian – it is the Indian who resists and fights who represents the point of reference. The democratic values of the Chiapan communities which caused governmental representatives to be so intrigued by the EZLN are not part of the pre-hispanic world, but rather represent a political culture forged through resistance to enslavement and attempted annihilation. The result is the paradox of a society which must undergo transformation in order to endure.

Urban Mexico is not attempting to go 'back to nature', as are certain millenarian groups who assume an Indian disguise upon adopting the Zapatista symbol. Rather the Zapatista symbol becomes the general equivalent of rebellion. Zapata is the figure closest to end-of-the-century Mexico to assume the values of deep Mexico in opposition to the project of a culturally monolithic Mexico, that which Bonfil called 'imaginary'. But, how indigenous was Zapata himself or the Zapatistas of 1910? The photograph of Zapata mounted on horseback, dressed as a *charro*,[16] or that of his soldiers entering Mexico City in 1914 bearing a standard of the Virgin of Guadalupe, cast doubt on the stereotype of the Zapatista struggle as one seeking to restore the idyllic pre-Columbian world. What has happened is that the popular world has dressed itself as the indigenous to the point that the two have become synonymous, whether as object of praise or of insult on the part of the power elites who, since Independence, have always used European- and American-style clothing.

Zapata makes revolution through his actions, not just by taking up arms but by subverting capitalist tendencies in the Mexican countryside, specifically the proletarianisation of the peasantry and the expansion of the *latifundio* through the absorption of communal land.[17] Not only does he counteract these tendencies but he deepens the people's traditional structures. In effect, he puts into practice the cry of the Zapatista Revolution in March 1911: 'Down with the haciendas, long live the people.'

Throughout the Colonial period, indigenous communities enjoyed their own rights as 'Indian Republics' (*Repúblicas de indios*), under the direct protection of the Spanish crown, as a counterweight to the creole landholding aristocracy. In spite of independence, this long tradition of self-government survived and fed indigenous resistance against the commercialisation of land promoted by successive liberal administrations. These peoples ruled themselves through consultations and debates in assemblies where all the affairs relating to the community were discussed. The Zapatistas revived this practice which during the dictatorship of Porfirio Diaz had been subordinated to the decisions of political chiefs, who were district officials named by the governor. In 1914–15, after the defeat of Huerta, the Zapatistas dominated and administered their region: 'This represented the violent transfer of power which had been taking place throughout the whole territory of the state. Down below the political turmoil which brewed on at those upper levels, this was the true seat of Zapatista power.'[18] The power of the Zapatistas, based in local assemblies, entailed the protracted use of time, the slow pre-capitalist time of the peasantry. This step-by-step political advance stands in contrast to the alleged, modern, *good use* of time, i.e. 'time is money', according to which power is delegated to save time. Hence the surprise of governmental negotiators in 1995 when the EZLN insisted on the slow path of constant consultation with their community bases of support.

The artisans and workers of 1914 Mexico had looked on with mistrust and a certain degree of anti-clerical hilarity as the Catholic Zapatistas occupied the streets of the capital. Some historians explain how this cultural diversity or even incompatibility opened the way for a pact between the unions and the Carranza administration which led to the formation of workers' regiments to fight the peasant armies. Urban Mexico of the mid-1990s looks on with sympathy and solidarity, supports and organises to the tune of what is happening in rural and indigenous Mexico. It appears to be a historical revenge for the episodes of 1914 and 1915.

End-of-the-century national history and Zapatismo
The Zapatismo of the end of the twentieth century is characterised, just as was its homonym when the century began, as a local movement. As such, it is felt that it can be brought to an end, suffocated, through isolation, confinement within the territory from which it originated. Certainly the method of isolation has a great

advantage: it is politically less costly than a military solution. Contemporary historians have often assumed this stance, asserting that Zapatismo was a movement without a national perspective, limited to local or even parochial problems. In our day, the same analytical perspective is used. Chiapas is said to be a faraway province which, precisely because of its lack of integration with the nation's destiny, experiences the greatest degree of marginalisation and poverty. The Zapatista rebellion thus represents, in this view, a desperate effort to join the train of capitalist modernisation accelerated by NAFTA. To this extent, and only to this extent, the government and its official ideologues justify the uprising and declare themselves willing to collaborate in achieving such an objective. The movement would end in the construction of a few hospitals, schools and highways, and this would guarantee the fidelity of the beneficiary population to a political regime which for more than 75 years has supported itself on this kind of relationship between government and the governed: power yields a few concessions and in turn the people promise not to question the networks of patronage-maintained domination.

It is beyond the thematic bounds of this chapter to explain why the objectives and nature of the Zapatista movement surpass the merely provincial. It is clear, however, that the EZLN sought from the beginning to demonstrate that the historical past of the indigenous rebels is that shared by the nation as a whole. Thus the first Declaration of the Lacandon Jungle commences with a reference to history to demonstrate that the nation's history, the history which Mexican children are taught at school, is also their history.

In Mexico perhaps more than in any other country in the Americas, history represents a mandatory point of reference for political discourse, a language familiar to all. Political confrontations are ventilated through opposing historical interpretations. Thus, for example, nineteenth-century conservatives had a high esteem for the Colonial period, while their political adversaries emphasised their pre-hispanic heritage. In the same way, for some time after the 1910 Revolution, criticisms of the political regime were made by praising or disparaging the revolutionary movement.

In Mexico, the development of a community of national interests has been based less on the proclamation of abstract values than on a historical past which has been invented, imagined and reconstructed. The declarations of the EZLN consistently make reference to history, and, through its review, kinship is established with movements and figures from a more or less remote past while distance is taken from others. A principle of identity and of difference or antagonism maintained for more than 500 years was the EZLN's letter of presentation on 1 January 1994:

> We are the product of 500 years of struggles: first against slavery, in the War of Independence against Spain led by the insurgents, then to keep from being absorbed by U.S. expansionism, then to enact our Constitution and expel the French Empire from our land, then the Porfirio Diaz dictatorship prevented the just application of the Reform laws and the people rebelled, developing their own leadership, Villa and Zapata emerged, poor men like ourselves.[19]

The same historical continuity is to be found in the case of their oppressors:

> They are the same as those who opposed Hidalgo, Morelos, those who betrayed Vicente Guerrero; they are the same as those who sold more than half of our land to the foreign invaders; they are the same as those who brought in a European prince to govern us; they are the same as those who formed the dictatorship of Porfirio Diaz and his scientists; they are the same as those who opposed the expropriation of the country's petroleum; they are the same as those who massacred the railway workers in 1958 and the students in 1968; they are the same as those who today are taking everything, absolutely everything away from us.[20]

The historical references are familiar to all Mexicans: the Independence, the Reform, the Porfirio Diaz dictatorship, Zapata and Villa, etc. By declaring themselves to belong to the defeated, to the underdogs of Mexican history, and not to a separate group, as they have frequently been understood to be in a mixture of racist paternalism and social marginalisation, the indigenous people of Chiapas assert that they are part of the nation. However, that nation is not the nation of the winners, of those who have written history, but rather of those who have fought and lost:

> It has been mistakenly said that the Chiapan rebellion has a different time, that it does not respond to the national calendar. That's a lie: the speciality of the exploited of Chiapas is the same as that of the exploited in Durango, the Bajío or Veracruz: to fight and lose.[21]

Chiapas is not a world apart because its history is the same as that of other regions of Mexico, the sole difference being that in this south-eastern province the wrongs suffered and shared have been more violent.

From this perspective, the rewriting of history consists in recovering the non-official past that has almost been wiped from official textbooks, but not completely from collective memory. This means recovering the dignity of the defeated rebels, but above all demonstrating that after 500 years 'when our struggle against slavery began',[22] history can be reversed: the *wind from below* is no longer a response to the *wind from above* which for 500 years placed and erased the clouds in a sky it dominated, but rather an initiative whose meaning, says the EZLN, is the hope that dignity and rebellion will turn into freedom and dignity. In sum, there is an attempt to recover history in a way that signifies both continuity and rupture, or rather the hope of rupture.

In any case, what is at issue is a critical recovery of history and thus an appropriation[23] which confers it with original meaning. Zapata is obviously a hero *par excellence*. That does not keep one of the indigenous comandantes from bringing the struggle for land up to date: 'We want new laws for land distribution, which might differ from what Emiliano Zapata meant when he said that each peasant should be given a piece of land. We now understand things differently.'[24] Likewise, the idea of a convention was taken from an event during the Mexican Revolution, whose sense of public and democratic dialogue had been erased or distorted by official and semi-official historiography. Once again, the recovery of history does not represent a nostalgic apology, nor the desire to return to a better past, but rather it is accompanied by a critical reflection on 1914:

> [In 1914] there was a need for a political organisation, many such things later led to the defeat of the Division del Norte, to the surrounding of the Ejército Libertador del Sur,[25] the assassination of Zapata and then that of Villa. But this country is not the same as the Mexico of 1914, it is better, I believe, much better.[26]

Tradition, archaism and modernity

The EZLN's updating of the collective memory leads us to some considerations regarding the relationship between tradition and modernity.

Too often historians tend to place the concepts of tradition and modernity along a *continuum* from less to greater development. What for Max Weber served primarily as a typological, categorical distinction, tends to be made into a chronological, evolutionary and restrictive distinction. The problem with such an approach is that it does not allow us to understand or explain phenomena of inter-penetration and interweaving between the two poles. Both participate in a creative dynamic.

Tradition is the set of representations, images, knowledge and behaviours which a group or a society accept in the name of the necessary continuity between the past and the present; it is the reserve of symbols and behaviours which establish a bridge between our collective past and our collective present, forging the new identity which the modern world requires. Tradition is never the mere repetition of the past in the present: it selectively reconstructs and updates the past according to the requirements of the present.

For historians, tradition is generally considered to be synonymous with archaism and the re-establishment of times gone by. From the perspective of tradition, no one disagrees, everything remains the same. These are the holistic communities which are currently so in vogue. In this case, the only possibility of bringing tradition into the present lies in observing it as pure reminiscence and 'relic' (Thompson), as a mere harvest of curiosities.[27] Tradition thus could never become an ingredient in processes of change, but could only promote identical reproduction over time.

Western modernity has demanded that there be a break with tradition as a condition for progress. Historical progress, in this view, is possible only when people free themselves from their traditions and atavisms since change can only come from the outside world. According to Eric Hobsbawn[28] and Edward P. Thompson, one characteristic of traditions is their flexibility in facing new challenges. Thus it is erroneous to characterise traditions as the resource of those who, unaware of current changes, brandish weapons belonging to a bygone epoch. This fallacy corresponds to a conception which identifies traditions as surviving remnants, and thus considers them ineffective, mere residues of a past whose death is merely a matter of time. On the contrary, their flexibility allows them to be renewed to confront current problems. Thus history can produce the paradox noted by Thompson: 'We find ourselves in a traditional and rebellious culture.'[29] The paradox is resolved if we free ourselves from the negative connotation which historiographic revisionism has assigned to tradition. This same stance has caused John Womack's famous epigraph to be hailed as the tightest synthesis of the idea that tradition requires conformism: 'This is a book about peasants who did not want to change and for that reason made a revolution.'[30] On the contrary, Zapatismo drew upon a progressive tradition, which provided leverage for rebellion. In spite of being strongly rooted in networks of ancient sociability which coexisted with systems of traditional loyalties such as family ties or ties of *compadrazgo*, Zapatista tradition integrated elements of modernity such as formal schooling and the need to produce an economic surplus beyond mere self-sufficiency.[31] Likewise, the legalism of Zapatista actions were reflected in the publication of written manifestos; they accepted the agrarian commissions and, above all, after Madero's assassination in 1913, they sought the protection of urban intellectuals. This image is quite different from that of a traditional society which by definition is turned in upon itself.

In similar fashion, it is frequently asserted that the Zapatista peasants were unable to transcend the limits of the micro-regions where they lived. This is used to argue that it would be impossible for them to make proposals of national scope or to feel involved in what was happening beyond their territories. Such an interpretation is in fact based on a confusion between two concepts which must be taken separately: patriotism (in the strictest sense of the word) and nation-building, that is, the construction of the nation state.[32] The peasants opposed the latter project, which emanated from the power elites, since it entailed political centralisation and threatened their systems of values, ideas and institutional forms On numerous occasions, however, they came out in defence both of their *patria chica*, or home area, as well as their country (*patria*) *tout court*. To the degree that the elites understand patriotism only to be a process of nation-building, the peasants could be considered to be recalcitrant anti-patriots; their access to full citizenship would necessarily require that they abandon their 'backward' and 'anachronistic' attitudes. In fact, political centralisation, concomitant with the Porfirista modernisation of power, progressively annulled local or regional political autonomy. Many traditional collective actors were heirs to and defenders of liberalism, whose modernity no one in nineteenth-century Mexico could deny. The federalism of the liberals combined well with their ancestral forms of political organisation which they were not willing to renounce.

Even when capitalism manages to perforate 'the tunic of custom, separating men from their accustomed social matrix and transforming them into economic actors freed from former social commitments to family members or neighbours',[33] the peasants are not mere puppets. Contrary to what Womack's phrase seems to suggest, the Zapatista struggle did not represent blind and stubborn resistance to capitalism – it was not a regressive utopia. Rather, it was a defensive rebellion against the loss of their lands and the suppression of the political autonomy of their villages.[34] The peasants forced their rights to be respected, they struggled to conserve their tradition of solidarity against the onslaught of a barbaric capitalism: 'Collective work, democratic thinking, obedience to the will of the majority represent more than a tradition among the indigenous – they represent the only possibility for survival, resistance, dignity and rebellion.'[35]

They had accepted economic transformations but they could not permit their own disappearance as a political entity. From the time of the Conquest, they had always coexisted with the haciendas, they had even sold them their labour power; but they continued to exist as neighbouring villages with their own lands, customs and cultural world linked to the land. The EZLN can be understood as part of this new understanding of the binomial of tradition–modernity as being composed of complementary and non-exclusive realities.

Chiapans live and assume their modernity by drawing from the stock of available national symbols. They have clearly chosen to claim kinship with Mexico's agrarian movements, given that the history of Mexico is the history of the struggle for land. These symbols allow them to establish a continuity between the past and the present. Their identity must find support within a collective memory, that is, it must insert itself within a tradition which provides them with a sense of belonging and which locates them within a network of sociability and of national symbols. This insertion provides them with a strong social identification, incorporating the Chiapans into a national lineage of defenders of the land.

Conclusion

End-of-the-century Zapatismo has been surprising for many reasons: the attire of the combatants, the ethnic and class composition of its adherents, the revival of images, names and events which were on the verge of being forgotten by history. But it has also been surprising because it demonstrated that politics need not inexorably be the austere terrain which it had become for several centuries. In fact, Mexican society took more seriously those who spoke irreverently and humorously of politics than those who wear serious faces and sombre dress to speak in a political language that few listen to and fewer still believe. Credible revolutionary political discourse appeals to poetry and jokes, to plays on words and metaphor. In the face of this, the professional political class has been disarmed. Perhaps a few members of this class understand that their formal or informal education has not prepared them to dialogue with society, but rather only among themselves in a code indecipherable to the uninitiated. That did not seem to matter: politics was for politicians. But the majority have yet not realised this; they continue to speak in the same codes as before to an ever smaller audience, unsuccessfully attempting to maintain their monopoly on the space for public expression.

Zapatismo, on the other hand, has politicised the language of society and its symbolic and historic content. It has managed to de-ritualise politics and make fun of its sacred forms, portraying, for example, the state party as a tarantula, and its opponent as a beetle. It has revived popular heroes and has desanctified them, showing, for example, the face of Zapata with Marcos's smoking pipe sticking out of his mouth.[36] That which would have been considered sacrilegious is today considered fun. The revolution in general is no longer imagined according to the patterns of socialist realism, that is, as men and women stoically marching behind a red, waving flag towards a luminous future: rather it has become a sort of carnival. And the revolutionary experience as carnival is probably closer to the Mexicans than its identification with the anthems of the Red Army choir. Historian Friedrich Katz tells of a cycle of lectures which he gave in Vienna on the Mexican Revolution. He asked students to listen to Mexican revolutionary songs:

> I played recordings of the most famous songs: 'Adelita', 'Valentina' and 'La Cucaracha'. As they listened to the music and the words that I translated for them, their faces became more and more incredulous. For Austrians, as for most Europeans,[37] revolutionary songs should be vibrant marches, filled with expressions such as 'Liberty or Death', 'The shining future' ... But what they were hearing was about someone promising Adelita that he would buy her a new dress, someone who told Valentina that if they were going to kill him tomorrow they should go ahead and kill him today, and someone who linked the names of revolutionary heroes like Pancho Villa and Venustiano Carranza with cockroaches high on marijuana.[38]

Contrary to the biblical precept which prohibited Lot's wife from looking back, on pain of being turned into a pillar of salt, Zapatismo constantly looks back. It does so not just to denounce a past of exploitation and racism and to demonstrate that such problems still exist, but also to draw from that past the values of struggle and resistance. Unlike the bronze statues which symbolised the revolutionary march towards a radiant future, Zapatistas do not hide the fact that they look back in order to walk forward. They want and expect the future to be different from the past but they do not programme the future of everybody and for everybody in the style of the vanguard parties. The future will be built collectively and not just from the trenches of the Zapatistas.[39] Peoples do not make revolution knowing in advance what the future society will be like; they make revolution because they do not want to continue living in the old regime.[40] This is also the meaning of the Zapatista cry: '¡*Ya Basta*!', 'Enough!'

Marx asserted that in all revolutions the dead are resurrected for the 'purpose of glorifying the new struggles'.[41] He noted that, in contrast with bourgeois revolutions, 'social revolution of the nineteenth century [and we would add that this is truer still in the twentieth century] cannot draw its poetry from the past, but only from the future'.[42] We insist that the poetry of the EZLN is inspired by the past, from which it draws its identity, its symbols and its heroes. Could it be, then, that Zapatismo is nothing more than the last and very stale edition of eighteenth and early-nineteenth-century bourgeois revolutions? We feel that we have demonstrated that the Zapatista reference to the past does not express the desire to return to the past. The elements of the past which are incorporated into its poetry are those which are building the future. Might not 'collective work, democratic thinking and obedience to the will of the majority' represent not only a tradition and source of resistance but also the guidelines for the kind of society for which men and women have been fighting for more than 150 years? If that be so, might not indigenous communities be closer to the *poetry of the future* than white or whitened urban Mexico?

Notes

1. Hero of the Mexican Independence, assassinated in 1815, author of the pamphlet *Sentiments of the Nation*, in which he defends the rights of the people.
2. Hidalgo was one of the most important popular leaders of the war of Independence; Juárez was the only president of indigenous origin: he led the resistance of the Mexican nation against the invasion of the French army (1862–1867).
3. The last Aztec king, defender of Tenochtitlan, tortured and assassinated by Cortés.

4. These *corridos* are collected and analysed in the book by Catalina H. de Giménez, *Así cantaban la Revolución* [How they Sang the Revolution] (Mexico City: Grijalbo, 1991).

5. A heroic episode of the War of Independence, led by Morelos.

6. Marciano Silva, a participant in the exploits of the Zapatistas and the greatest bard of their feats, wrote, on the death of his leader in 1919 a *corrido* entitled *Duelo de Zapata* (Lament for Zapata) which ends thus: 'With their grief various families demonstrated their gratitude and affection for Zapata who, like Christ, had come to the end of his labour to free our people from oppression.'

7. Maurice Agulhon, *Histoire vagabonde* [Vagabond History] (Paris: Gallimard, 1988) p. 186.

8. 'If I could have chosen my condition, says Adriano at the end of his life, I would have chosen to be a centaur' (Marguerite Yourcenar, *Memoirs of Hadrian* (London: Secker & Warburg, 1955).

9. Agulhon, *Histoire*, p. 313.

10. A Villista *corrida* reflects well this popular sentiment: 'I am a soldier of Francisco Villa, of that man of world renown who, although he was seated on the chair, did not covet the presidency.'

11. See Armando Bartra, *Los herederos de Zapata. Movimientos campesinos posrevolucionarios en México. 1920–1980* [The heirs of Zapata. Post-revolutionary peasant movements in Mexico 1920–1980] (Mexico City: Era, 1985). The author shows that, in spite of the defeat of the peasants and the prophecies, from the right and from the left, of their imminent disappearance, they continued to be an active force throughout the twentieth century.

12. The *ejido* is property in land, belonging to the nation, which grants possession to the peasants. Before the constitutional reform, the *ejido*'s status prevented the sale of the land and compelled its free transfer along family lines or, where there were no heirs, through redistribution.

13. Guillermo Bonfil, *México Profundo. Una civilización negada* [Deep Mexico. A civilisation denied] (Mexico City: Grijalbo, 1989).

14. The adjective 'imaginary' is, nevertheless, ambiguous, since this Mexico is real too, just as the *deep* Mexico produces myths which feed the collective imagination.

15. Translator's note: The Spanish word 'tierra' means both 'land' and 'earth': both words have been used here to render the sense of the argument.

16. A *charro* was named after a special suit worn by hacienda owners in the nineteenth century and later by horsemen when they *caracole* or tame horses.

17. Alan Knight, 'La Revolución Mexicana: ¿burguesa, nacionalista o, simplemente una "gran rebelión"'['The Mexican Revolution: bourgeois, nationalist or simply a "great revolution"?'], *Cuadernos Políticos* No. 48 (octubre–diciembre 1986).

18. Adolfo Gilly, *La Revolución Interrumpida* [The Interrupted Revolution] (Mexico City: Era, 1994) p. 296.

19. 'Declaración de la Selva Lacandona. Hoy decimos ¡Basta!' (Declaration of the Lacandona Jungle, Today we say Enough!) in *La Palabra de los Armados de Verdad y Fuego. Entrevistas, cartas y comunicados del EZLN* [The Word of those Armed with Truth and Fire. Interviews, letters and communiqués of the EZLN] (Mexico City: Fuenteovejuna, 1994) p. 5.

20. EZLN, *La Palabra*, p. 5.

21. EZLN, *La Palabra*, p. 32.

22. EZLN, *La Palabra*, p. 53.

23. 'If it is necessary to know history, it is ... rather to liberate ourselves from it, to avoid having to obey it without knowing or to repeat it without wanting to.' Pierre Bourdieu, 'Sur les rapports entre la sociologie et l'histoire en Allemagne et en France' ('On the relation between sociology and history in Germany and in France'), *Actes de la Recherche en Sciences Sociales*, No. 106–107 (1995) p. 117.

24. EZLN, *La Palabra*, p. 131.

25. The names of the armies of Villa and Zapata, respectively.

26. EZLN, *La Palabra*, p. 227.

27. It is not by chance, indicates E.P. Thompson, that the study of customs has been appropriated by the more conservative historians, in the face of the indifference of left historians who prefer to 'occupy themselves on innovative and rationalising movements': 'Folclor, antropología e historia social', in *Historia Social y Antropología* (Social History and Anthropology) (Mexico City: Instituto Mora, 1994) p. 59.

28. Eric Hobsbawn, *Labouring Men. Studies in the history of labour* (London: Weidenfeld and Nicolson, 1964).

29. E.P. Thompson, 'Eighteenth Century English Society: Class struggle without class?', *Social History*, Vol. III, No. 2 (May 1978).

30. John Womack, *Zapata y la Revolución Mexicana* [Zapata and the Mexican Revolution] (Mexico City: Siglo XXI, 1969) p. xi. Very aptly, Armando Bartra amplified the original sentence: 'Perhaps

at first the peasants rebelled because they did not want to change, but, once they started, they decided to change everything': Bartra, *Los herederos de Zapata*, p. 15.

31. Zapata insisted on maintaining the haciendas as physical units of production, not as nuclei of social relations of exploitation. Their destruction was the work of Carranza, conceived as a means of defeating Zapata's army.

32. Alan Knight, 'Peasants into patriots: thoughts on the making of the Mexican nation', *Mexican Studies*, Vol. 10, No. 1 (Winter 1994).

33. Eric Wolf, *Peasant Wars in the 20th Century* (New York: Harper & Row, 1969) p. 379.

34. 'Not every economically conservative movement is socially reactionary, especially when material progress and the development of the forces of production do not signify a liberation, even partial, but a reinforcement of the old yoke through the addition of new chains' (Bartra, *Los herederos de Zapata*, p. 12). Bonfil follows a similar line of argument when he distinguishes the 'culture of resistance' from 'a sort of culture of immobility' (*México Profundo*, p. 191).

35. EZLN, *La Palabra*, p. 32.

36. The video *Consulta Nacional por la Paz y la Democracia* (National Consultation for Peace and Democracy) ends with this image.

37. Or people of any part of the world who have a conception of revolutions as events made possible by austere personalities like those who appear in statues.

38. Preface to Hans Werner Tobler, *La Revolución Mexicana. Transformación social y cambio político, 1876–1940* [The Mexican Revolution. Social Transformation and Political Change, 1876–1940] (Mexico City: Alianza, 1994) p. 9. In the demonstrations in support of Zapatismo, people dance to the rhythm of cha-cha-cha: 'Subversión, qué rica subversión' ('Subversion, lovely subversion').

39. This is the deeper sense of the organisation by EZLN in August 1994 of the National Democratic Convention.

40. One of the most lucid ideologues of the Revolution of 1910 captured this phenomenon very well: 'The truth is there is no revolution in the world that has been undertaken seeing in advance the means of reconstructing the social order or of substituting the regime which it is intended to destroy'. Luis Cabrera, 'La revolución es la revolución' ['Revolution is revolution'] (1911) in Eugenia Meyer, *Luis Cabrera: teórico y*

crítico de la revolución [Luis Cabrera: theoretician and critic of the revolution] (Mexico City: SEP/80 – Fondo de Cultura Económica, 1982) p. 73.

41. Karl Marx, *The 18th Brumaire of Louis Bonaparte. Marx Engels Collected Works*, Vol. 11 (London: Lawrence and Wishart, 1979) p. 105.

42. Marx, *The 18th Brumaire*, p. 106.

2

Chiapas and the Global Restructuring of Capital

Ana Esther Ceceña and Andrés Barreda

Chiapas: an illustration of the contradictions of capitalism

Chiapas has become one of the most vivid expressions of the contradictions of the Mexican economy, and to a large degree, of the world economy as well. Chiapas is such an extreme case, very diversified and rich: in Chiapas, the past and present become one, and all the polarisation and heterogeneity that capitalism has to offer are revealed to their fullest extent. In spite of the magic with which it surprises us at every turn, Chiapas is marked by contradictions that paint a gross picture of underdevelopment – contradictions that NAFTA and the process leading up to it have only served to accentuate.

In addition to becoming a prime example of political impunity, Chiapas depicts the most eloquent synthesis of Mexico's position in the new international division of labour. It is a classic case for viewing the impact of the global restructuring of capital on Mexico's prospects for development and its use of territory and productive resources. In Chiapas we can also catch a glimpse of the redefinition of hegemonies, geo-economic integration, and the rebuilding of a world-wide proletarian army.

Capitalist reorganisation has put into motion all the mechanisms within its reach in order to relaunch accumulation on a new technological basis, focused on electronically generated information. It seeks to subjugate labour to a new set of conditions and fortify the foundations of world hegemony and hierarchial power structures. In this context, Chiapas has become in many ways a strategic arena, but it also constitutes an objective limit to the general process of exploitation and lays bare the two faces of capitalist modernity – the relentless simultaneous generation of both wealth and poverty.

Historical link to the world market

Chiapas is an effervescent, captivating state, characterised by enormous geographic, cultural and economic wealth, but also by contrasts that transform it into a wellspring of contradictions. Chiapas extends from the coastal area to the high mountains, and its many rivers provide an abundant water supply. The land is fertile and bountiful, and the subsoil is rich in valuable resources. The geographical and biological diversity undoubtedly had some degree of influence on the cultural mosaic formed long ago by the many different branches within the Mayan culture. The ethnic groups we know today are a small, but representative sample of the previous diversity and richness of the cultures in this region. Some groups have been eliminated in the difficult struggle for survival, but those who have endured have maintained the rebellious spirit of their cultures, vindicating their rights from a national, citizen and class-based perspective.

Most of the region's productive activities are at the primary level: specifically, agriculture, livestock and forestry production. Each of these has its own specific work relationships as well as its particular impact on the environment and the population. From the time of the conquest, a wide variety of tropical products from Chiapas rapidly made their way into the world market. There was a high demand in European markets for cacao, cochineal and precious woods. These products were the basis for the semi-slave labour relations introduced into the region. Over the years the close ties to the world market have been maintained, although the products have varied somewhat according to the general development of the productive forces. Products such as rubber, wood and, more recently, coffee and oil have provided links to the rest of the world, and changes in labour relationships have taken place around these products.

The period of 1530 to 1550 is known for a surge in the region's cacao production, but also for the beginning of one of the most voracious, bloodthirsty regimes of indigenous exploitation. The customary cacao tributes required of the native inhabitants, which previous to the Spanish Conquest had been based on productive capacity as well as their own needs for food and commerce, were raised drastically during this period. As a result, cacao production spelled the death of many indigenous people.[1] Research on the period speaks to enormous profits derived from the sale of cacao on the national and European markets. These profits were gained, however, to the detriment of the native populations, in terms of their health, their numbers and their community life,[2] which was disrupted by the new demands and forms of subjugation.

There are records of the forced relocation of whole communities to meet the growing need for labour to produce cacao and other tropical goods. Increasing numbers were required to replace the many workers who died, to meet the rising demand on the market, and to satisfy the insatiable greed of commercial brokers.[3] There are also many references to plantations owned by friars, mainly in the Grijalba valley (in the region known as the Frailesca because of the religious order), where the native populations were cruelly and relentlessly exploited in the production of corn and beans.

In spite of the differences between the two types of agricultural regions, one producing tropical and the other basic crops, they had a common need for a temporary labour force. Thus both participated in creating a system of symbiotic equilibrium with the indigenous communities – a system that persists today. The fertility of the soil provided profits based on the differential rent value of the land. As long as there was land to be expropriated from the communities and a supply of cheap submissive labour – guaranteed by the force of racism and the exercise of power – it was not necessary to change methods of production.[4] The introduction of significant technological innovations is recent, and still very limited.

The plantation owners and agricultural entrepreneurs disrupted community life, partially incorporating the people into forced or wage labour in forms ranging from the *encomienda* and *repartimiento* (institutions used by the Spanish crown to subjugate indigenous peoples and take over their lands, forcing them to work for the benefit of colonial landlords) to forced recruitment[5] and the relatively recent free wage labour. The temporary character of the work and the fact that the abundant indigenous communities were defenceless created a system that alternately attracted and rejected workers. It relied on the community as a fundamental context for reproducing the labour force, but under very precarious conditions, so that people would be obliged to work.

With the disintegration of communities and the deterioration of their living conditions, the mechanisms for subjugating the labour force have become internalised over the years. This has been reinforced by the arrival on the scene of new capital which, not familiar with forced recruiting, has introduced wage labour, and has gradually exerted social pressure to generalise it beyond its own use. Thus workers who were previously recruited by *force* now work *voluntarily* since they cannot survive in what remains of their communities.

Indigenous communities have been gradually, and nearly always violently, expelled from the most fertile regions with the best climatic conditions, to the most inhospitable and least fertile ones, like the highland region known as Los Altos. They have very little land left, which is therefore densely populated. Their reproductive equilibrium has been broken and, to a large extent, their relationship with the environment as well.

Plantation owners do not have to concern themselves with the reproduction of the labour force as long as the communities exist, since work on the plantations is only seasonal. Thus, capital takes advantage of precapitalist forms of production and the relatively abundant population to guarantee a steady supply of labour with the necessary conditions: misery and willingness to submit to any humiliation or excess. The pay is not enough to survive on without the existence of the communities, where the primary responsibility for reproduction lies. However the communities are so precarious that they cannot survive by themselves either.

The incursions of big capital and the products through which the region is linked to the world market have contributed to the systematic impoverishment of the indigenous population. At the end of the nineteenth century the Mexican government promoted immigration from the United States and Germany in an attempt to promote technical development for the region's tropical crops, such as coffee. Since then, the agricultural growth of the Soconusco region, based not only on coffee but also bananas and other tropical goods, has increased the demand for labour. This has promoted population growth in the indigenous communities of Los Altos which have provided, until recently, the human support for these production units.

Throughout the whole period, the region has also been penetrated by exporters of precious woods. Although the exporters provide work for part of the indigenous population, they mostly accelerate the deterioration of the indigenous population's living conditions and environment. The introduction of modern equipment such as the chainsaw has brought significant benefits to this industry, but has also led to the devastation of three-quarters of the jungle in a period of only 30 years.

From the time of the Conquest, the perverse relationship between the plantations and communities, combined with the development of livestock production which has slowly taken over the lands, has been destroying the living space of the communities. As Antonio García de León writes:

'Land without men and men without land': this was the formula to define the tributary regions that served as reserve forces for great extensions of uninhabited, inhospitable land or expansive valleys where cattle were more abundant than men. Tribute-paying indigenous were confined to the steep terrain, while the open areas were left for the communities' secular enemy – cattle.[6]

Cattle raising has been one of the most buoyant activities of the Chiapas bourgeoisie. This economic activity has created a profoundly racist ruling group, whose interests are diametrically opposed to those of the communities. Livestock production requires very little labour, especially in this area where farming is extensive, but it constantly requires more land. Under these circumstances the communities represent more of an obstacle than an advantage. Racism, which in the case of the plantations serves basically to lower the cost of labour and reinforce its employment for the most inhuman tasks, is oriented here towards the extermination of the indigenous communities, which represent one of the limitations – although until now the least threatening one – for the expansion of grazing areas.[7]

Chiapas's economic profile has changed over the last two decades. There are new national and international interests seeking to take advantage of some of the other enormously rich natural resources such as oil, biodiversity and water. A very important change took place when the Mexican government decided to harness the region's hydraulic power and make it the principal source of electricity for petrochemical complexes in Tabasco and southern Veracruz. The flooding of land in the Grijalba River Basin forced peasants to abandon their homes, and while the dam construction brought employment to many workers, they were later left unemployed.

In addition to the 'traditional' economic contradictions in the region, there are now new ones resulting from pressures to modify the use of the territory and its population, which lead to a qualitative evaluation of the region that differs from the one that prevailed until recently, and to new demographic policies as well.

The maturing of capitalism in the region thus conditions the fate of a super-exploited, semi-salaried and surplus indigenous peasant population. Whether because of their own population growth, the precariousness of their agricultural activities, or the greediness of the cattle ranchers, they are being pushed from the highlands into the jungle region. There, once again, they will be forced to confront other ranchers and, above all, the Mexican state, which owns the region's vital strategic sources of wealth.

Today, it appears that the groundwork is being laid for a new incursion of major international capital in Chiapas. Thanks to the current neoliberal government's privatisation policies, powerful transnational firms are preparing to buy all of Mexico's strategic natural and technological resources, along with the public enterprises in charge of exploiting them. Such a process will no doubt reorganise all the previously existing forms of capital such as farming, ranching, etc.

Strategic resources

Mexico was the world's fifth largest oil producer in 1995 (2.86 million barrels of oil daily) and the eleventh largest producer of natural gas (3.625 billion cubic feet daily). The country holds eighth place in existing hydrocarbon reserves (54.1 billion barrels), but even more significant are its potential reserves, which PEMEX[8] calculates at 250 billion barrels, but which Jorge Diaz Serrano, a former PEMEX director, has estimated at more than 600 billion barrels.

Three-quarters of the current crude oil output is concentrated in what PEMEX calls the 'marine region' of the Gulf of Mexico. One-fifth comes from the 'southern region' (mainly from Tabasco and Chiapas) and only 3.6 per cent from the 'northern region'. The southern region provides half of Mexico's gas production, while the marine and northern regions produce 36.9 per cent and 13.2 per cent, respectively. It should be pointed out, however, that there is a difference between the geographical distribution of current gas and oil production and proven hydrocarbon reserves. Forty-seven per cent of these reserves are in the marine region (Mayan-type oil, mainly), while the southern region seems to have only 20 per cent (but it is Olmec-type oil) and the northern region has 33 per cent (mainly gas).[9]

According to prominent national and international geologists, most of the potential oil reserves in Mexico are located in six large deposits, the most important of which is in the Gulf of Mexico near Tabasco and Campeche. The oil fields in the north-east region of Chiapas should also be considered part of this deposit.[10] The second most important region appears to be just next to the first: known as the Petén Basin, it is situated to the east of Chiapas and the north of Guatemala and Belize. Up to now it has been maintained that the reserves in this second region are not comparable to the previously mentioned one, but both the abundance and quality of the oil already found make this a strategic spot for the world's major oil companies. The Chiapas portion of this deposit is called the Cuenca de la Sierra de Chiapas (Basin of the Chiapas Mountains),[11] and is the most recently discovered oil-producing region in Mexico.[12]

Precise figures are still lacking – since there is no reliable official information available – so we will mention here only some of the most significant examples of evidence for evaluating the strategic importance of oil in this region currently embroiled in conflict. For George Baker, an American specialist on the subject, the most important oil resources discovered on land are located in a new zone which he calls the 'Ocosingo field' located in the Lacandon Jungle near Guatemala.[13] There are also numerous scientific studies and direct testimonies which confirm the existence of a vast oil region,[14] in which one of the most notable areas is located in the heart of the Lacandon Jungle and identified by some Mexican geologists as the 'Anticlinal Bonampak'; another is the 'Comitan-Pedregal' area located in Los Altos and Las Cañadas. This information was confirmed when the Mexican press made public an official report addressed to the US Congress in which PEMEX officials mention 'recent discoveries of vast oil deposits in the state of Chiapas near Ocosingo'.[15] Official information that PEMEX has provided to the Mexican public rounds out the picture, acknowledging oil reserves in still another region, located in Simojovel Municipality, where 36 exploratory wells have been drilled over the past ten years (whereas in Ocosingo PEMEX only admits to drilling one dry well for the production of gas!).

The withholding of information and the recent plugging of exploratory wells in Ocosingo[16] is evidently linked to the neoliberal privatisation policies promoted by the government in recent years, aimed at selling off the country's strategic resources (oil, electricity, water, railroads, airlines, urban public transportation, highways, seaports and airports, telephone lines and telecommunications, etc.). The information has been withheld, no doubt, to cover up exploratory activities carried out by private national and international corporations (Comesa, Perforadata, Compañia Mexicana de Geofisica, the French company Général de Geophysique and the US company Western) between 1992 and 1993.[17]

Finally, the prospects for this region and its strategic importance become more evident if we recall the exploration and exploitation policies adopted by the large international oil companies during the last 20 years in neighbouring Guatemala.[18] First of all, the areas chosen by these companies for oil exploration are especially revealing. Curiously, the areas explored since the end of the 1970s are located along the Mexico–Guatemala border (covering approximately 60 per cent of it), and such exploration currently covers nearly half of the Petén Jungle. Secondly, it seems that several oil pipelines begin along the Usumacinta River section of the border, in addition to the one originally acknowledged by the Guatemalan government at the beginning of the 1980s, running from the Chixoy River section of the border to the refinery in Puerto de Santo Tomas de Castilla on the Caribbean.

In our opinion the oil transported in these pipelines could come from deposits located in both countries, such as the 'Anticlinal Bonampak' area mentioned earlier. The pipelines – which may be the result of a longstanding agreement between Guatemala and Belize – seem to run diagonally through the Petén Jungle in Guatemala and across Belize until they reach the Caribbean Sea. At any rate, what is publicly acknowledged is the network of highways built during the last ten years which begin from a number of points along the Guatemalan–Mexican border: an increasing flow of tanker trucks transporting oil has been observed along these roads.

For nearly 20 years now, both civilian and military governments in Guatemala have mysteriously and systematically veiled the exploitation of their energy resources. This fact, along with constant activities in the region of important international oil companies, lends support to researcher Jacobo Vargas Foronda's suspicions regarding the existence of a huge black market in oil, not mentioned in either national or international official reports. This suggests that the Chiapas region may be more important than is claimed in the above-mentioned geological studies. And, in the light of some of the recent scandals and revelations in the national press, we are led to wonder if Mexico may be involved in such a black market.[19]

Because of the strategic wealth involved, an inevitable question arises: in recent years, how have the neoliberal Mexican state and the big international oil companies viewed the tens of thousands of indigenous peasant farmers who have been migrating to the jungle and the Las Cañadas region since the 1950s in search of new agricultural lands? To answer this question, the following factors must be considered.

First, when an entire territory is devoted to oil production, it is impossible to predict the exact locations where drilling will be most productive, in spite of increasingly refined methods for geological detection. The final phase of exploration requires a great deal of drilling, much of which will be fruitless. Thus, the territory involved is enormous. The state of Tabasco, where practically all the rivers and agricultural and grazing lands have been ruined by contamination, offers the most poignant example of how Mexico tends to exploit its oil resources.

The current reorganisation of territories dedicated to oil production must, however, be viewed in relation to the type of administration (state or private) dictated by capitalism. We must remember that while the Mexican state has managed the country's oil exploitation for the past 60 years, this way of doing things is being questioned. The technocratic elite presently in power wants to pursue its own interests through a privatisation policy that involves selling off the country's strategic resources to big international corporations. The motives behind this dramatic change in economic policy must be sought not only in the structural indebtedness of the national economy, which has led to selling off some of the nation's principal sources of wealth, but also in the gradual but alarming and steady depletion of US oil reserves. This depletion is occurring just when a new surge in international oil prices appears likely to take place, as China and other Asian Pacific countries become incorporated on a massive scale in production for the world market.[20]

That is the only explanation for the persistent efforts on the part of private capital and the US government to promote the ideological and moral decomposition and corruption of entrepreneurs, politicians and intellectuals, with the aim of re-establishing monopolistic ownership of all nationalised oil industries (Arab, Russian, Latin American, etc.). Only in such a historical context can we begin to imagine the criminal motives behind the Mexican government's economic and political harassment of the indigenous population in the jungle over the last six or seven years. The intention must be to promote a migration process that will facilitate denationalising and privatising the oil deposits.

While oil is extremely important in strategic terms, the jungles of Chiapas have another resource that might prove to be of even greater importance in the near future: biodiversity. Biotechnology is at the forefront in the development of a new world-wide technological base, with genetic engineering as its strategic nucleus. The genetic codes of all living creatures are acquiring increased value as the new raw material at the service of this new technology, which is based on the identification and matching of existing genes in order to artificially design functions in living beings. This technical revolution will probably provide major innovations in the production of means of subsistence (agricultural and industrialised foodstuffs as well as medicines), and may have applications in other branches of production, including microelectronics, as well. Therefore there is a growing appreciation of the diversity of biological species as a genetic bank from which billions of genes may be extracted to design and produce new anatomical and physiological properties in living things. This means not only new technical instruments and new items for consumption, but also a whole new global pattern of raw materials.

For this reason, the regions of the planet with the greatest biodiversity are gaining strategic importance today. As of yet, there are no clear criteria for evaluating biodiversity or imagining how it will be used in industry. None the less, government research departments in the United States, Canada and the European Union, as well as those in the World Bank, the International Monetary Fund and big transnational corporations, have painstakingly financed environmental organisations dedicated to the research and conservation of these areas, perhaps as the first step toward the privatisation processes that will take place in the near future.

Mexico is currently considered to be the third most biodiverse country in the world; most of this biodiversity is concentrated in the jungle areas in the south-east part of the country, especially in the state of Chiapas.[21] The Lacandon Jungle, which represents only 0.16 per cent of national territory, actually contains more than 20 per cent of this biodiversity. Overall, Mexico has an immense variety of plants and animals and contains each of the 32 different ecosystems identified for the planet as a whole. In spite of terrible devastation, the Las Cañadas region, which borders on the Lacandon Jungle, contains a third of these ecosystems. This region is located right between the Nearctic and Neotropical floral domains. Transnational capital is interested in privatising not only the richest part of the jungle, known as the Montes Azules biological reserve, but also the neighbouring Las Cañadas region, which is considered by biologists as a buffer zone necessary to the survival of the Montes Azules region. This zone happens to be precisely where the Zapatistas' strength comes from.

Chiapas has the country's heaviest rainfall and also receives the water flow from much of Guatemala's rainfall. It is not only Mexico's primary hydroelectric producer (55 per cent), but is also the principal region where water reserves can be found. Because of the many large, swift rivers in Chiapas and its uneven terrain, even more energy could be generated. The Usumacinta River system, which has more volume than any in the country and marks the border with Guatemala, is included in binational projects for irrigation and for electricity production.[22] Proposed projects for the Grijalba River (the longest in Chiapas) would provide the production of 20,982 gWh/year, compared to the current 13,099.

Most of the 20 dams programmed for increasing the hydroelectric capacity of the Usumacinta River are located right in the Las Cañadas region. These dams would increase output by 9,947 gWh/year, which is 53.8 per cent of the overall potential of the Usumacinta system and 22 per cent of the entire state's possible future output. This presents additional elements of conflict and pressure on the area's indigenous groups, who settled there about 30 years ago after being displaced either from Los Altos or the southern part of the state.

Racism at the core of social contradictions

In 1524, when Pedro Alvarado and his troops arrived in this natural paradise called Chiapas, there began a long and painful history of resistance and submission. It took more than a century for the *encomenderos* to make slaves of the Mayan princes who survived the battles. Chiapas was one of the hardest places to conquer. The strong and determined resistance was expressed in a series of rebellions that have changed in character over time. The territorial struggle against foreign invaders turned into class conflicts with farmers and landgrabbers who benefited from the agreements on colonisation and the alienation of communal lands which date from the times of Benito Juárez and Porfirio Díaz.

Through this historical process the indigenous people of Chiapas have been defined as the natural labour force for agriculture and ranching, and at the same time, as the constant offenders who have forced landowners to repeatedly reassert themselves as the authentic *coletos*,[23] and to postulate their racial and cultural superiority.[24] For 500 years, racism has provided justification for the extreme social contrasts that continue to exist, attributing the misery and ignorance forced upon the indigenous populations to 'natural' conditions or cultural differences, when, in reality, their illiteracy and apparent inability to assimilate alien cultural patterns, or to further develop their own culture, is in fact part of a deliberate policy of segregation carefully promoted in Chiapas to keep this part of the population as a captive labour force.

Racism has become an economic factor used to deny the indigenous peoples their rights and to validate their inferiority.[25] By this means, it has been possible to reject systematically their litigations for land, and to gain acceptance for the brutal methods used to transform them into a seasonal labour force.

The *encomienda* and *repartimiento*, as well as the various methods of forced collaboration, all developed by the Church in the past, are like a cloud hanging over the present-day mechanism of forced recruitment and the different types of slavery which continue to be practised today, although in a more limited, camouflaged way.

All the land in Chiapas is so rich in resources that the limits of indigenous territories have been ill-defined and at times have reflected contradictions. Since the 1950s, the frictions generated by the appropriation of the best lands and their conversion into pasture by the large landowners have been resolved by opening the jungle up to colonisation. Sizeable groups of landless indigenous people migrated to Las Cañadas and the Lacandon Jungle. Today, interest in the biological reserves, the oil and the water of the jungle (as was previously the case with precious woods) has created new risks and tensions for these same indigenous communities. In some instances there has been a deliberate policy to allow indigenous peoples to clear areas and then force them to move on to other regions. In other cases, the incipient development of the productive forces meant that the people were unable to exploit the resources or, as in the case of the biological reserve, they lacked the know-how.

Force and racism have been the arms used to uproot the indigenous communities – or, more precisely, the use of force justified by racism and contempt.

The nature of these communities has been the subject of much discussion. The Consejo Nacional de Población (National Population Bureau) classifies them as marginalised communities, and therefore expelled or on the outside. That is to say, their impoverishment is explained by the fact that they remain outside the country's and their own region's development process. However, while these communities do indeed lack the most basic services, they are part of the productive structure of Chiapas and constitute one of its most important foundations. So, while they may be on the outside in terms of public services and the benefits of capitalist development, they are not on the outside with respect to the accumulation of capital in Chiapas. This process systematically uses and expels them because it cannot do without them.

It cannot be easily assumed that their supposed marginalisation is a result of cultural differences, generated by a particular world vision that prevents them from assimilating modern Western culture. That argument places the responsibility on indigenous people and ignores the contradictory mechanisms which, throughout history, have included them productively but excluded them socially. These mechanisms create conditions which maintain a labour force available for capitalist exploitation: a rudimentary form of exploitation, however, in which there is little development of productive forces, so that reproduction of the labour force takes place mainly within the domestic economy, based on limited self-sustained subsistence. Actually, the mestizo culture has grown at the expense of the indigenous one and has no interest in recuperating it. To do so would deny their own superior authority over natural and human resources and would limit their possibilities for exploitation, thus affecting their profit margins. Thus, their predatory spirit reaches also into the cultural realm.

In these 500 years of mestizo domination, indigenous peoples have become an organic labour force for Chiapas's particular style of capitalist development. It is not because they are indigenous that they have been bestowed with this privilege, but rather because a contradictory culture has been established in the region – one that maintains the class structure by means of racism. It is not because they are indigenous that these groups suffer poverty and apparent marginalisation, but rather due to their class position within the regional economic structure and the level of development of the productive forces.

But, how is the poverty of the indigenous communities related to the capitalist forces of production? To what extent do they truly constitute the proletariat that corresponds to such a level of development? Can the indigenous communities really offer that kind of labour force?

Certainly, indigenous communities share with other rural communities the isolation imposed by capitalist development and the confinement to a subsistence economy based on their relationship to the environment. The concrete elements of subsistence are always delimited by the particular characteristics of the local ecosystem. When the channels for exchange with the rest of the world are interrupted and the ecological balance is broken, as occurred with the conquest of Mexico, not only is the relationship between humans and nature altered, but the environment itself suffers changes, depending on the magnitude of the impact. In the case of Chiapas, however, it is the development of specifically capitalist relations of exploitation that has provoked the greatest changes.

Previously, even though the communities' subsistence was starting to become precarious, they still had the foundations and organisation required for their own reproduction.[26] Capitalism in Chiapas was established from the outset on the basis of the land and its prosperity. In other words, its development has been primarily extensive, and productive forces have therefore not been developed. It is, by definition, usurping, monopolising and predatory. Profits are derived from appropriating as many resources as possible, and appropriation is basically by means of force. It is not even a matter of competing with other capitals, but rather of dismantling prior modes of production to then cast their technological and human resources on the market. When profits are determined by external conditions – which cannot yet be produced by capital – such as the fertility of the land, weather modifications, etc., they are more dependent on quantity than quality. In this case, the more land, the closer it is located to water sources, and the more accessible it is – the better and more abundant the production. In the same way, the more workers there are, the less they are paid and the easier they are to replace. The possibility for reducing costs, therefore, is not based on increasing productivity but rather on what can be seized from one place or another, from an advantageous position of strength. In this situation, any opportunity to shore up or validate relationships based on power serves to enhance profits.

These are the particular circumstances that distinguish the indigenous population from other rural populations. Capitalism in Chiapas has inherited from colonial times the sanctioning for extortion, super-exploitation and devastation of the native peoples in these lands. These peoples are integrated into the society only as a dominated, scorned class. Thus, racism acquires its modern characteristics as it becomes part of the process of accumulation of capital in Chiapas.

In this situation, capital in Chiapas does not particularly concern itself with the issue of reproducing the labour force. This attitude in relation to indigenous communities sets the tone for social policies at both the state and federal levels. The state of Chiapas has the highest degree of marginalisation in the country. The indigenous zones have the worst overcrowding conditions in the state, and among the worst in the country.

Of the 112 municipalities in Chiapas, 38 are classified as highly marginalised areas. Among the latter, 30 have a primarily indigenous population and are located in the Los Altos region or in municipalities surrounding the part of the northern zone where oil is found. The rest are located in the highest mountain region, where inhabitants are impoverished, but not indigenous. Nevertheless, 79 per cent of the zone characterised by a high degree of marginalisation includes municipalities where more than 75 per cent of inhabitants are indigenous.

More than half the population in this zone is illiterate. Of the rest, 83 per cent did not even complete primary school. About half the population lives in housing with no sewage systems, toilets, or running water. In a state which produces half the electricity consumed by the entire country, only about half the inhabitants have electricity in their homes. More than 80 per cent live in overcrowded conditions in dwellings with dirt floors. The income received by 90 per cent is less than two minimum wages (as established in Mexico), an amount which is officially used as a parameter in assessing living conditions: 'monetary incomes of up to two minimum wages are insufficient for covering the basic needs of households'.[27]

A substantial percentage of deaths in indigenous regions are caused by illnesses related to malnutrition. The main cause of death is registered as gastrointestinal infections or diarrhoea, which are provoked by unhealthy living conditions, eating unsafe food, insufficient nutritional intake, or the classic syndrome of malnutrition.[28] Many other deaths are caused by congenital malformations, many of which are related to pregnant women's poor nutrition, or by respiratory illnesses which are, once again, closely linked to poverty.

The climate in the areas occupied by the indigenous communities is cold, very rainy and generally inclement. When the communities have been uprooted from their homes, it is often difficult for them to adapt to their new environments. Inhabitants from the coastal plains along the Gulf have been resettled in the jungle region. Communities from the Los Altos highland region have suffered a similar fate, or have been displaced towards the jungle, settling in the Las Cañadas region, as we have previously mentioned. These are difficult changes for populations whose only defence is their knowledge of their environment and the establishment of a harmonious balance with that environment. Thus, they are often left without this important link and furthermore, without the possibility of incorporating new technologies that would allow them to develop favourable living conditions in these areas. As a result, they suffer more illnesses, and because they are unfamiliar with their new environments, they are unable to use their traditional healing methods. In summary, they no longer have adequate knowledge of their living environment and have lost any control over it.

Many of the respiratory illnesses suffered are a result of this lack of adaptation to the environment or the lack of resources for protection from the environment, such as construction materials for adequate housing to shelter them from the rain and cold.

Thus, the causes of death among children and the elderly are related to malnutrition, unhealthy living conditions and the lack of protection from inclement weather. However, beginning in 1990, accidents became the second highest cause of death, reaching a level of incidence nearly as high as that of infectious intestinal illnesses.

This second cause of death, however, affects those in the productive age range, between 15 and 50 years of age. The incidence is so high that it claims more deaths than pulmonary tuberculosis,[29] an illness causing more deaths in Chiapas than anywhere else in the country.[30] This particular combination of causes of death is provoked by the process of ruthless accumulation of capital in the region.

These causes of death are also undoubtedly related to the precariousness and violence that characterises the struggle for survival in Chiapas. Through the deliberate, harmful use of racism, poverty is concentrated and exacerbated in order to sustain a desired level of productive output. In addition, the federal health authorities have treated this situation with disdain and neglect. In 1990 measles caused more than a thousand deaths in Chiapas. This is an extremely serious matter, if one considers that this illness can be prevented or eradicated with an adequate vaccination programme. While such programmes are deficient in many areas of the country, they are nearly non-existent in Chiapas. The infant mortality rate in Chiapas is 51.7 deaths per 100,000 inhabitants, compared to 34.8 for the country overall.

Consistent with this panorama – of which we have described only some of the most significant factors – we find that while the fertility rate in Chiapas is the highest in the country (4.6 per cent compared to 3.2 per cent nationwide), the high death rate (6.73 per cent compared to 5.18 per cent nationwide) means that any population growth is limited.

Economic contradictions and the conflict

Contemporary capitalist restructuring is being built upon a more developed technological base, and this has modified the relationship between capital and the environment, redefining the universe of raw materials and its corresponding hierarchies. Raw materials that were not even previously considered are now being incorporated into the nucleus of the strategic needs of world capitalist reproduction, others have acquired new dimensions, and still others have lost relative importance. All of this is taking place in accordance with the new technological fields and initiatives which have entered into practice, and with the new articulation of world capitalism.

As the new technological pattern redefines the areas of valorisation, this also brings significant modifications in social relations. This is especially the case in situations where the impossibility of separating labour power from the worker becomes complicated by the fact that the worker is, in a way, part of what is being appropriated, such as in the case of ecosystems. The rearticulation of the world-wide process of accumulation upsets the labour market and brings into question the quantitative and qualitative configuration – active and reserve; industrial, rural and intellectual – of the world proletarian army.

During periods of crisis and restructuring of the conditions for accumulating capital, there is in effect a purging which consists of eliminating inefficient capitals which have become an obstacle to the continuation of the general process. This purging drives capital to seek the destruction of the labour force which, during these times characterised by sweeping exclusions, appears to be a dysfunctional surplus since it is more than what is necessary to carry out the tasks of the industrial reserve 'army' (reducing wages and encouraging a more docile labour force). At the same time, however, this contributes to the increasing political risks confronting capital.

The process of capital accumulation in Chiapas appears to have entered into contradiction with the accumulation of international capital, as it has reached the limits of devastation (of the labour force and of nature). Any further ravaging of the natural reserves in Chiapas could be irreversible and could eliminate the potential for future genetic or medical exploitation. However, international capital itself is seeking to exploit the area's oil fields, and this will necessarily lead to future destruction of the jungle. As well, the despoiling suffered by the population of Chiapas cannot be carried any further because it has already passed biological and humanitarian limits and, in fact, has reached such heights as to provoke a conflict which – although not defined as a class conflict – threatens the whole of capital.

The capitalist exploitation of biodiversity aimed at developing the productive forces and at appropriating and exerting control over nature are currently the basis for new possibilities for expanding capital. Thus biodiversity is among the new resources making it possible to break through obstacles and extend the limits for the historical end of this mode of production. The global restructuring of capitalist society is founded on a new technological initiative which, while it presents electronically generated information as its visible core, seeks to use that information to appropriate the essence of life and creation more directly.[31] The current potential for genetic engineering is nearly infinite, but not yet well defined. Therefore, the needs for raw materials still cover a broad spectrum.

Oil, on the other hand, is an indispensable and exhaustible commodity. According to experts' estimates, there are enough proven reserves to meet world demand only until the year 2030. But the deposits described in Chiapas represent the possibility of expanding that limit. Since this area is within the region covered by the North American Free Trade Agreement, they would clearly enhance the hegemonic control of the United States. However, if these resources are exploited, it will spell the destruction of the indigenous population of Chiapas and the area's environmental wealth.

The natural resources of Chiapas which make it one of the world's paradises, characterised by unparalleled conditions for the development of life, also turn this region paradoxically into one of the most inhospitable environments for human life. The great variety of cultures represented in this region should, without a doubt, be considered part of its great wealth. But, according to government figures, the indigenous population of Chiapas no longer accounts for even a third of the total population (27.6 per cent)[32] and indigenous territories have been gradually reduced by a variety of economic activities and by the violence of racism.

Chiapas's recent history, which still includes some forms of forced labour, demonstrates the persistence of policies based on dispossession – although now with a modern face. Land continues to be the primary productive force for the type of activities carried out in this zone, including agriculture, cattle ranching, oil drilling and biotic exploitation.

This fact, together with the objective limits of territorial expansion, presents a difficult situation not only for the indigenous and peasant populations, but also for ranchers and the local dominant class who find themselves confronted by a world-wide process of valorisation which defines them as inefficient and encourages them to exploit even more brutally the productive forces at their disposal: land and the peasants, most of whom are indigenous.

The existing contradiction between the accumulation of capital and the reproduction of labour power refers to the historical limit of the extensive development of exploitation. Capitalism has resolved this problem through technological development, which has the effect of reducing the value of commodities in general, including that of labour power. None the less, this general tendency of capitalist development is combined, in any given moment or space, with the particular way in which the relationship between capital and wage-labour is established, as well as the articulation – also contradictory – of the capitalist area as a whole. The particular relationship with the indigenous population, which we have discussed here, has made capitalism in Chiapas an easy and bloody process: easy, because it has taken what the land has to offer, and bloody, because the only way to reduce costs is by cutting wages and dispossessing the people of their lands.

Chiapas and its indigenous population are currently in the midst of a dispute over land and resources – with the population contradictorily included as part of the latter category. The issues of continuity and readaptation of the accumulation of capital in this region are not resolved, and the violence with which they have been posed is the cause of an immense social conflict, which is pointing to the limits of capitalist development itself. Many conflicting signs are revealing the different prospects for reordering the exploitation or use of resources and redefining the relationship with indigenous communities. The general tendency of capitalist development, which guides large-scale movements and the definition of technical and material conditions, and the bases for organisation and domination, does not seem to coincide with the intentions of the local capitalists who were previously the main link with the world market and for whom NAFTA and the process leading up to it have created serious problems.

Even for international capital there is a conflict between its most immediate needs and the building of alternatives for the future. While the most immediate needs make it necessary to increase the devastation of material and human resources in the region in order to extract the wealth contained in the subsoil as rapidly as possible, the prospects for the future are dependent on preserving the environment and the land's inhabitants.

Something similar happens among the local entrepreneurs and pillagers. There are conflicts of interest over the methods for using the land and its resources between ranchers, farmers, and traffickers of wood and exotic animals, etc.

The conflict in Chiapas expresses the contradiction between two modalities of accumulating capital, between two technological eras, each with their particular way of organising the world and its resources. It is much more than a conflict over new political relationships between indigenous populations and the *caciques* or local powerful landowners. It is much more than a problem regarding effective land reform. In Chiapas – a region of strategic economic and geopolitical importance – what is at stake is the rearranging of the material bases of US hegemony in the world. But also involved is the capacity of the population to rebel against the capitalist depredation of human beings and to open the way for liberating alternatives. Therefore, it is not an issue of land, but of territoriality and sovereignty. It is not an issue of whether policies are more or less generous in public spending, but rather an issue of self-determination, democracy and justice. It is a conflict that questions the polarising, predatory way in which capitalism develops in the world. It questions the expansion of poverty which inevitably accompanies the technological perfection of capital and the establishment of its domain throughout the world.

Since labour power cannot be dissociated from the worker, it becomes a subject in the process and is thus able to modify it. The surplus population that confronts capital can be understood from two points of view: numerical and political. Chiapas is the expression of the synthesis of these two contradictory processes, and at the same time, it is the first organised response to the purging of capital. In any case the question that must be asked is: if there is truly a surplus population, who are the excess ones? At least two opposing viewpoints will be found.

Notes

1. This problem is repeatedly referred to in a study by Antonio García de León, *Resistencia y utopía. Memorial de agravios y cronica de revueltas y profecias acaecidas en la provincia de Chiapas durante los ultimos quinientos años de su historia* (Mexico City: Era, 1985), 2 volumes, and another by Nélida Bonaccorsi, *El trabajo indígena en Chiapas, siglo XVI (Los Altos y Soconusco)* (Mexico City: UNAM-CIHMECH, 1990) p. 37, both of which are based on information from codices and contemporary documents. Nélida Bonaccorsi states: 'In the last decades of the sixteenth century there is a reduction in the native population due to diseases introduced by the Spaniards and to excessive work. Documents show that in 1576, one thousand eight hundred indigenous persons had to pay a tribute of six hundred and fifty cargas [a unit of measure equal to about 50 pounds], and in 1609, two thousand indigenous persons paid one thousand one hundred and fifty-seven cargas.'

2. '... the tributes reached impossible proportions: from 400/500 cargas in 1573, they rose to 1,133 cargas in 1613. According to the British pirate John Chilton, the Soconusco exported 8,000 cargas in 1570,' says Antonio García de León, *Resistencia y utopía*, p. 58. According to Nélida Bonaccorsi in *El trabajo indígena*, p. 29, 'The tributes were not only taken from the communities' surplus production. On the contrary, they were forced to pay an amount that notably changed production methods. The tributes became impossible to fulfill due to the ongoing decrease

in population provoked by epidemics, excessive work, wars, etc., and this seriously affected community life.'

3. 'Many Indians from Los Altos [the highland region] of Chiapas were forced to go to Soconusco, where labour was needed, in order to earn cacao beans or silver coins to pay their local tributes. Many people died from the long journey, the climatic change or the coastal diseases, so the shortage of labour was constant,' Bonaccorsi, *El trabajo indígena*, p. 37.

4. In our opinion, the best-known studies on racism have left out its economic dimension, which constitutes one of its most solid explanations. In the case of Chiapas, racism has become the principal element of justification for the plunder, subjugation and extermination of the autochthonous populations. The cultural refinement of the Mayan groups that lived in the area was notably superior to that of their conquerors, who used racism as an ideological defence for the impunity and bestiality with which their weapons imposed the domination of European capitalism. We believe that the regime of cruel and predatory exploitation that continues to exist today in Chiapas is only possible through the justifying force of racism. This problem is discussed in Ana Esther Ceceña and Andrés Barreda, 'Chiapas y sus recursos estrategicos', in *Chiapas*, No. 1, (Mexico City: ERA, 1995).

5. Forced recruitment was the mechanism used by plantation owners to recruit enough workers during planting and harvesting. For this purpose the owners kept a man with two or three helpers close to the indigenous communities: '...they were in charge of recruiting the temporary workers and taking them back and forth; sometimes they had to catch the deserters, but there were officials and the public forces to help with this task,' Armando Bartra, 'Modernidad, globalización y trabajo forzado,' in *Chiapas*, No. 1 (Mexico: ERA, 1995) p. 47.

6. García de León, *Resistencia y utopía*, Vol. 1 (1985), p. 54.

7. The following quotation gives an idea of the indigenous peoples' living conditions and the treatment they received from plantation owners: 'During the early years of Spanish domination in Soconusco, a slave was worth two pesos in gold, pigs were sold for twenty gold pesos each and a carga of cacao was worth ten gold pesos. The *encomenderos* in this region abusively used indigenous slave labour for mass production of cacao.' Nélida Bonaccorsi, *El trabajo indígena*, p. 21.

8. Mexico was the first peripheral country to claim national sovereignty over its oil reserves (1938). Thus, petroleum

production and refining have been carried out by Petroleos Mexicanos (PEMEX), a state-owned enterprise that also progressively took charge of exploration and petrochemical production. Today, PEMEX is among the world's top ten oil companies even though, unlike its international competitors, it has subsidised Mexico's industrialisation for over 50 years.

9.   Unfortunately the Mexican government does not provide official information on regions where major oil reserves are likely to be found. PEMEX classifies three types of oil according to its viscosity: Olmec is the lightest and thus commands the best price on the international market; Mayan is the heaviest and has the lowest price; Isthmus is really a mixture of the other two.

10. This basin in the Southeast, better known as Chiapas-Tabasco, is today the major producing zone (2,414,379 barrels per day, 1992) and has 62 per cent of the country's verified reserves.

11. In *Oil and Gas Journal*, 1 June 1992.

12. The discovery of the Nazaret field, located near Altamirano, was reported in 1986. In 1990 another important oil field was discovered near the Lacantun River.

13. In 'Oil Deposits in the South-east of Mexico', a paper presented by Baker, of UCLA, on 4 September 1991 at the UNAM (Universidad Nacional Autónoma de México) School of Engineering.

14. See also James A. Peterson's references to various small oil fields trapped under anticlinal salt domes in '*Petroleum geology and resources of south eastern Mexico, northern Guatemala and Belize*', a paper presented at the American Association of Petroleum Geologists (AAPG) Annual Convention, 15–18 June 1986, Atlanta, Georgia.

15. Miguel Angel Sanchez, 'En Chiapas, ricos yacimientos petroliferos' [Rich oil deposits in Chiapas], *El Financiero*, 17 January 1995.

16. Fabio Barbosa, 'Pozos petroleros en la selva Lacandona', *Memoria*, No. 50 (Mexico City: Centro de Estudios del Movimiento Obrero) January 1993.

17. Captain Julian of the EZLN (in *La Jornada*, 24 February 1995) speaks of the precise location of important oil and gas reserves in the Las Cañadas area, as well as in the region bordering on the Montes Azules biological reserve. His testimony is particularly interesting since he refers to regions not even reported as important by the geologists just mentioned. This gives us an idea of the immense difference which may exist between the geological reports to which we as university researchers have

access, and the comprehensive but secret reports provided to the oil companies.

18. Jacobo Vargas Foronda, in his important study, *Guatemala: sus recursos naturales, el militarismo y el imperialismo* (Mexico: Claves Latinoamericanas, 1984), mentions the following companies: Getty Oil Guatemala Inc.; Texaco Exploration Guatemala; Amoco Guatemala Petroleum Company; Texas Eastern Guatemala Inc.; Monsanto Oil Company of Guatemala; Elf Aquitaine Guatemala; Hispanica de Petroleos (Hispanoil); Petrobras Internacional, S.A. (Braspetro); Basic Resources International; Halliburton Company; Shenandoah Guatemala Inc.; Saga Petroleum, S.A.; Petrolera Internacional and Texaco Canada Resource Ltd.

19. M. Dornbierer 'Contaminación=corrupción,' *El Financiero*, 27 January 1996, p. 13.

20. Richard S. Teitelbaum, 'Your last big play in oil,' *Fortune*, No. 21, 30 October 1995.

21. In Chiapas, there are currently eleven protected areas, covering a total of 751,353 hectares and representing 10 per cent of the state's territory. We should add to that another 31 reserve areas that have not yet been formally recognized as protected areas.

22. The problem with this project is that a significant part of Guatemalan territory would be flooded, submerging not only important archaeological sites but also probable oil deposits.

23. '*Coletos*' is the term used to refer to those born in San Cristóbal de las Casas. It is however also used by the dominant classes to 'claim' their original rights to the land.

24. In the writings of Emilio Rabasa, we find an eloquent sample of the ideology used to justify actions. To explain the inevitability of electoral fraud in Chiapas, he said: 'to conduct elections, fraud was necessary; to fulfill the function stipulated in the Constitution, it was necessary to violate the Constitution [since] Indians were included among voters, and nearly all of them not only were and continue to be incapable of the judgement and freedom necessary for the civic act par excellence, but they know nothing of the ways of government and lack even the most indispensable notions for understanding them, if someone would attempt to explain them'. Emilio Rabasa, *La evolución histórica de México* (1920) (Mexico City: Porrúa, 1986) cited in Catherine Héau-Lambert, 'Rabasa y el liberalismo histórico en México', *Relaciones*, No. 5–6 (Mexico City: UAM-X, 1991), p. 141. Héau-Lambert captures the essence of Rabasa's racist, liberal thinking when she writes on p. 143 that an Indian 'will always be incapable of understanding what is read, because reading is

an act of intelligence *par excellence'*. Rabasa manages to summarise superbly the feelings, not only during his time but throughout history, of the white or non-indigenous population that settled in Chiapas.

25. In a review of the theory of democracy and the writings of Weber, Mabel Piccini tells us that: 'The problem lies in *being able* to legitimate and *knowing how* to legitimate order, even when such order is – in one way or another – the result of an imposition: How can inequality be legitimated and harmony be promoted among the sides involved, in order to achieve the stability that will allow for equilibrium and the integration of a social system? ... In summary, how can beliefs be produced which will cause those in the position of obeying – the absolute majority – to obey?' 'Estructuras simbólicas y acción social', *Relaciones*, No. 5–6 (Mexico City: UAM-X, 1991) p. 77.

26. Here we are not referring to those indigenous persons incorporated into the *haciendas* or *repartimientos*, but rather to those who remained in community groupings and were to be severely affected by the implementation of the Leyes de Reforma (reform laws).

27. Consejo Nacional de Población (CONAPO), *Indicadores socio-económicos e indice de marginación municipal* (Mexico City, 1993) p. 24.

28. The only states which report infectious intestinal illnesses among the five highest causes of death are: Chiapas and Oaxaca, as the highest cause; Puebla, third highest; Guerrero, Quintana Roo, Querétaro, Tabasco and San Luis Potosí, fifth highest. Secretaría de Salubridad y Asistencia, *Atlas dela Salud* (Mexico City, 1993), statistical annex.

29. Instituto Nacional de Estadística, Geografía e Informática (INEGI), *Estadistícas vitales del estado de Chiapas* (Mexico City, 1994). The statistics we have referred to here are based on data from official registers available to the public. We can assume that the existing problems are underestimated, given the isolated conditions in which indigenous populations live. There are a number of studies conducted by field researchers but they usually provide only partial information, since they cover only a certain region, or study only one type of illness. The information they do provide, however, makes it possible to discern the serious health situation facing these populations.

30. Secretaría de Salubridad y Asistencia, *Atlas dela Salud*, statistical annex.

31. The strategic importance of microelectronics, computer sciences, biotechnology and specifications regarding the term 'electronically generated information' is addressed in Ana Esther Ceceña and Andrés Barreda (coordinators), *Producción estratégica y hegemonía mundial* (Mexico City: Siglo XXI, 1995).
32. This figure is probably an understatement generated by the measurement criteria used. Just how 'indigenous' a person may be is difficult to determine precisely, especially given the existing racism. Figures from INEGI, *XI Censo general de población y vivienda* (11th general demographic and housing census), (Mexico City: 1990).

3

Zapatista Indigenous Women

Márgara Millán

One of the things that surprised the world about the Zapatista uprising was the number of women, mostly young, among the insurgents who took over San Cristóbal de las Casas at the dawning of 1994. As this novel, end-of-century indigenous movement became better known, it also became clear that a large number of women participated in the Zapatista Army of National Liberation (EZLN). Although the press paid scant attention, the Woman's Law was included among the proclamations published on 1 January 1994 in the EZLN's official publication, *El Despertador Mexicano* (The Mexican Awakening). Women's voices were also promptly heard. Captain Elisa, Captain Laura, Major Ana Maria and comandante Ramona made statements to the press. These women were eloquently photographed, and their serious, smiling eyes behind the balaclavas, the directness of their gaze, the handkerchiefs that cover their mouths combined with the clasps in their hair never cease to surprise me.

The massive presence of women among the Zapatistas has undoubtedly been visible in different ways and is something the insurgents have had to deal with. It is not a joke when Subcomandante Marcos says the women are not there because the Zapatistas are feminists, but because they have won the right to be there. They have opened up a space for themselves and combined it with specific demands, and this begins to make them visible in a new way, even – and especially – to themselves. This chapter will look at some of these new ways of making indigenous women visible and how they have begun changing the traditional order of gender relations and redefining the experience of feminine indigenous subjectivity.

The socioeconomic and organisational environment and the first horizon of visibility of indigenous women

The presence and participation of women in the conflict in Chiapas is not limited to the EZLN. Alongside the armed uprising, many other sectors of the peasant movement who identify with the Zapatista demands have mobilised and carried out a series of actions: land takeovers, closing city halls, hunger strikes, organised voting and boycotts. They have also organised civilian protection of the dialogue process, surrounding the negotiations site with a permanent indigenous human ring no matter where they take place. They have gone on marches in which the majority of the participants are women of all ages, many with small children. Approximately 30 per cent of EZLN members are women, but the percentage is higher among their base of support.

Chiapas peasants have a long tradition of organising and struggle, and have answered the Mexican state's 'modernisation and development policies', which are nothing short of blatant attempts to exterminate the poor and indigenous population, with a lively social response. Statistics reveal a desperate situation in which congenital malnutrition and high mortality rates from preventable diseases are a constant. Chiapas is not only geographically at one of the extreme ends of the country, but is also an extreme in terms of culture and exploitation. While it is one of the states richest in natural resources, it also has the highest poverty and marginalisation rates. It is the extreme of a racist, discriminatory society, the extreme too of the contradictory nature of capitalist modernisation. Here, the law that the poorest among the poor are women is clearly borne out.

In Las Cañadas, for example, the average rate of fecundity of women during the period of fertility is very high, 7.32: a woman is likely to have more than seven children. More than half the population show some degree of malnutrition, the highest levels being among girls. Among twelve-year-old girls, for example, none presents a normal nutritional condition, while for boys of the same age the percentage is 39.4 per cent. The source for this is two studies done by the *Fideicomiso para la Salud de los Niños Indígenas de México*, AC (Trust for the Health of Indigenous Children of Mexico), one on health and nutrition in indigenous hostels and another on the health of indigenous children in Mexico. The *Centro de Investigaciones Históricas de Mesoamérica y el Estado de Chiapas* (CIHMECH) has shown in its studies the problem of hunger and malnutrition in the region, and the persistence of patterns of illness and death due to preventable illnesses, the so-called deaths of poverty. Bad feeding and congenital undernourishment have affected the size of the indigenous people, particularly of women. Life expectancy in the indigenous communities is 44 years, as compared with a national average of 70 years.[1]

In Chiapas, poverty is combined with cultural phenomena specific to a frontier region. The forced migration of indigenous populations from different ethnic groups to the Lacandon Jungle has spurred interchange and the construction of a new life that combines the affirmation of the community with pluralist forms and ways of political, cultural and productive organisation. This has also combined with the action of groups which, from different ideological positions, share what we could call 'grass-roots politics'. What has been happening in Chiapas is very like a huge social laboratory, combining many elements: a broad gamut of inter-indigenous mixes, together with leftist and progressive ecclesiastic ideologies (sometimes even within the state), but all rooted in the defence and reconstruction of the communities.[2] This has spurred an unprecedented force for cohesion and community organisation and activity, which puts traditional forms into action, alongside with what we could call the best components of modernity. These communities are combining their traditional structures of authority and cohesion with fundamental demands like democracy, justice and dignity. All these demands are an affirmation of indigenous life and culture while at the same time trying to bring them up to date. Indigenous matters become contemporary, thus demanding that the rest of society become as contemporary as indigenous reality, with its economic, political, legal and cultural forms.

A very important part of this process has been the construction of new spaces of identity, where indigenous men and women are changing their forms and cultures.

This social laboratory is not homogeneous; rather, it combines many contradictory experiences and has its own 'geopolitics': regions, sub-regions and borders. The space opened up by the EZLN is precisely what we could call the limit or outer borders of this social laboratory. It is a space which includes not only the Zapatista Army, but also serves as a magnet (a symbolic and cultural reference point) in broad areas of the social movement.

During the 1970s, several peasant organisations were founded in Chiapas and in turn joined three national organisations: the Emiliano Zapata Peasant Organisation (OCEZ), National Plan of Ayala Coordinating Committee (CNPA) and the Independent Peasant and Farm Workers Confederation (CIOAC). Women began creating their own organisations, particularly of artisans and Christians. For the last ten years, women from the universities and non-governmental organisations (NGOs) have worked from a gender perspective on questions of reproductive health, civil and human rights and against sexual violence. Some mixed organisations have also put forward women's demands, for example, the Christian Base Communities (CEBs) and the Organisation of Indigenous Doctors of the State of Chiapas (OMIECH) as well as autonomous groups working within the CIOAC and the teachers' movement and organisations, like the Independent Organisation of Indigenous Women (OIMI), the Women of Motozintla, Women of Margaritas, Women of Ocosingo, Women of Jiquipilas and the Organisation of Artisan Women of Chiapas, J'pas Joloviletik, in the Highlands. Particularly outstanding is the human rights defence network organised by women from the CEBs in the Lacandon Jungle and Highlands. Another important experience has been the contact with the organisations of Guatemalan refugee women, who have also combined demands linking ethnic origin and gender.

In the last few years, organisations have been founded like the San Cristóbal Women's Group, the Centre for Research and Action for Women (CIAM), the San Cristóbal Centre for Ecological and Health Training (CCESC), Chiltak, and, since the beginning of hostilities, the NGO Coordinating Committee for Peace (Conpaz), which supports communities and women's organisations with a clear gender focus.

Women in the communities have taken up tasks in the public sphere through cooperatives, as health promoters, in village banks, and often they have had to negotiate directly with the authorities. Little by little, all this has changed women's position in the community and provided them with a series of experiences which have created the space for developing their own specific women's demands as part of more general ones. Although experiences differ from one region to another, this has happened everywhere at least to some degree.[3]

In the milieu surrounding Zapatista women, as we can see, indigenous women were already becoming part of social and political tasks. Indigenous women from Chiapas, while supporting and mobilising around community and ethnic demands like the struggle for land, for justice, for democracy, also began to put forward gender demands: democratic relations within the family, the community and the organisations themselves; their participation as women in decision making in communal and organisational bodies; the right to inherit land; the right to decide when and whom they marry; the right to work and study and, when in a position of authority, the right to be respected by men. This implies the need to change customs and traditions wherever customs and traditions also mean domination and gender segregation, inequality and mistreatment.

The workshop 'The Rights of Women with Our Customs and Traditions,' held 19 and 20 May 1994 in San Cristóbal de las Casas, produced a document which clearly enunciates the way in which this gender consciousness questions the patriarchal 'common sense' of both the state and the community, as well as a discourse of women's new experiences. The workshop was organised by Chiltak and attended by more than 50 Tzotzil, Tzeltal, Tojolabal and Mame women from very different communities.[4] The document says:

We talked about poverty, discrimination and the injustices indigenous people suffer and also about violence against and mistreatment of women. We talked about what we cannot do now, what they won't let us do. We talked about the rights that are denied indigenous people and women, the rights denied us by the authorities, the cashelanes (mestizos), the poverty. We also talked about the rights denied us by the community, our husbands, children, fathers and even by women ourselves. From the time we were very small, we have been taught to be obedient, not to protest, to be quiet, to take everything, not talk, not participate. But now we don't want to be left behind; we don't want to be stepped on. We demand respect as indigenous people and as women and that our rights be recognised. We want respect for our customs, those customs that the community considers positive for all women, men and children. We also want to participate in making the laws that involve us and our peoples and that respect our rights.

The document not only clearly evidences the subordination of everything indigenous, but also the place in which the gender system situates women, a place women no longer want to occupy. This document is the interior reflection of the EZLN's Women's Law.

In the workshop, the women said that they want to hold posts in the community and in their organisations; they want to hold positions of authority, to have the right to work, to good wages and good prices for their products. They want the right to decide how many children to have and when, to go to school, to retain their own language as well as to learn Spanish. Regarding some important points, they manifest self-affirmation and place value on themselves with regard to men: 'Not only the men know how to think. We also know how to think, just like the men, or even better, because the majority of women don't drink *posh* [an alcoholic drink common to the Highlands of Chiapas].'

The women talk about the combination of tradition with modern/Western practices on different levels, such as the proposal of making gynecological attention available from doctors and midwives working together. On other levels, they question tradition and propose the need to act differently:

Parents think that working in the fields is more useful than going to school. We don't agree because knowledge allows us to work better ... Sometimes in the communities they force us to get married; sometimes they trade women for cows. The way they treat us isn't fair. It is mistreatment when they force us to marry. They should respect their daughters' decisions and marriage should be voluntary. When a woman is married against her will, the couple fights and the man is more likely to mistreat her. The parents are the ones to blame for forcing her to marry. That's part of our tradition. Sometimes the father-in-law wants to take the bride as his woman for a while, and does not want her for the bridegroom ... We women have the right to choose our husbands and they can't force us to marry someone we don't love, or take us by force or sell us. Our husbands, our children, our fathers, our mothers, our fathers-in-law or our mothers-in-law, our brothers-in-law cannot mistreat us or beat us: neither can the police or soldiers or anyone else ... We have the right to defend ourselves from rape, whether we're married or single. Even our husband cannot force us to be with him if we don't want to ... It is important that women support each other ... We propose there be a law that demands that women be given land because we also work, eat and have needs ... We should have the right to inherit land, the right to credit and to have our own decent house, the right to start and direct productive projects.[5]

They clearly distinguish the different levels of violence, including violence within marriage, and put forward the need for solidarity among women. They propose changing the addition to Article Four of the Constitution,[6] which reinforces a custom countering their right to the land, since the patriarchal community tradition prevents women from inheriting or buying land.

The patriarchal nature of the family structure makes it contradictory: it is simultaneously a unit of solidarity which implements cooperative strategies to ensure the survival and reproduction of its members, and a power structure which establishes its own internal relations and the position of women within them, creating inequalities by sex and age. This is what gives older males the power that they, as heads of households, wield over women and the younger generations, both in the domestic and the political-religious-community spheres. This power is exercised to control sexuality, material resources, work and participation in decision making and government institutions. Masculine control of resources is, first and foremost, control of the land. The other important area of control is the decision about when and whom their daughters and sons will marry:

> Women's position with regard to the hierarchy of authority also varies according to the stage of the domestic cycle they are in and their age and marital status. But, women's lives are not the same as men's. The overwhelming majority of the women never become a head of household, nor do they ever control an important part of the most valuable resources. As long as a male head of household (father, father-in-law, husband) is over them, 'they do not run their own lives.'[7]

The nature and depth of the changes that the women propose involve a process of construction and redefinition of subjectivity that changes the content of family and community relations to resignify gender. Family structure could continue to function as a solidarity survival unit, but the power structure that accompanies it will have to change because the needs that indigenous women today put forward touch the heart of that domination: the loss of the head of the family's control over his children's marriages, the transformation of the marriage pattern, women's access to control over resources, above all the land, and participation in community government.

Women are the ones who are posing most sharply the question of the relationship between change and tradition, rethinking them from a perspective that reveals the complicity between 'respect for tradition' and continued marginalisation. For example, they say, 'It is not true, as some mestizos think, that it is our custom to eat only vegetables and pozol [ground corn]. We want the right to eat meat and drink milk, and our children not to die of malnutrition or women to die in childbirth.' That is, there are practices which are not tradition: they are the practices of marginalisation. But the women also say that tradition has to change, and they establish an ethical norm for that change: 'We also must think about what new things should be incorporated into our customs. The law should only protect and foster those usages and customs that the communities and organisations think are good. Our customs should do no harm to anyone.'

The women insurgents: the second horizon of visibility of Chiapas indigenous women

The EZLN opened up a sphere in which women and men can have new experiences. There is a gap, in a certain sense, between the indigenous women who continue in their communities and the insurgents. The experience of command, of egalitarian, non-sexually differentiated work and of control over one's own sexuality are three practical dimensions of the change in, and redefinition of, gender. Paradoxically, it is an exceptional situation in which women, as Marcos says, 'have had to stop being women to become soldiers', but in which they can also step from that negation of 'being a woman' toward finding a new norm of femininity.[8]

Zapatismo as a life option
Captain Elisa, one of the twelve women who together with 100 armed militia and insurgents gave a press conference on 19 January 1994 said:[9]

> When I lived at home with my family, I didn't know anything. I didn't know how to read. I didn't go to school. But, when I joined the EZLN, I learned to read. I learned all the Spanish I know. I learned to read and write, and I trained for combat.

Laura, a 21-year-old Tzeltal and captain of assault troops for three years, said,

> I only studied up to the fourth grade in primary school. I was very young when I heard about the EZLN. I worked the land with the women, and we got together to produce food. That's where we began the talks about [our] poverty and why we couldn't live any better ... I began [on this road] dictated by my conscience, to fight for the poor because it's not right for children to keep dying.

The vast majority of women who join the army are young, practically children themselves. Faced with the options of going to San Cristóbal to work as a servant or staying in the community and being bartered as a bride, many prefer to join the Zapatistas.
Marcos relates:

> When the women insurgents went into the mountains, the old women of the villages accused them of going to be free to play

around sexually and said that no one would be there to keep an eye on them. But the young women of the town were enthusiastic. They asked the women insurgents how women were treated. 'If you don't want to be "taken" do they punish you? [The answer was] 'No, they can't "take" you if you don't want to be taken.' [Then they asked] 'If you don't love a man can you refuse to marry him?' 'Yes, [they answered]. If you don't want to, you don't get married.' Then, a shitload of women started coming to us.[10]

Something similar happened with the men. They could go and hire themselves out at some job and bring money home, but going to the Zapatistas began to be a more interesting option. One young man told the story that he had gone home to his community for his identification papers to join the Mexican army and his family convinced him it would be better to join the EZLN.

The EZLN rose out of the communities. Its ties are blood ties. Parents have two, three or more of their children in its ranks. The community reserves food for them; it makes sure that whatever is needed for the army to continue existing is provided. The families in the community have given their sons and daughters to the EZLN.

When a woman insurgent goes back to the community, she looks different. She is a woman of 18 or 20 who has not already had several children, who has eaten well, knows how to speak Spanish, has learned to read and write. She is sure of her words. This difference is illustrated by Herman Bellinghausen in his report from a Zapatista area in the jungle on 4 April 1994:

Captain María Elena, a young woman, goes with me. We visitors can go wherever we like and talk to whomever we like, but we can never be alone. About the poverty here, my companion says to me, 'This is nothing. Further down it's worse ...' The women look at what is happening with a certain fatalism, but they do not disapprove of everyone being a Zapatista. María Elena speaks Tzeltal, even though she is a Chol. EZLN women are healthy and educated. For years they have led a Spartan existence, but with health services and regular meals. Just like Amalia, María Elena thinks she is better off than if she had stayed in her village. She would be like those sad mothers, barefoot and skinny, surrounded by sick children. Any mother over 20 has lost one or several children and speaks with a fixed sadness that María Elena does not have. There is no fatalism or rigidity in her conversation. She speaks freely; but, when asked specifically, she answers that she is fighting so people can live better. Dying in battle does not worry her, and she was already close in Ocosingo 2 January [1994]. For three months now, she has been living on borrowed time.[11]

Insurgent Major Ana María, of the infantry, appeared together with Comandante Ramona at the first dialogue meeting in San Cristóbal. Ana María, about 25, says that she joined the EZLN when she was about 12 or 13:

> The EZLN is in my personal interest. We joined this struggle for more than ten years ago. First they were peaceful struggles in which I participated with my sisters and brothers ... When I joined, there were only two women, out of a total of eight or nine people in the mountains. The compañeros taught us to walk in the mountains, to load the guns, to hunt. They taught us combat exercises and when we learned that, they taught us politics. Then we went out into the communities to talk to our people, to tell them about our struggle and how we could solve things, and many people began to join us, men, women and children. Most of us are young ... We need support from the women because we are the ones who suffer the most. It is very painful to watch children die, die of malnutrition, of hunger, of curable diseases. Women suffer very much. And that's why we fight.[12]

Women's place inside the EZLN

> Captain Laura, 21, talks to reporters sitting on a small rock with her rifle on her lap. They ask her about Marcos and she says he is 'a man of struggle, even if he is mestizo, as you have seen'. The reporters ask how she achieved her rank. 'Well,' she answers, 'rank is won by the experience you have in the mountains, your ability to work hard and how you carry out your duties. When you start to work as an insurgent, you're just another soldier. The commanders watch your progress ... On the way they begin making you responsible for people and you lead them, you command them. That's how I moved up in the ranks. They began putting people under my command. They saw that I could handle it and so they began raising my rank.' Captain Laura has 150 militia members under her command.[13]

Women earn their place in the military by sheer effort. Major Ana María was the commander of the operation to take the San Cristóbal City Hall. But undoubtedly what showed the Zapatistas women's military importance was the clash in Ocosingo:

Before the war, the men were suspicious and uneasy with a woman in command. Things were crazy; I spent all my time patching up quarrels. It was, 'I'm not taking orders from her because she's a bird. How am I going to do that?' That's the way they've been taught ... The fighting in Ocosingo put an end to that because the best combatants were the women officers. They got the wounded out of the trap. Some of them still have pieces of shrapnel in their bodies. They got people out; they got them out alive. That was the end of the problem of whether women were fit for command or not.[14]

There are other indications that work among the troops is egalitarian: everyone has to do cooking and cleaning. This gave rise to Marcos' joke that he eats rice made by an inexperienced cook. These relationships are being described by the women as the new norms to which the men have to adhere.

Laws as consensus or 'command obeying'

Equal status has also been won by the women due to the way the Zapatistas make decisions. The revolutionary laws, among them the Revolutionary Women's Law, rule the Zapatistas' lives in the liberated zones.

These laws went through a long period of consultation and consensus-building in the Zapatista communities. They are the result of a broad consensus, not something imposed by the EZLN, but rather the agreement of the communities that the EZLN implements through 'command obeying'. The Zapatista consultation about the revolutionary laws is a vehicle to articulate the demands of the different community sectors. It is a method for building power (the power of the word) with the sectors themselves as the starting point, thus giving rise to plurality.[15]

The national press did not cover or analyse the Revolutionary Women's Law read on the radio as part of the EZLN's first proclamation on 1 January 1994. The law was published in *El Despertador Mexicano* (Mexico's Awakening), the EZLN's official paper on that first day of January, next to the *First Declaration of the Lacandon Jungle, Today We Say 'Enough!'*, and as part of a larger body of laws under which the insurgents live. The following is the full text of the law:

In its just fight for the liberation of our people, the EZLN includes women in the revolutionary struggle without regard to race, creed, colour or political affiliation. The only prerequisite is that they make the demands of the exploited their own and that they abide by and enforce the laws and regulations of the revolution. In addition, and taking into account working women's situation in Mexico, their just demands for equality and justice are included in the following Revolutionary Law for Women:

Article One: Women have the right to participate in the revolutionary struggle wherever and to the degree that their own conscience and abilities dictate, without regard to race, creed, colour or political affiliation.

Article Two: Women have the right to work and receive a fair wage.

Article Three: Women have the right to decide the number of children they can have and care for.

Article Four: Women have the right to participate in community affairs and hold posts if they are freely and democratically elected.

Article Five: Women and their children have the right to basic health care and decent food.

Article Six: Women have the right to education.

Article Seven: Women have the right to choose their partners and not be forced to marry.

Article Eight: No woman may be struck or physically mistreated by either family members or strangers. The crimes of attempted rape and rape shall be severely punished.

Article Nine: Women may hold leadership posts in the organisation and military rank in the revolutionary armed forces.

Article Ten: Women will enjoy all rights and obligations established in revolutionary laws and regulations.

Part of a letter sent by Subcomandante Marcos to *La Jornada* writer Alvaro Cepeda Neri reveals more about this law and its meaning for Zapatistas, both men and women. The idea is that it is within the Zapatista ranks that the first uprising, the first revolution, took place:

In March 1993 we were discussing what would later be the revolutionary laws ... Susana was assigned to visit dozens of communities to talk with women's groups and develop the women's law. When the CCRI [Indigenous Clandestine Revolutionary Committee, the Zapatista high command] met to vote on the laws, the commissions on justice, agrarian law, war taxes, the rights and obligations of peoples in struggle and the women's law each came before the meeting in turn. Susana read out the proposals that she had gathered from the thinking of thousands of indigenous women ... She began to read, and as she read, the CCRI assembly became more and more disquieted. Murmuring and remarks became audible. Comments in Chol, Tzeltal, Tzotzil, Tojolabal, Mam, Zoque and Spanish buzzed from one end of the room to the other. Susana did not shrink from her task, but forged ahead against everything and everyone. 'We do not want to be forced to marry anyone we don't want to. We want to have the children we choose to have and are able to care for. We want the right to hold posts in the community. We want the right to say our word and to be respected. We want the right to study and even to be drivers.' And she went on like that until she finished. At the end, there was a heavy silence. The 'women's laws' that Susana had just read were a true revolution for indigenous communities. The men looked at each another, nervous and disturbed. Suddenly, practically simultaneously, the translators, all women, finished and the compañeras began increasingly to applaud and talk among themselves. Needless to say, the laws on women passed unanimously. One Tzeltal representative said, 'The good thing is that my wife doesn't speak Spanish. Otherwise ...' One woman insurgent official, a Tzotzil major in the infantry, counter-attacked, saying, 'Well, now you're fucked because we're going to translate it into all the dialects.' The compañero lowered his gaze. The women were singing. The men just scratched their heads. I thought it prudent to call a recess ... That's the truth. The first EZLN uprising was in March 1993 and it was headed up by the Zapatista women. There were no casualties and they were victorious. That's how things are in this part of the world.

The law integrates women and Zapatismo. It incorporates women as a sector, recognising the specific discrimination they suffer, and makes consensus a norm for basic questions. In this sense, the law has a double impact: it fosters a sphere for consensus (for the formulation of a proposition) and then makes it into law. It exercises the 'respect for our word' that the women request as a form of decision making. But, the law is only the formal representation of a broader process in which women are taking the floor to express themselves.

The body, maternity and sexuality

Zapatista women can marry in two ways: deciding with their partners to do so and notifying the command, or requesting a ceremony. What they cannot do is have children, 'because we are at war'. If they do have children, the mother, the father, or both, return to their community with the child or leave it in the care of their families. The most common contraceptive, besides the rhythm method, is the pill, although such young women often have difficulty tolerating it.

Making the decisions about their own bodies, about when to become a mother, about marriage is one of the most innovative experiences Zapatista women go through compared to traditional community practice. Sexuality and maternity are being divorced. This is not revolutionary celibacy, but rather an experience of liberation in which sexuality is practised by indigenous women from a different standpoint.

In Point 29 of the demands put forward in the Dialogue of San Cristóbal, called 'Women's Demands',[16] they request 'the immediate solution of all our urgent needs which the government has never provided for'. These are demands for economic support, medical attention, nutritional aid, not the demands put forward in the Revolutionary Women's Law:

> Why do the demands we make on the bad government not include the Women's Law that the Zapatista WOMEN IMPOSED UPON US [capitalization by Marcos] on March 8, 1993? The Zapatista women responded, 'Some things are requested and some things are imposed. We request minimum material conditions ... Our freedom and dignity is something we impose, whether the compañeros or the government recognize them or not.' They are doing it despite the newspapers, the churches, the criminal code and what it is only fair to acknowledge is our resistance as men to being thrown out of the comfortable sphere of domination that we have inherited. There is a long way to go, they say, but I cannot see even a minimal sign of their tiring.[17]

What is happening in Chiapas is enormous. It is also having an enormous impact on what happens around it. The most significant feature of the women's experience seems to be that they have begun a process which could be stopped only with great difficulty, either by the Zapatistas or by our preconceived ideas about the absolute subordination of indigenous women and the immutability of ethnic groups. These and other out-of-date, fatalistic ideas are demolished when faced with the vitality of a movement which gives expression to its actors, both men and women.

Notes

1. *Fideicomiso*'s study was reported in *La Jornada*, 5 October 1994; the CIHMECH study was reported in *La Jornada*, 8 April 1995 by Juan Antonio Zuniga.
2. In one of the regions of the 'zone of conflict' people speak up to four languages, 'related directly to their political, economic and religious activities': Xochitl Leyva Solano, *La Jornada*, 1 February 1994.
3. The region of the Highlands appears much more traditional than the Lacandon Jungle. There it has been through the craftwork cooperatives that the participative experience of the Tzotzil women, mostly monolingual, has advanced. In other zones other spaces have been created, such as the 'Women's Houses' in the Tojolabal villages of Santa Martha and El Porvenir, both in the municipality of La Trinitaria, and in Poza Rica, in the municipality of Las Margaritas. These are projects that have arisen with the support of the CCESC, with the aim of creating community pharmacies. See Rosalva Aida Hernández Castillo, 'Las Voces de las mujeres en el conflicto chiapaneco: nuevos espacios organizativos y nuevas demandas de género', December 1994, mimeo; 'Reinventing Tradition: the Women's Law' in *Akwe:kon*, 'All of us', Vol. XI, No. 2, Summer 1994; and Mercedes Olivera Bustamente, 'Aguascalientes y el movimiento social de las mujeres chiapanecas', in Silvia Soriano Solis (ed.), *A Propósito de la insurgencia en Chiapas*, (Mexico: Asociación para el Desarrollo de la Investigación y Humanística, 1994).
4. 'El grito de la luna. Mujeres: derecho y tradición', *Ojarasca*, August–September 1994.
5. The majority of peasant women work in all the stages of cultivation – sowing, weeding and harvesting – as part of the famly agriculture, without pay. They also hire themselves out for work on other land, especially in the harvest season.
6. The reform of the fourth article of the Constitution was published in the *Diario Oficial* on 28 January 1992. The first paragraph says: 'The Mexican nation has a pluricultural composition based originally on its indigenous peoples. The law will protect and promote the development of their languages, cultures, uses,

customs, resources and specific forms of social organisation, and will guarantee their members effective access to the jurisdiction of the state. In the judgments and agrarian proceedings in which they take part, their practices and juridical customs will be taken into account in the terms established by the law.'

7. Soledad Gonzalez Montes, 'Los ingresos no agropecuarios, el trabajo remunerado femenino y las transformaciones de las relaciones intergenéricas e intergeneracionales de las familias campesinas', in Vania Salles and Elsie McPhail (eds), *Textos y pretextos: once estudios sobre la mujer* (Mexico: Colmex-PIEM, 1991) pp. 225–257.

8. 'Why is it necessary to kill and to die so that Ramona can come and you can listen to what she says? Why is it necessary that Laura, Ana María, Irma, Elisa and so many other indigenous women should have to take up arms, make themselves soldiers instead of becoming doctors, lawyers, engineers, teachers?' Report by Marcos on the second day of the Dialogue of San Cristóbal, 22 February 1994, in EZLN, *La palabra de los armados de verdad y fuego* [The Word of Those Armed with Truth and Fire], Vol. 1 (Mexico City: Editorial Fuenteovejuna, 1994) p. 223.

9. All the information is taken from *La Jornada* unless otherwise indicated.

10. Martha Durán de Huerta (ed.), *Yo Marcos. Entrevistas y pláticas del Subcomandante* (Mexico: Ediciones del Milenio, 1994) pp. 33–34.

11. *La Jornada*, 4 April 1994.

12. *La Jornada*, 7 March 1994.

13. *Proceso*, 18 April 1994.

14. Durán de Huerta, *Yo Marcos*, pp. 32–33.

15. This plural intention can be seen in the famous ten demands, in which the great majority of the world's population can recognise themselves. The demands are basic: health, housing, education, land, employment, justice, food, freedom, independence and democracy. As Julio Moguel points out (*La Jornada*, 28 March 1994) this is 'a non-sectarian indigenous movement, a movement which feels itself to be part of a process of global transformation of many heterogeneous social forces'.

16. Point 29: Petition of the indigenous women: We the indigenous peasant women demand the immediate solution of urgent necessities, which the government has never solved:
a) birth clinics with gynecologists so that peasant women receive the necessary medical attention;
b) the construction of creches in the communities;

c) we demand that the government send sufficient food for the children in all the rural communities such as milk, corn flour, rice, corn, soya, oil, beans, cheese, eggs, sugar, soup, oats, etc.;

d) the construction of kitchens and dining rooms for children in the communities with all the facilities;

e) that there should be corn mills and *tortillerías* in the communities, depending on the number of families they have;

f) that they should give us farms with hens, rabbits, sheep, pigs, etc., with technical consultants and veterinarians;

g) we demand bakeries which have ovens and material;

h) we want craft workshops with machines and raw materials;

i) for the crafts, there should be a market where it is possible to sell at a fair price;

j) schools should be constructed in which women can receive technical training;

k) there should be nursery schools in the rural communities where the children can entertain themselves and grow morally and physically;

l) as women, we should have sufficient transport to move ourselves and to transport our products from the different projects that we have.

17. Letter from Marcos to Marta Lamas, 5 May 1994, published in EZLN, *La palabra*, p. 178.

4

The Zapatistas and the Electronic Fabric of Struggle[1]

Harry Cleaver[2]

In the narrow terms of traditional military conflict, the Zapatista uprising in Mexico has been confined to a limited zone in the southern state of Chiapas. However, through their ability to extend their political reach via modern computer networks the Zapatistas and their supporters have woven a new electronic fabric of struggle to carry their revolution throughout Mexico and around the world.

Initially the Mexican state tried to restrict the uprising to the jungles of Chiapas, through both military repression and the limitation of press coverage (most Mexicans get their news from the state-controlled TV network, Televisa). Those efforts failed. First through written communiqués and personal interviews with independent journalists which were flashed around the world by fax and electronic mail, then through more detailed reports by Mexican and foreign observers circulated in the same manner, the Zapatistas were able to break out of the state's attempted isolation and reach others with their ideas and their programme for economic and political revolution. As vast numbers of Mexicans responded with sympathy and mobilised in support, the Chiapas uprising kindled a more generalised pro-democracy movement against the centralised and corrupt Mexican economic and political system. Inspiring many others outside of Mexico, the Zapatista uprising set in motion a new wave of hope and energy among those engaged in the struggle for freedom all over the world.

Despite its initial defeat, a key aspect of the state's war against the Zapatistas (both in Mexico and elsewhere) has been its ongoing efforts to isolate them, so that they can be destroyed or forced to accept cooptation. In turn, the Zapatistas and their supporters have fought to maintain and elaborate their political connections throughout the world. This has been a war of words, images, imagination and organisation in which the Zapatistas have had surprising success.

Vital to this continuing struggle has been the pro-Zapatista use of computer communications.[3] While the state has all too effectively

81

limited mass media coverage and serious discussion of Zapatista ideas, their supporters have been able, to an astonishing degree, to circumvent and offset this blockage through the use of electronic networks in conjunction with the more familiar tactics of solidarity movements: teach-ins, articles in the alternative press, demonstrations, the occupation of Mexican government consulates and so on. Over time the state and its strategists have become acutely aware of the effectiveness of this new form of struggle and have begun to take steps to counteract it. Both sides are now active in the cyberspacial dimension of a war which has raged out of Chiapas across Mexico and the world. The ways in which these networks have been effectively used within the larger framework of struggle deserve the closest attention by all those fighting for a democratic and freer society. The measures now being taken by the Mexican state to counter them also need to be understood in order to be dealt with effectively. The description and analysis of this new dimension of revolution and counter-revolution are the objects of this article.

The Zapatistas' new frontier

When the Zapatistas suddenly appeared in San Cristóbal de las Casas and several other cities of Chiapas in the early hours of 1 January 1994, they brought with them a printed declaration of war against the Mexican state and for the liberation of the people of Chiapas and Mexico. News of that declaration went out through a student's telephone call to CNN; then, as journalists arrived to investigate, stories went out via the wire services, newspaper reports and radio and television broadcasts all over the world. For the most part, however, readers and viewers of that reporting saw and heard only excerpts from the Zapatista declaration of war. They never saw the whole declaration, with all of its arguments and explanations for what were obviously dramatically surprising and audacious actions. Except for the rare exception, such as the Mexico City daily newspaper *La Jornada*, they only got what the editors wanted them to get, according to their own biases.

As the Mexican state poured 15,000 troops into Chiapas and the fighting escalated, this kind of reporting continued. Even after the cease-fire, when the emphasis of the Zapatista offensive shifted from arms to words, the commercial media overwhelmingly refused to reproduce the striking and often eloquent communiqués and letters sent out by the EZLN. With the distribution of *La Jornada* – which did continue to publish Zapatista material in full – sharply limited, especially outside of Mexico City, this refusal of the world's media was a serious blockage to the ability of the Zapatistas to get their message out.

For those in Mexico who read those messages and found them accurate and inspiring, this blockage was an intolerable situation which had to be overcome in order to build support for the Zapatistas and to stop the government's repression. What they did was very simple: they typed or scanned the communiqués and letters into e-text form and sent them out over the Net to potentially receptive audiences around the world. Those audiences included UseNet newsgroups, PeaceNet conferences, and Internet lists whose members were already concerned with Mexico's social and political life, humanitarian groupings concerned with human rights generally, networks of indigenous peoples and those sympathetic to them, those political regions of cyberspace which seemed likely to have members sympathetic to grass-roots revolt in general and networks of feminists who would respond with solidarity to the rape of indigenous women by Mexican soldiers and to the EZLN 'Women's Revolutionary Law' drafted by women, for women, within and against a traditionally patriarchal society. Again and again, friendly and receptive readers spontaneously re-posted the messages in new places while sometimes translating the Spanish documents into English and other languages. In this way, the words of the Zapatistas and messages of their communities have been diffused from a few gateways throughout much of cyberspace.

As journalistic, humanitarian, religious and indigenous observers have visited the conflict zone in Chiapas and written about what they have found, their reports – often embarrassing to the Mexican government and its supporters because the reports confirm Zapatista statements – have been circulated through the same computer networks providing vital material for the growing network of solidarity organisations. When grass-roots groups came together at the behest of the Zapatistas in early August 1994 at the new Aguascalientes carved out of the jungle to form the Convención Nacional Democrática, and then again later at San Cristóbal, Chiapas (11–13 October 1994), Tuxtla Gutierrez, Chiapas (4–6 November 1994) and Queretaro (1–5 February 1995), speeches, reports and convention documents were circulated on the Net. The same occurred in 1996 and 1997 before, during and after the continental and intercontinental 'Encounters' called by the Zapatistas. The on-line postings of dozens of papers, follow-up reports, digital audio recordings, digitised photographs of the meetings and a World Wide Web (WWW) forum carried the discussion from these meetings of thousands to cyberspace and a much larger audience. Much of this material certainly deserves being labeled with the term used by Italian militants: *'contro-informazione'* (counter-information), that is, opposed to the official reports of governments and commercial mass media.

As the number of people involved in these processes of uploading, re-posting, translating, etc., has grown, so has their self-organisation. What began as, and to a degree still is, an interlinked set of spontaneous actions has become more organised. On some lists, for example, a cooperative division of labour has emerged so that a dozen or more people take individual responsibility for tapping and re-posting relevant material from particular sources to a single site in cyberspace.[4] Moreover, a number of groups of activists have posted regular summaries of news stories and other information available on the Net, along with the URLs for those wanting to read the original materials.[5] In this way the skills and resources of many separate individuals and computer systems are connected in ways that benefit everyone who needs the pooled information. In another case, the best material from a few such poolings is re-posted to those who need the information but don't have time to sift through the whole flow.[6] As a result of such cooperation, the work of culling the Net has been drastically reduced for the vast majority of those needing and using information about the struggles in Mexico for purposes of mobilisation and solidarity.

Such cooperation has also made it possible to crystallise some of this continuing flow of useful information into new, hybrid electronic products. One such is the electronic book *Zapatistas! Documents of the new Mexican Revolution* which was put together by an e-mail coordinated team translating material largely gathered from the Net. Although the anti-copyrighted, electronic book was subsequently published in hard copy, it first became available, and continues to be available in its entirety on the Net.[7] A second such collaboration produced an electronic English translation of the first collection of materials on the activities and thoughts of women in Chiapas since the uprising began.[8] A third collective effort is the construction of a multimedia compact disk on the Zapatistas that draws much of its textual material and many images from the Net while combining them with music and video and other, newly created material. The resultant package of information is organised to permit a free-ranging exploration of nearly a gigabyte of information on the Zapatista uprising, its background and its effects.[9]

Throughout this whole process, the circulation of Zapatista materials and reports from independent observers on the Net has been accompanied by increasingly systematic re-posting of commercial media stories. While the commercial media has largely ignored the Net as a source of information and understanding about what has been happening in Chiapas, the reverse has not been the case.

On the contrary, given the obvious bias and incompleteness in such reporting, those circulating material on the Net informally adopt the practice of posting *everything* available. As a result, those who have tapped the Net for their organising around the issues of the Zapatista struggle, and the movement for democracy in Mexico more generally, have been far better informed and far more able to shape critical assessments of any given event than the consumers of a limited sampling of mass media. Where casual readers may have access to one story in a local newspaper (often purchased from the *New York Times* or the *Washington Post*), those subscribing to the relevant conferences or lists will receive anywhere from two or three to more than a dozen stories, both from the media and from unpublished sources. Good stories by independent reporters, for example, those written by John Ross for the small circulation *Anderson Valley Advertiser*, have been made as accessible as those of *New York Times* reporters Tim Golden and Anthony DePalma. Otherwise totally obscure reports from human rights groups both local (for example, the *Centro de Derechos Humanos Fray Bartolome de las Casas* and *La Liga Mexicana por la Defensa de los Derechos Humanos*) and international (for example, Amnesty International and Human Rights Watch) have been made as available as Mexican and US government propaganda.

Beyond this access to more diverse and critical sources of information, the various conferences and lists in cyberspace have generally archived all this material, making it permanently available for reference and study. Whereas the single story in a local or national newspaper or newsmagazine usually disappears into the trash or recycling bin in fairly short order, the archives of reg.mexico or Chiapas95 can be accessed through the Net easily and efficiently. Throughout most of this century, old newspaper stories or published reports had to be painstakingly dug out of microfilm files or book stacks by the few dedicated people who could make the time; in contrast, this material is now kept available – for reading, downloading, or forwarding – via a few keystrokes. Such archives have generally been stored as easily transferable files at FTP and gopher sites.

As World Wide Web browsers such as Netscape Navigator and Microsoft Explorer have become more widely available, Web pages have facilitated the interface with archived and other materials. These Web pages are not only more colourful – often containing photographs, graphic images, interactive forums for the exchange of opinions and analysis, audio and even video – but their hypertext programming makes movement among them wonderfully quick and easy through a click of the mouse button.[10]

All of this thorough and rapid circulation of news and observer reports of the situation in Chiapas led quickly to analytical and critical assessments of the origins and meaning of the Zapatista uprising. Cyberspace provided forums for informal discussion and debate. Alongside editorial pieces from the print or sound media appeared questions and opinions from a wide variety of concerned participants. Unlike 'letters to the editor', every single one of these comments and feedback appeared in electronic 'print', not days later but hours or even minutes after an original story or argument. The repressive response of the government, with its torture and killing, was subjected to widespread condemnation, while being very feebly defended, mostly with lies that were quickly exposed. Unlike government or editorial 'retractions' which might be buried in some obscure corner of a newspaper, the exposure of lies within an ongoing 'thread' of discussion in cyberspace emerges right up front where everyone can see it. Within this context of open debate, the Zapatistas were condemned by some and praised by many, dismissed by the apologists of the state and treated with great seriousness by those who studied their communiqués. Wild charges of 'terrorism' (echoes of state propaganda) were dissected and demolished in plain public view.

At first, the most pressing issues concerned the shooting war. Mass mobilisation to stop the state's military repression and force a withdrawal of the Mexican army was organised on the basis of outrage generated by detailed reports on the bloody character of that repression. Information was downloaded from the Net, gathered from other sources and transformed into flyers, pamphlets, newsletters, articles and eventually books detailing the torture, rapes, summary executions and other violence being perpetrated by the military, the various police forces and the private 'white guards' – hired goons of the big ranchers.

Such material fuelled the organisation of mass marches in Mexico City, San Francisco, New York and other cities around the world. They fired passions that led people to candlelit vigils, letter-writing and fax campaigns, Mexican consulate takeovers and other forms of protest. Stories of these actions (often ignored by the media) were then uploaded to the Net and as the reports multiplied they encouraged local militants who could see their own efforts as part of a larger movement. Taken all together, this explosive movement of solidarity certainly forced the government to back off its military solution and to negotiate with the Zapatistas. This was true in January and February of 1994 and a year later in February and March of 1995 after the Zedillo government unilaterally ruptured negotiations with the EZLN and again resorted to military violence.

Over the months separating these dramatic events, the issues the Zapatistas were raising, for example, NAFTA, poverty, land rights, justice, exploitation, environmental preservation, women's rights, democracy and so on, tended to become more and more the subject of discussion. Issues such as the democratisation of the Mexican political system, which was initially dismissed as a fantasy, became – through a multitude of political meetings, including such national events as the Convención Nacional Democrática (CND) so central to public discourse as to dominate Mexican politics – to the utter dismay of the very undemocratic ruling Partido Revolucionario Institucional (PRI). A pro-democracy movement developed the power to force a reformation, if not total revision, of the formal electoral system. Faced with the popular excitement stirred by the Zapatistas' vision of an open democratic system no longer monopolised by professional political parties and recognising the autonomy of indigenous ethnic groups, the PRI (so internally divided as to assassinate its own leaders) began to cede ground. Both grass-roots groups and opposition parties moved quickly to occupy the space given up. The Partido de Acción Nacional (a conservative opposition party) and the Partido Revolucionario Democrático (a more liberal party) first gained control of some state governments and then, through the 1997 elections, replaced the PRI's stranglehold on the Mexican Congress by an oppositional majority.

As the dual phenomena of a rapidly growing pro-democracy movement and an increasingly unstable and desperate ruling party have became more and more apparent, people's sense that things could change significantly in Mexico has grown. As the multiplying flows of information, analysis and debate have provided the sense of collective concern and organising necessary for committed forms of action, caravans bringing material aid and observers have gone to Chiapas, less to 'learn what is happening' than to curb state abuses and bring support and solidarity to those suffering the brutalities of the state's counter-insurgency strategy of so-called 'low-intensity warfare', that is, a generalised terror campaign against all viewed as sympathetic to the EZLN and radical change. In turn, political innovation in Chiapas has circulated to the rest of Mexico and beyond through the CND, the EZLN-organised general plebiscite on its programme in 1995 and the EZLN-called continental and inter-continental encounters of 1996 and 1997.

The result for business, the state and the ruling class generally is a continuing crisis of 'governability' wherein virtually every historical mechanism of domination is being challenged and ruptured from below. The old combinations of repression and cooptation have not been working and the traditional elite coalitions are splitting apart. The PRI has had to accept electoral reforms, cede state governments, tolerate public denunciations from its own human rights commission, suffer repeated exposures of massive state corruption, while watching the centre of gravity of public political debate and action shift toward radical groups like the EZLN or moderate groups like Alianza Civica. Desperate in the face of so many crises, the fragmenting ruling alliance has struck back with its usual violence: military repression in Chiapas, police state repression all over Mexico, but especially in indigenous communities. At the same time, unfortunately, it has not collapsed and is hardly without resources – both financial and human – even *in extremis*. As a result we have begun to see some new efforts to fight back on various fronts, including that of cyberspace.

Capitalist counter-attacks against the appropriation of cyberspace

The capitalist response to the autonomous appropriation of cyberspace has had many dimensions. To begin with, there has been increased monitoring, reporting and analysis of our use of cyberspace in ways designed to delegitimise and inform counter-strategies. In February 1995, for example, there were several mass media stories on the use of the Net to spread the word of the Mexican government's attack on the Zapatistas and to mobilise opposition. For example, the *Washington Post*, *Newsweek* and *TV Globo* all ran original stories about the new 'high-tech' guerrilla war.[11] Such reporting, often biased, has had contradictory effects. It has made both enemies and friends of the Zapatista solidarity movement more aware of what has been going on, stimulating both more opposition and more support.

In less public view, researchers in universities and think tanks have been paying much closer attention and have seen serious threats to the current political order. Even before the role of the Internet in the Zapatista struggle was recognised, analysts were beginning to call the attention of policy makers to grass-roots uses of electronic communications. One widely quoted report was Sheldon Annis's 1991 'Giving Voice to the Poor' published in *Foreign Policy*, an influential American journal in that field. Annis provided details of how grass-roots utilisation of the Net was 'empowering' and 'emboldening' the poor by undermining elite control of information. Generously, if somewhat naively perhaps, he recommended that state institutions such as local governments and the World Bank shift expenditures toward increasing flows of information which can assist the 'political empowerment' of the poor and 'processes of democratisation'.[12]

In the summer of that same year, Cathryn Thorup, then Director of Studies and Programs at the Center for U.S.-Mexican Studies at the University of California, San Diego, published an assessment of 'cross-border coalitions' in the *Columbia Journal of World Business*.[13] Her primary focus was on the actions and impact of the anti-NAFTA network. She traced the development of opposition to and lobbying against the government's 'fast-track' approach to railroading NAFTA through Congress as well as elite efforts to divide and conquer that opposition. While calling the debate 'healthy for both societies' (the US and Mexico), she also highlighted the 'tremendous vulnerability' of the state to such organising and discussed how state policy makers might seek to convert such opposition into 'valuable political allies' by consulting with them and cutting deals. Her vision of how the political system might cope with the emergence of these new rogue networks would seem to lie squarely in the tradition of pluralism, that is, integrate and coopt the new forces into a slightly modified fabric of governance.

In a more recent paper written for RAND, Thorup analysed the development of US and Mexican NGOs (non-governmental organisations) organising around immigration in the San Diego–Tijuana border area and its interaction with the US and Mexican governments.[14] Here again she explores both the threat of such grass-roots 'wild cards' to elite policy making as well as the possibilities of harnessing NGO activity: 'Both governments [US and Mexican] will find it necessary to complement efforts to cultivate and nurture their official relations with a more vigorous pursuit of direct communications with a variety of non-governmental actors in both countries.'[15] One example she cites is the Mexican government's success in harnessing NGOs' 'moral authority' to use them as mediators between itself and immigrants who are 'fearful of government entities'.[16] She notes how such efforts have 'enabled the Mexican government to demonstrate its concern for the plight of its nationals in the United States and, in passing, to make political gains with first, second and third generation Latinos residing in the United States'. Strengthening its support among Mexicano communities across the border is certainly important to a Mexican state-in-crisis all too aware that such communities have been prime sites of mobilisation in support of the Zapatistas.

One of the more thoughtful of these analyses to come to light, so far, has been that by national security analysts John Arquilla and David Ronfeldt working at RAND Corporation.[17] In a 1993 report entitled 'CyberWar is Coming!', they formulate two related concepts: cyberwar and netwar – in both of which the role of information is central and critical. The former refers to military war making while the latter refers to 'societal-level ideational conflicts waged in part through internetted modes of communication', 'most often associated with low intensity conflict'. Their examples of cyberwar range from the Mongols to the Gulf War. One of their primary examples of netwar is how 'advocacy movements' are 'increasingly organising into cross-border networks and coalitions, identifying more with the development of civil society (even global civil society) than with nation-states and using advanced information and communications technologies to strengthen their activities'. In that paper Arquilla and Ronfeldt cited movements concerned with environmental, human rights and religious issues. In a later publication called 'The Advent of Netwar' they cited the pro-Zapatista movement as a prime example of the kind of activity they are concerned with.[18] In their discussion, the 'other side' of such 'netwar' is the state and its traditional hierarchical institutions of governance. With their writing directed primarily at the US government – with which they clearly identify – they warn that new forms of warfare must be developed appropriate to this new arena of power.[19]

Arquilla and Ronfeldt defend their use of terms like 'cyber'war and 'cyber'space by pointing out that the Greek root 'kybernan' means to steer or govern. They like this prefix because it 'bridges the fields of information and governance better than any other available prefix or term'. Their discourse on threats to institutional power, especially that of states, therefore, fits within an older discourse on the contemporary problems of 'governability'.[20]

The theme of 'governability' was widely discussed in the wake of the Trilateral Commission Report on *The Crisis of Democracy: Report on the Governability of Democracies* that was published in 1975.[21] That controversial report located the roots of the economic and political crises of the 1970s in the ways grass-roots movements in the late 1960s and early 1970s had generated too much 'democracy'. Its authors called for a restoration of the balance in favour of elite 'governance'. The theme resurfaced in Mexico in the wake of the Zapatista uprising and prior to the August 1974 presidential elections as a variety of political analysts and pundits worried about the possible collapse of the PRI party-state. As that state has continued to disintegrate, as its corruption has become more and more apparent and as it has allowed both regular crime and police lawlessness to spread unchecked, the worries about 'governability' have continued.

While the spectre of 'ungovernability' haunts capitalist policy makers, many of us are fighting for just that: to make it impossible for those who would 'govern' to do so, and to open space for a recasting of democracy in which there are not governors and governed but rather self-determination. When Joel Simon of Pacific News Service reported on Arquilla and Ronfeldt's views, their 1993 paper was circulated on the Net and provoked considerable discussion. How influential the report has been among national security strategists is hard to say, but it did provide the occasion for self-reflection and evaluation among those they warned against.[22]

Such thinking about the emergence of cyberspace challenges to governability have also drawn on the currently popular concept of 'civil society' to contemplate how such threats might be tamed and integrated. In these formulations, 'civil society' is conceived as that part of society dominated by neither state nor market and often best represented by non-governmental organisations (NGOs), for example, human rights, environmental, consumer, women's groups. In a recent RAND paper available through the RAND web site, Cathryn Thorup and David Ronfeldt joined forces to provide a sketch of the problems of integrating the increasingly powerful networks of 'civil society' into a workable balance with the state (hierarchy) and business (market). For those whose understanding of democracy sees the state and business as fundamental obstacles to its realisation, such a conceptualisation can only lead to formulae for cooptation, neutralisation and defeat.[23]

In another sector of RAND, even more closely integrated with the US military, analysts have incorporated Arquilla and Ronfeldt's 'netwar' preoccupations into war-game modelling. A war game called 'The Day After ... in Cyberspace' includes the activities of a fictional NGO called the Committee for Planetary Peace – 'an Internet-intensive, anti-U.S.-military group with suspected Iranian fundamentalist ties'. In the game scenario this NGO is portrayed as 'mobilising all its chapters to thwart the U.S.'s "mad dash" to war'.[24] The parallels with pro-Zapatista, anti-war efforts to block the Mexican government's military actions in Chiapas are striking.

On the side of the computer industry, rogue activity in cyberspace has provoked renewed efforts to enclose as much of that space as possible via commercialisation and the enforcement through the state of 'intellectual property rights', for example, attacks on software

· piracy or copyright violations. With the growth of the commercial and governmental use of the Net, a burgeoning 'operational security' industry has also emerged to create and defend new kinds of electronic 'barbed wire' around enclosed cyberspaces.[25] The infrastructure of the Net has been taken over by private capital (for example, Sprintlink, MCI) and is no longer managed by public institutions such as ARPA or the National Science Foundation.[26] Today all access to the Net is via some commercial gateway. Institutions such as universities pay large fees, individuals pay smaller ones. Computer magazines are filled with advertisements of companies such as America On-line, Prodigy, Delphi and now Microsoft offering competing gateways to the Net and charging varying rates depending on the enclosed services to which access is provided.

With respect specifically to Chiapas, at least two of us who are active in circulating counter-information have separately received lucrative proposals to sell out by funnelling our information to corporate investors. The proposals came in the wake of the peso crisis in December 1994 when many investors lost money in a devaluation they had not foreseen and the government was blaming its moves on the Zapatistas. The proposals, made by an editor of a major business magazine, were for us to provide 'relevant information' from 'alternative sources' that could be sold to capitalists anxious to be on top of things so as to avoid such unexpected crises and losses. We would 'get rich', he said, and of course we could do what we wanted with our money, for example, support the Zapatistas. This entrepreneurial editor foresaw eventually generalising this service from information about Mexico to other countries in Latin America and beyond.

On the side of the state, besides backing up the 'legal rights' of corporate private property, governments struck first against hackers who dared to penetrate the state's own enclosures, for example, military computer systems. The best known cases in the US have been well-publicised FBI arrests of hackers and seizures of equipment. The strategy has been terror: prosecute a few to intimidate others.[27]

The state has since extended its repression to those using the Net to challenge its political hegemony, sometimes charging others with its own crimes, such as terrorism. One good example was the March 1995 Carabinieri Anti-Crime Special Operations Group raid on the Italian 'BITS Against Empire' BBS whose members were accused of 'subversive association with intent to subvert the democratic order'.[28] The 'Omnibus Counterterrorism Act of 1995' submitted to Congress after the Oklahoma bombing threatened to facilitate such repressive tactics in the US. The 'Communication Decency Act' to mandate FCC

(Federal Communications Commission) censoring of the production and circulation of pornography threatened to provide the state with an opening wedge for legal repression. How and whether such censorship can be enforced is still very much an open question. The battle against such legislation has involved widespread mobilisation throughout the Net by those who saw their freedom of speech menaced, even indirectly.[29] More recently, the front line in such struggles has shifted from censorship to encryption with the state wanting 'keys' to all encrypted messages while vast numbers of Netizens (including businesses) are opposed to this invasion of privacy.[30]

Unhampered by legal restrictions in its overseas operations, the CIA is reported to have supported the US invasion of Haiti through psy-ops (psychological operations) warfare via the Internet. As part of a broader set of actions, it sought to undermine resistance to US policy by sending 'ominous e-mail messages to some members of Haiti's oligarchy who had personal computers'.[31]

In the case of the Zapatistas and Mexico, it is clear that the Mexican state is well aware of the way the Net is being used to undermine its credibility and challenge its policies. This became publicly evident when Jose Angel Gurria, Mexican Secretary of State, told an April 1995 gathering of businesspeople at the World Trade Center that the conflict in Chiapas was a 'war of ink, of the written word and a war of the Internet'.[32] How the Mexican government has chosen to fight this 'war of the Internet' has become a hotly debated subject on the Net itself.

There have been assertions of the Mexican government tampering with computer communications and more concrete evidence of government efforts to create a counter-presence on the Internet. One charge has concerned the Profmexis network going down at critical moments such as the elections in August 1994 when upheaval was feared. Another was the disruption of opposition communications in the Mexican Congress.[33] In neither case, however, has any hard evidence been forthcoming. The frequent interjections of a few rabid anti-EZLN commentators on some of the Internet lists have raised suspicions that they are PRI operatives, but so far, the simpler conjecture – that they are just fellow travellers – seems more likely.

A more documented case has involved the Canadian Security and Intelligence Service interviewing members of the Mexico Solidarity Network (MSN) supposedly as part of an investigation of interference of Mexican diplomats in Canadian affairs. MSN organisations, however, think that the interviews were the product of collaboration between Canadian and Mexican intelligence agencies and their real purpose was to intimidate Canadian activists and visiting Mexicans reporting on events in their country. The result of such doubts about the covert intentions of the Mexican and Canadian governments have been protests and a call for a commission of inquiry.[34]

On the other hand, there can be no doubt that the Mexican state has been expanding its overt presence in cyberspace both in Mexico and in the rest of the world. The number of government agencies accessible on-line has been growing. The Consulate General of Mexico in New York and the Mexican Embassy in London have created colourful Web pages offering information about government services and information on Mexico undoubtedly, at least in part, to offset and counter the massive flow of negative information about the Mexican government's actions and policies.

These pages are dominated, naturally, by the usual government propaganda (statements by Zedillo and press releases by various agencies) and public relations material designed to draw tourists and lure investors (pretty pictures, travel information, recipes for Mexican dishes, pointers to business Web sites). The information offered about the situation in Chiapas is minimal and consists of a handful of government pronouncements.

Thus, at present, the Mexican government's public propaganda strategy on the Internet is no different from its more general strategy *vis-à-vis* the EZLN: by minimising public attention it seeks to create the illusion of stability and at the same time maximise the possibilities of either neutralisation or suppression. This strategy is a familiar one and so far the traditional rigid structures of the PRI party-state are merely reproducing their old habits in this new sphere. As a result, visiting such state-sponsored sites is largely a waste of time if not a total dead-end. If, as a result, official spaces in the Net are bypassed and ignored, their political usefulness will be reduced. Clearly the government has not yet been able to achieve anything like an active counter-insurgency presence on the Net.[35] The same can be said, as far as I can see, about all other governments, including that of the United States.

The state of the struggle in cyberspace and beyond

Despite scattered attacks by governments in various countries, the initiative in this area still lies almost entirely on the side of those using the Net for the circulation of struggle. So far, those attacks have been rather crude – police raids and censorship – and caused little disruption to the myriad flows of information and mobilisation that continue to criss-cross the globe. The most effective capitalist initiatives in cyberspace have been the commercialisation of the Internet and the use of electronic communications for organising transnational corporate operations. These efforts, however, have not directly impeded the kinds of struggles I have been describing. Indeed, if anything they have provoked greater international organising to offset the power of multinational capital, for example, the coordination of widespread strike and protest actions in ports around the world in support of Liverpool dock workers. Similarly, efforts to introduce legislation in the US to regulate and control information flows have provoked widespread counter-organisation and mobilisation.

Similar observations hold *vis-à-vis* the Zapatistas and the pro-democracy movement in Mexico. While multinational corporations have used electronic networks in tandem with NAFTA to reorganise themselves against North American workers and consumers, the anti-NAFTA movement and then the Zapatista solidarity networks have elaborated extensive and effective networks of their own. Available evidence suggests that efforts by the state to counter these networks inside the Net have been limited and ineffective.[36] The initiative continues in the hands of the solidarity networks providing support to the Zapatistas.

Nevertheless, it would be dangerous to become complacent in this situation. Just because the state has not found effective ways of countering these struggles does not mean that it will not be able to come up with better tactics in the future. We have seen that our struggles are being observed and studied by the analysts and strategists of the state and of capital more generally. We must continue to monitor their monitoring to see where it leads them. We have seen that Arquilla and Ronfeldt have suggested that the US government 'may want to design new kinds of military units and capabilities for engaging in network warfare'. *Are* such new kinds of units and capabilities being created? Will the US military go beyond war-game scenarios to develop the means to 'penetrate, monitor, disrupt, deceive and dominate any computer or any communications system for any length of time, ideally without being detected', as one CIA veteran has suggested?[37] Obviously, it is in our interest to attempt to keep track of efforts to create such capacities.

At the same time, such analysts see that 'netwar' is quite different from traditional forms of either guerrilla warfare or intelligence and counter-intelligence warfare. Arquilla and Ronfeldt clearly understand that the broad-based, grass-roots struggles being carried on in cyberspace (such as the pro-Zapatista efforts) primarily involve the open circulation and open discussion of political ideas, news about events and detailed reports about ongoing situations. Any kind of politically effective state response would have to go beyond covert disruption to sophisticated overt intervention. While this has yet to happen – to all appearances – it would hardly be without precedence.

The epoch of the Cold War provided ample experience of how a sophisticated propaganda apparatus could be formed and wielded against ideological enemies, both real and imagined. The covert operations of military or intelligence agents were complemented by very overt and much larger-scale anti-communist, counter-revolutionary intellectual warfare. Fighting the wave of revolutionary energy that boiled up in anti-colonial movements and continued in anti-*neo*colonial, pro-national liberation struggles required the new post-Second World War American empire to create a whole new body of foreign policy elites and a research apparatus to support them with information and ideas.[38] It also required the creation of a sophisticated propaganda machine, both public (the United States Information Agencey (USIA), for example) and private (such as think tanks and the mass media).[39] Similarly, in Mexico, the PRI has, over the last decades, built its own apparatuses of ideological warfare and information control.

While the collapse of the Cold War and the disintegration of the ruling coalitions in Mexico have left both of these sets of institutions in some disarray, they have continued their work, albeit perhaps with less unity and consistency than before. This was apparent in the battle over NAFTA where both US and Mexican capital were able to field substantial teams of apologists to attempt to control the debate. It has also been true with respect to the Zapatistas – but with less success.

The differences in the two situations are worth noting. In the case of the battle over NAFTA, capital had the initiative and two hundred years of free-trade arguments at its disposal. The anti-NAFTA networks were forced to create, virtually from scratch, a set of arguments and mass of information to counter that initiative. That they lost is not surprising; that the next round of battle will be on a more even terrain is certain. In the case of the Zapatistas, the *campesinos* of Chiapas and then their supporters had the initiative, first on the ground, then in the world of ideas. Unable to fit the Zapatistas, their organisation and ideas into familiar boxes, the Mexican state has been flailing around defensively, and losing. Its campaign of low-intensity warfare terrorises many *campesinos* in Chiapas, but it continues to lose the broader battle over the future of Mexico. Its failure to cripple the ability of the Zapatistas to present their arguments against the status quo has forced it to cede more and more ground, if not to the Zapatistas directly then to the democratic reform movement that has taken up their banner.

At this point the reform movement itself is probably the key terrain of struggle between the Zapatistas and capital. Those forces within the movement pushing for the Zapatistas to convert themselves from a revolutionary force into one more traditional political party can be seen as the embodiment of the Mexican state's traditional strategy of cooptation (repression via assimilation).[40] As Ronfeldt and Thorup's joint work suggests, the conversion of the Zapatistas into a political party might not even be required for their neutralisation. It might be enough to merely convert them into one more 'independent' organisation among others in a domesticated, neutralised and all too 'civil' society.

To some degree, the forces pushing for such non-revolutionary solutions are already present on the terrain of cyberspace. For the most part they have not yet become active participants but their voices are regularly heard through articles taken from the political battles in the written Mexican press. With the PRI and its official government increasingly discredited, it would seem that the main threat to the development of the Zapatista struggle and to the elaboration of its ideas of real change will come from the ranks of such reformers.

What all of this means is that as the struggles on the Net have expanded from mobilisation against military repression to the circulation of Zapatista ideas and the discussion of their political visions and programmes, the conflicts in this electronic fabric of connections will increasingly take on all the complexity of the more general political, economic and social crises in Mexico.

The future elaboration of flexible, interlinked, uncontrollable networks must be worked out at these increasing levels of complexity. While the experience of the circulation of the Zapatista uprising can teach us much about the ways in which rhizomatically organised, autonomous but linked groups can replace 'the organisation' with its rigidities and hierarchies, we must still grapple with the problem of creating and recreating effective connections along a growing number of dimensions and directions of movement.[41]

The rhizomatic pattern of collaboration has emerged as a partial solution to the failure of old organisational forms; it has – by definition – no single formula to guide the kinds of elaboration required. The power of the Net in the Zapatista struggle has lain in connection and circulation, in the way widely dispersed nodes of antagonism have set themselves in motion in response to the uprising in Chiapas.

The limits to that power lie both in the limits of the reach of the Net (it does not connect everyone) and in the kinds of connections established. There is already an enormous amount of information in the Net about all sorts of struggles which have not yet been connected, not to the Zapatistas, nor to each other. The availability of information and a vehicle of connection does not guarantee either that a connection will be made or that it will be effective in generating complementary action. Even political activists fully capable of tapping all the sources of information about social struggles available on the Net are regularly overwhelmed by the sheer amount of information. As the Net grows, and as the number of groups involved in struggle that are capable and willing to use it grows too, this problem will grow apace. We have seen how the Net helps to overcome isolation and division. It can dramatically accelerate the circulation of struggle. Yet, because the number of divisions are so great and the points of isolation are so numerous, it is clear that no individual, nor any one group, can competently grasp the whole in its particulars.

Those who have sought to govern have long recognised this problem. Arquilla and Ronfeldt think of it in terms of the relationship between hierarchies and networks: 'Our preliminary view is that the benefits of decentralisation may be enhanced if, to balance the possible loss of centralisation, the high command gains topsight ... the view of the overall conflict.'[42] Those of us who are seeking to develop new forms of democratic social relationships should only try to 'solve' this problem in a limited sense. We must abandon the perspective of command and control in favour of consultation and coordination. The problem then, is not to substitute a better 'high command', but to create a world with no command at all. Such a world would have many different 'views' of the whole and be involved in an endless dialogue about its nature, but without the object of control. If the cooperative networks of indigenous peoples have demonstrated the possibility of such a world, continuing invention of the Net has shown how the sinew, or communicative nerve-fibre, of such a world might function. Thus the problems in Chiapas and in the Internet are similar: how to continue the elaboration of new kinds of cooperation and self-determination while preventing the imposition of centralised monopolistic control.

Notes

Technical Note: In several of the footnotes below addresses of various web sites are provided for the interested reader. Because many of the sites are maintained on UNIX servers which are 'case sensitive' it is essential to use the addresses exactly as given with lower case and capital case letters as indicated.

1. This chapter elaborates a theme first laid out in a February 1994 article written for the Italian journal *Riff-Raff*. The English language version is available on-line (gopher:// mundo.eco.utexas.edu:70/11/fac/hmcleave/Cleaver%20Papers).
2. e-mail: hmcleave@eco.utexas.edu homepage: http:// www.eco.utexas.edu:80/Homepages/Faculty/Cleaver/index.html
3. Computer communications constitute only one aspect of a sophisticated use of various forms of electronic technology. The Zapatista solidarity movement has also proved adept at the speedy production and circulation of videos, the genesis and compilation of pro-Zapatista interviews and music on audio tapes and CD-ROM and the use of radio (both legal and pirate) and community-access TV to outflank scanty and biased coverage by the mainstream media.
4. This is the situation with the group whose members constitute MexNews and who gather material for posting on Chiapas-l and Mexico2000 on the Internet. Information on MexNews can be obtained from its coordinator José A. Briones at brioneja@ttown.apci.com
5. Early on, the Latin American Data Base at New Mexico State University issued a regular compendium of Chiapas News. Later Equipo Pueblo began, and continues, to publish Mexico Update in English and Spanish which provides summaries of the latest news about Mexican politics, the Mexican economy and the conflict in Chiapas. The MEXPAZ network of such groups in Mexico (including Equipo Pueblo) now issues four different series of postings on news, human rights, Chiapas and analyses of current events. Other regular postings of news and current article summaries include those of Nuevo Amanecer Press, of the Frente Zapatista de Liberación Nacional (FZLN), of the Centro de Información y Analisis de Chiapas (CIACH), of Melel Xojobal, a service aimed specifically at the indigenous but which now publishes also in English to reach a more global audience.
6. Such as Chiapas95 which is managed by Acción Zapatista de Austin (Texas). Information on Chiapas95 and access to its archives can be found at gopher eco.utexas.edumailinglists/ Chiapas95 or http://www.eco.utexas.edu:80/Homepages/ Faculty/Cleaver/chiapas95.html

7. The electronic version can be found at gopher://
    lanic.utexas.edu:70/11/1a/Mexico/Zapatistas/ The subsequent
    hard-copy version was published with the same title by
    Autonomedia in Brooklyn, New York later in 1994 (ISBN: 1-
    57027-014-7).
8. Rosa Rojas (ed.), *Chiapas, y las Mujeres Qué?* (Mexico: Ediciones
    La Correa Feminista, 1994). A second volume has been published:
    Rosa Rojas (ed.), *Chiapas, y las Mujeres Qué?* Tomo II (Mexico:
    Ediciones La Correa Feminista, 1995).
9. For information on this project, whose CD should eventually
    become commercially available, contact Tamara Ford at
    tamara@home.actlab.utexas.edu
10. A report, compiled by the author in the Fall of 1996 and regularly
    updated, provides a one-stop gateway to over 30 such pages. It
    can be accessed at URL: http://www.eco.utexas.edu/
    faculty/Cleaver/zapsincyber.html
11. Tod Robberson, 'Mexican Rebels Using a High-Tech Weapon:
    Internet Helps Rally Support,' *Washington Post*, 20 February
    1995, p. A1. Russell Watson et al., 'When Words are the Best
    Weapon. Revolution: Information can undermine dictatorships,
    and the faster it flows, the more trouble they're in. How Rebels
    use the Internet and satellite TV', *Newsweek*, 27 February 1995,
    pp. 36–40. *TV Globo* Report, Sunday February 26, 1995; re-run
    by CNN on their weekend World Report the same day.
12. Sheldon Annis, 'Giving Voice to the Poor', *Foreign Policy*, no. 84,
    Fall 1991, pp. 93–106.
13. Cathryn L. Thorup, 'The Politics of Free Trade and the Dynamics
    of Cross-border Coalitions in U.S.-Mexican Relations', *Columbia
    Journal of World Business*, Vol. XXVI, No. 11, Summer 1991,
    pp. 12–26.
14. Cathryn Thorup, 'Redefining Governance in North America:
    The Impact of Cross-Border Networks and Coalitions on Mexican
    Immigration into the UnitedStates', RAND, DRU–219–FF, March
    1993. The paper can be ordered from the RAND through its
    website (http://www.rand.org//).
15. Thorup, 'Redefining', p. 8.
16. Thorup, 'Redefining', p. 53.
17. John Arquilla and David Ronfeldt, 'Cyberwar is Coming!'
    (http://gopher.well.sf.ca.us:70/0/Military/cyberwar). Originally
    published in *Comparative Strategy*, Vol. 12, No. 2, 1993,
    pp. 141–165.

18. John Arquilla and David Ronfeldt, *The Advent of Netwar*, Prepared for the Office of the Secretary of Defense, Santa Monica: RAND (National Defense Research Institute), 1996.

19. Arquilla and Ronfeldt's identification with the US government is clear both directly and indirectly. Their whole essay is concerned with how the government can cope with all threats, from the blatantly military to more subtle informational challenges.

20. There is a certain irony in their logic, in as much as the current popularity of the term cyberspace derives not from its Greek root, but from William Gibson's 'cyber'punk novels which portray a future of governance through the control of information in the bleakest possible manner.

21. Michel J. Crozier, Samuel P. Huntington and Joji Watanuki, *The Crisis of Democracy: Report on the Governability of Democracies* (New York: New York University Press, 1975).

22. Some of this discussion can be found in the archives of Chiapas-l at http://profmexis.dgsca.unam.mx:70/11/foros/chiapasl My own contribution was posted on 20 March 1995 as 'Cyberspace and "Ungovernability"' to Chiapas95 and can be found in its archives.

23. The RAND Corporation web site can be found at: http://www.rand.org// See also: Howard Frederick, 'Computer Networks and the 'Emergence of Global Civil Society', in Linda M. Harasim (ed.) *Global Networks. Computers and International Communication* (Cambridge: MIT Press, 1993).

24. Mark Thompson, 'If War Comes Home: A Strategic Exercise Simulates an Info Attack on the U.S. and its Allies', *Time*, 21 August 1995, pp. 44–46.

25. See: Daniel Brandt, 'Infowar and Disinformation: From the Pentagon to the Net', *Namebase Newsline*, No. 11, October–December 1995 (gopher://ursula.blythe.org/00/pub/NameBase/newsline.11)

26. Glenn Fleishman, 'The Experiment is Over' uploaded to Mexico94 on 4 May 1995. Fleishman is president of Point of Presence Company, an Internet presence provider.

27. Bruce Sterling, *The Hacker Crackdown. Law and Disorder on the Electronic Frontier* (New York: Bantam Books, 1992).

28. 'State Charges Italian Computer Bulletin Board with "Subversion"', European Counter Network, March 1995. The Italian state has become an old hand at such ludicrous charges

since it began using 'anti-terrorism' in the late 1970s to repress its political enemies.

29. For background and updates on the struggle against these censorship proposals see the homepage of the Center for Democracy and Technology at: http://www.cdt.org/cda.html

30. For further information on the debate about encryption, also see the homepage of the Center for Democracy and Technology at: http://www.cdt.org/

31. Douglas Waller, 'CyberWar: The U.S. Rushes to Turn Computers into Tomorrow's Weapons of Destruction. But how Vulnerable is the Home Front?' *Time*, 21 August 1995, p. 40.

32. Rodolfo Montes, 'Chiapas es Guerra de Tinta e Internet', *Reforma*, 26 April 1995, posted at http://www.infosel.com.mx on 26 April 1995.

33. See the report posted to Chiapas-l by the National Commission on Democracy in Mexico on Federal Deputy Carlota Botey's claims of interference with her e-mail (24 February 1995 under the Subject: *Sabotage in Internet*).

34. 'CSIS onto Mexican Activists' newsgroup misc.activism.progressive 4 May 1995.

35. The outcome of current battles within the government over its redesign and 'modernisation' will undoubtedly affect its ability to intervene in the Net. To the degree that Zedillo and other reformers succeed in breaking down old patterns of power, they may create space for new and more imaginative interventions in this sphere as in others.

36. Unfortunately, the efforts outside the Net have been more effective. Fast-track and NAFTA were successfully pushed through by the governments of North America and despite the best efforts of humanitarians in the Net and elsewhere, the Mexican government has been all too successful at keeping reports about its campaign of terrorism in Chiapas out of the mass media.

37. Major Robert David Steele (USMCR) 'The Transformation of War and the Future of the Corps', Cleared for publication 28 April 1992 (http://gopher.well.sf.ca.us:70/0/Military/4_warriors)

38. On the creation of post-Second World War elites and their research apparatus see: David Horowitz, 'Billion Dollar Brains' and 'Sinews of Empire', *Ramparts*, 8, 1969, pp. 33–41.

39. On the character and operation of the post-Second World War propaganda machine see Noam Chomsky, 'Foreign Policy and the Intelligentsia,' in Noam Chomsky, *Towards a New Cold War* (New York: Pantheon Books, 1982).

40. Nevertheless, this 'modern' embodiment should be seen as a sign of weakness of the PRI. In earlier years it would have either annihilated or absorbed the opposition into its own organisation.
41. The term 'rhizomatic' is taken from the essay by Gilles Deleuze and Felix Guattari on 'The Rhizome' which appears in their joint work *Thousand Plateaus* (Minneapolis: University of Minnesota Press, 1987). In that imaginative essay they think through the metaphor of the rhizome as a new way of conceptualising horizontal, non-hierarchical networks of relationships.
42. Arquilla and Ronfeldt, 'Cyberwar is coming'.

5

Breaking the Blockade: The Move from Jungle to City

Patricia King and Francisco Javier Villanueva

'This city is sick', said Durito – excuse me, I mean Don Durito. Don Durito, a little beetle of a fellow, a knight errant from somewhere in the Lacandon Jungle, is one of the many imaginary characters created by Subcomandante Marcos. Durito was on a visit to Mexico City, and was writing to Marcos with a diagnosis which could be applied to all big cities, whether modern, postmodern, or submodern:

> This city is sick with loneliness and fear. It's a huge collectivity of lonelinesses. It is many cities, a different one for each of the people who live here. This isn't a sum of individual anguishes (do you know any loneliness that is not anguished?), but anguish raised to a power: each loneliness is multiplied by the lonelinesses that surrounds it ... Each loneliness is a mirror reflecting another loneliness, which, like a mirror, bounces back lonelinesses.

And Marcos remarks: 'Durito has begun to realise that he's on alien ground, and that the city is not the place for him.'[1]

So what is Don Durito's place, the Zapatistas' own home ground? If we can begin to answer that question, even if we open up others, we'll have gone some way towards defining what it means to be a Zapatista, and what commitment that involves.

Zapatista strength lies in the power of work: community and transformation

If Durito discovers that the city is no place for him, it is not because he rejects its glut of riches, knowledge and power, in favour of the poverty of the countryside. That glut and that poverty are the two sides of the same coin. The Zapatistas cannot demand integration into modern society because they are already integrated, not through society's excesses but through its corresponding deficiencies.

104

So Durito is not turning his back on the city as such, he is rejecting the collectivity of loneliness and fear. He finds his home in the struggle, and in community (common-unity): the community of work and struggle. We might ask why that community has developed in the countryside, rather than in the city. But if we study the relationship between the Zapatistas and the city, the distance between city and countryside is not what matters, so much as the gap between the community of struggle and work on the one hand, and the collectivity of loneliness and fear on the other.

Loneliness works on the term 'community' to give it a romantic and sentimental meaning: newspapers speak of the European community, governments of the national community, and bankers of the financial community. Yet their talk only seeks to put a shiny wrapping on groups of lonely beings who pay homage to the notion of 'competitiveness'. Here each loneliness is competing with all the others to see which can exclude the others. In this world individuals are representatives of nothing but what they own and serve, be it their business, their job, or their knowledge: they spend their whole lives trying to maintain and expand it, cost what or whom it may. Loneliness is living like a thing in a world of things.

In contrast, when the Zapatistas speak of community they are talking about the real thing. They may be speaking seriously, or joking about it, but they never use the word in a demagogic manner. And while it is true that their base is made up of small, indigenous communities which have managed to survive and bring to the movement their wisdom and capacity for resistance, it is also true that these same small communities have transformed themselves to create the Zapatista movement, and are sketching out a vision of how larger communities of a new type might be organised in the future. Besides, the privilege of defining what *community* means should not be left to those living in loneliness, since it is as important or more important for the future than any other category, economic, sociological or historical. The most rigorous and demanding definition is the one formulated by Sartre developing Marx's ideas in the light of the experience of this century and of the critique of anthropology and sociology.[2] Taking this definition, Durito's diagnosis can be seen to be better-founded than one might think.

A community group forms as a result of a need or danger affecting all its members in a global way. Such a community defines itself by the common goal which guides the *collaboration* between its members, whereby they aim at a collective resolution of the situation which caused them to unite ('unity comes with struggle, unity comes with action'). Need, objective and transformation are all decisive *in so far*

as they are shared by all members of the group: each finds his or her own
need reflected in the need of the other; each recognises the objective
as a goal *to be achieved for all and by all, or not at all*; each respects the
other's work as part of the whole, and answers to the rest for his or
her own work. This is the idea captured so precisely by the Zapatistas'
two central slogans: 'everything for everyone, nothing for ourselves';
and 'command obeying'.[3]

The thinking which springs from this cannot be a repetition of dead
clichés. The Zapatistas are having to find material ways of overcoming
the material situation which threatens them, and that means *creating*
a new situation. It means using the tools which are to hand, products
themselves of the situation they are rebelling against. This sort of
community *praxis* can have several different outcomes (there is no
longer destiny, only a future to be created). The thinking and language
which characterise the movement must be open-ended, not without
echoes of the past and a consciousness of inertia, but also laden with
fecund promise.

The community group only takes on massive dimensions in
moments of revolution, when it becomes the characteristic feature
of such moments.[4] Of course, there are communities and there are
communities. We can distinguish them by their social content, their
form of organisation and their size, etc. But the essential difference
lies in the direction of their movement. All of them tend to be
surrounded by a sea of lonelinesses; but whereas for a state community
the collectivity of lonelinesses is the condition of its power ('divide
and rule'), for the revolutionary community the collectivity of
lonelinesses is a suffocating gag ('the people united, will never be
defeated'). So if the Zapatistas have proved to be intransigent in one
thing, it has been in seeking unity with any collectivity of lonelinesses
that begins to move and realign itself against the party state.

The real struggle is between the revolutionary community and the
statist community. In this struggle, the collectivity of loneliness
plays an ambiguous role: on the one hand it is a barrier containing
the revolutionary community and defending the statist community,
but, on the other hand – precisely because, as Durito says, there is
no loneliness without anguish – the collectivity of loneliness is a
potential for the generalisation of the revolutionary community, one
which threatens to isolate the statist community. When the
collectivity of loneliness is subverted by *its own members*, and
transformed *by them* into a revolutionary community, the days of
the statist community will be numbered. Conversely, when the
revolutionary community disintegrates and relapses into a collectivity
of loneliness, the statist community will have reaffirmed its power.

This brings us to the issue at the heart of the Zapatista movement and, in fact, of all revolutions: the question of power. If power is understood as the effectiveness of one praxis against another, then the confrontation between the statist community and the revolutionary community is clearly a confrontation between powers: communal insurgent praxis can only be born and grow, in so far as it proves itself effective against government praxis; similarly, government praxis can only survive as long as it succeeds in reducing – controlling or eliminating – any other communal praxis which appears within its territory. It is, necessarily, a struggle between powers. The Zapatistas are a community of communities in arms, with their own set of social relations (command structures, laws) and their own territory. They reproduce themselves and interact with society in spite of and against the arms and orders of the state community. The Zapatistas are a nascent power, the embryo or one of the atoms of a new power. Thus their struggle develops by successively breaking the bounds intended to separate them from the collectivity of loneliness, with each outbreak appearing as the emergence of new communes liberating themselves from loneliness and fear.

Yet the struggle is not about *taking* power. The efficacy of one praxis over another is not something which can 'be taken', as you might pick up a tool; it must, and can only, take shape from the material through which it works. Power in action takes form in the political institutions it creates and shapes to extend its rule. Taking power means that a new community takes control of the institutions formerly used by the old community to exercise its power, thus displacing and reducing the old community. A revolutionary community cannot do this, because the efficacy of such institutions lies in their capacity to maintain the collectivity of loneliness and eliminate revolutionary communities. For reasons of immediate 'efficiency', the revolutionary community may feel tempted to manipulate the collectivity of loneliness against the state community – or may feel it has no alternative. But in so doing, it transforms itself into another state community, losing its own revolutionary character in the act. The revolutionary community also needs 'tools', not for building barricades, but for breaking them down.

The Zapatistas do not propose to take power, but rather to develop the community they represent to the utmost. The power which this implies is a form of power based on the direct democracy ('command obeying') of all those seeking community satisfaction of communal needs ('everything for everyone, nothing for ourselves') and developed with nothing more than their hands and their voices. This power can only be the power of their work: it is a democratic power, both deliberative and executive, open to everyone so long as they do not claim property of the products of communal work.[5] It is a power which exists only to break bounds, and which carries inside it the extinction of itself and of all power. It is a power which necessarily criticises itself and power in general, all power. Yet it does not cease to be power: it has to prove its efficacy against the praxis of those whose interests are based on their claim to privileged property over the products of common work. It must be effective against the power deployed through those products of labour, concentrated and accumulated in the hands of a few.[6]

It is a power struggle, therefore, between the power of work and the power of the things which, torn from the work that produced them, are turned against it and subjugate it: the power of capital. If we do not consider carefully the force of things, there is a risk that the Zapatista movement might be misread as a re-bound version of utopian communism – either idealising it ingenuously or condemning it meanly. In order to recognise that the Zapatistas are not only proposing to develop the revolution they represent to its ultimate conclusion, but also that they are doing so consistently with what is historically possible, we need to attribute due weight to the huge gravitational mass whose symbol continues to be industry.

The power of capital lies in the force of things: loneliness and inertia

The loneliness of which Durito speaks is not the absence of social relations, but rather an enormous abundance of relationships buried beneath the relations between things. That is why he discovers loneliness to be an epidemic not of the countryside – where one might expect to find isolation – but of the city, which is the seat of power of the kingdom of things, whether they be commodities, machines, texts, institutions or any other product of social labour.

The power of things is overwhelming: it is there in the city's power to attract migrants and swallow them whole; in the factory's power to concentrate and mechanise the workforce; in the power of machines to bring workers together and prevent their association; in the power of housing to compartmentalise families and silence them; in the power of a video-player to isolate us in a room; in the power of alcohol, ingested or inhaled, to trap us in a fantasy world, in the power of ... Certainly, electronic networks, with their e-mail and discussion groups, as well as videos have gone some way towards undermining the power of the radio and television chains, as their role in the Zapatista movement has clearly shown. But as quickly as they spread, they are blocked by the traffic of loneliness and by images of fear.

Things dictate their own laws. In their kingdom, all actions have a predetermined outcome. History is known in advance, and the men and women of flesh and blood who make it, never make an appearance. They are the mass-produced creatures of history, made to execute its dictates. There is no room for thought or action to come alive, or for human beings to relate in community; only for the following of instructions and pre-set scripts. It is the things themselves that, like chains, 'unite' each person with others, be it in production, distribution or communication. Rules and roles. This is the power which shuts each one off from the others. Loneliness becomes a refuge, where solitary beings are so terrorised by their own powerlessness, that they can no longer recognise their loneliness and fear for what they are.

For those city-dwellers who have abandoned the struggle to make homes, factories, neighbourhoods, sports, videos and information super-highways into tools for community communication, there remains only one option. They buy something which allows them to escape from their reality, which transports them to a virtual reality where people neither miss nor fear one another, where the other is neither present nor absent but simply does not exist, where there is no such thing as a human subject. Just as you can have junk food, you can have junk communities. Nearly everything in these cities serves the same purpose: to subjugate human beings to things – and make them feel at ease in their subjugation.

Durito's condemnation is very specific. He does not condemn a state of mind, but the existential reality underpinning all social relationships under this system. Capital is a social relation, a relation which is at the same time economic, political and cultural, a relation between real, live, flesh-and-blood human beings, a *relation produced by them*. And we human beings can only relate to one another through things, whether they be words or bullets, gifts or commodities, creations or rules. The important question is what dominates the relationship between people: human beings or the things they produce. In capitalism, the social relationship is dominated by the products of labour (economic, political and social). The product controls the worker rather than the other way about.

So Duritos's condemnation hits at the very heart of capital. It hardly matters whether we choose to look at a factory or a football match, a financial system or a school of thought. In each case, capital is present wherever the living work of people acting together is made subservient to the extended reproduction of the labour objectivised in the particular thing. This is the point at which the owner of the thing becomes a businessperson, and the worker turns into a wage slave (need we spell out the worker's political and cultural counterparts?). Here the production of wealth becomes the exploitation of the producer, and cooperation for a common goal is transformed into competition among producers and the things they produce. Rational planning in the production of each thing is replaced by anarchy in the production of everything. In short, social coexistence turns into class struggle, and the production of wealth is transformed into the production of economic, political and cultural misery. Or, to put it in Durito's terms, the community of work and struggle turns into the collectivity of loneliness and fear.

At the start of this chapter, we asked why the revolutionary community had developed in the countryside first, rather than in the city. We can now rephrase the question: why is it that this condemnation which strikes at the heart of capital originates in the most impenetrable depths of the jungle, instead of coming from the centre of industry, finance, culture and power? And if before we asked whether the Zapatista project might not be seen as just another manifestation of utopian communism, we now have to ask if the condemnation of the existential reality of capitalism would be understood by industrial and urban workers as the condensation of all the economic, political and cultural condemnations of the system of wage slavery.

A sizeable number of people from the intellectual and militant Left – especially those in the city – have reacted defensively to these paradoxes. Their 'knowledge' of this Left has come into conflict with the experience of the rebellion. Instead of revolutionising their knowledge to raise it to the level of praxis, they have laboriously tried to reshape the uprising in Chiapas so as to make it fit their preconceived ideas. They believe that if the jungle communities live in the rearguard of economic and political development, they simply cannot be the vanguard of democratic, economic and cultural transformation. That's the end of the argument, so far as they are concerned. All the rest is just a question of fitting the evidence to support their basic premise, dismissing as irrelevant any evidence which might call it into question. This kind of subjugation of thought to knowledge is another example of how things dominate praxis, and of how objectivised labour dominates living labour.

With few exceptions, thinking on the Left has been trapped in domination of this kind, since the time of Stalin. It has caused a paralysis of knowledge, and a growing process of disintegration which has led many to abandon the movement. Because of it, the conflict between knowledge and experience, which normally would be considered natural and positive, has developed in these conditions into a crisis which is extremely difficult to resolve. The inertia of the traditional Left has been one of the hardest barriers to overcome, in the Zapatistas' struggle to reach an understanding with their brothers and sisters in the city.

Durito did not take long to identify the barrier. If you go to the city and start talking about 'community', the traditional Left will take it as a confession of backwardness and an attempt to find followers among indigenous groups and peasants, abandoned housewives, liberation Christians, and romantics of all hues who still lament the lost community. Their response will depend on how much mileage they think they can get out of the slogans. Talk of 'command obeying' might win votes, but calls into question electoral practice. Likewise, the phrase 'everything for everyone, nothing for ourselves' condemns the privileges of government and employers, but also strikes at the root of trade union practice. So long as the Zapatista slogans are confined discreetly to banners, this Left will welcome them. But turn them into criteria for action or for living, and you will find the door closed in your face. They are acceptable only for as long as they stay limited to clichés, as long as they are not brought to life in action.

The Zapatistas have called the theories and organisational strategies of the traditional Left 'outworn and tarnished robes'. There is a clear relationship between these 'robes' and the kind of moribund thinking characteristic of the lonely, frightened individual who seeks to adapt his or her life to the dictates of the kingdom of things. The traditional Left believes that the Zapatista uprising is just one more peasant battle in the struggle to resist the savage development of capitalism. It is another example of what has always happened: everything comes down to a redistribution of things. The traditional Left is corporativist: it believes in organising 'the masses' along the lines of a machine. It does not organise itself alongside the rest, but administers the masses like an exercise in social engineering. It believes in the vanguard, not as an inference drawn from the dynamic process of reflection on action, but as something that is fixed, as the premise of all thought. This Left is a profound believer in the State: the State is, of course, the supreme machine, which subjects the masses through the powerful forces of inertia.

And yet it is the very force of things that, by its development, has made it possible that from a place like the Chiapas jungle there should be launched those challenges which go to the heart of capital, although this possiblity has become reality only thanks to the will and intelligence of the Mayan Zapatista communities. Thus, there is already present in the knowledge of the Left the possibility of resolving the dilemmas that the Zapatista challenge has created for it, without abandoning its principles or tampering with the evidence.

Two features of capitalist development are relevant here, one geographical and the other temporal. The domination of objectivised labour is spread geographically through a kind of network, which leads to an increasing concentration of things in industrial centres; the communication and transportation of things between these centres gets faster and faster, embracing also the outlying regions connected to each centre by a network of 'free-floating' threads. It remains true then that the strongholds of capital are principally in the industrial centres, and it is not possible to conceive of its overthrow without the urban proletariat joining in revolutionary community among themselves and with the rural proletariat. Yet the 'revolution' in information and transport has made a qualitative difference to geographical and social distance. During the 1910–19 Revolution, the Zapatista and Villista forces had to take the cities by storm and they were often surprised by the behaviour of the 'doctors' and even of the workers. When they entered the City of Mexico, it was as much an event for the revolutionaries themselves as for the city's population. Nowadays that has changed: today's Zapatistas know the streets of the centre of the capital better than many of its own functionaries; they have lived and worked as migrants all over the country, as well as in the United States and Central America; they speak two or three languages; they suffer the same television channels and radio stations as most of the workers in the city. In 1910, workers were quite familiar with life in the countryside, while peasants knew nothing about the cities. In 1994, it was the other way about, with the Zapatistas knowing the city much better than the urban proletariat knew the countryside. There is, then, nothing to stop a revolutionary community of communities in the depths of the jungle, from launching a strategy of struggle directed at the very heart of capital, based on an understanding of the essential features of capitalist domination as a whole.

Temporally, capital's domination develops like a series of pulse beats, with democratising waves and fascistic backwashes. The bottlenecks in the concentration and circulation of the products of labour are broken to the extent that the interests that come into contradiction with the functioning of the system as a whole are swept aside. But the room for manoeuvre of the handful of financial magnates has grown enormously, both spatially and temporally, independently of whether the sum of properties has grown or not.

And now it is not just finance capital that is capable of rapid movement: directly productive capital is as well. At the beginning of the century, the decisions of an investor might have been capable of upsetting or precipitating a crisis in one branch of industry; now they can bring about the economic collapse of entire countries, across several continents. Before, years might pass before the effects of their decisions were fully felt; now the process takes place in a matter of days. Thus, it took until the 1910 Revolution for the end-of-century agreement between the Mexican government and English railway entrepreneurs to meet resistance from the then Zapatista communities. By 1994 this had changed, and the NAFTA agreement was met by the current Zapatista rebellion on the very day of its entry into force. The extended reproduction of the system as a whole still requires the breaking of bottlenecks, but the quantity and diversity of the interests vested in each possible bottleneck are of such a scale that it becomes more and more difficult to threaten a single one without engendering the immediate and massive resistance of a vast coalition of interests, in the face of which the reproduction of the system appears as a particular interest. There are now more and more things which, as soon as they are touched, are immediately revealed as being of common interest to more and more lonelinesses (from city, countryside and jungle) and which draw them together, urging them to form a democratic community in the face of the increasingly fascist power of financial capital.

This is the point where the collectivity of loneliness and fear enters into articulation with the community of work and struggle. Just as the kingdom of things over work translates into the repression of struggle and disintegration of community, so the same kingdom not only signifies the possibility of constituting ever-larger communities, but also constantly stimulates their constitution, as a necessary condition for the expansion of the kingdom of things itself. This brings us to the stage foreseen by Marx, when capital – like a vampire – becomes so dependent on the community which it seeks to suck dry, that it cannot help but generate the conditions for the birth and reproduction of community. It is another apect of the way in which accumulated labour feeds on living labour. The power of labour is the keystone of all this.

The lonelinesses form themselves into a community by breaking through boundaries

Not all commodities are opiates within the kingdom of things – a sign of the power of labour; and not all people can leave off resisting a domination which for most of us means death. There is also a force in things which pushes towards struggle. This is why loneliness and fear are afflictions, not permanent conditions. Mexico City has seen many large-scale mobilisations: there were the big trade union uprisings in 1958–59, and 1972–76; the student movement of 1968; the 1981–83 uprising of rural peasants and teachers, together with the urban popular movement; the civic rebellion, following the earthquake of 1985, and the electoral fight of 1988 to oust the Party which held power for 70 years.

The most graphic example is the 1985 earthquake. The very floor of the city shook, bringing down buildings and burying thousands of bodies beneath the heavy walls. The same force of things, which before had trapped people in tragic isolation, now brought them face to face with a huge and spiralling collective tragedy. There was an urgent need for action, and the very weight of things meant that people had to act collectively. The civil protection services did not arrive, so people had to work together without them; we had to take charge of the situation and direct actions ourselves. Communal praxis sprang into being, through the cracks opened up by the disintegration of buildings and services. Autonomous rescue groups were formed, appearing like a flash of freedom in the darkness of the kingdom of things. When the services did turn up, they brought conflict. Instead of strengthening the rescue effort, they obstructed it. Soon it was clear that they were more concerned with controlling the crowd than with rescuing victims. They were working against living praxis and its struggle to win the race against death. People had to work collectively, outside the institutions and against them.

Beginning there, the autonomous rescue groups formed communities with objectives which went beyond the rescue of those buried in the quake: their aim was to rescue the living labour buried underneath the institutions. Large numbers of groups began permanent work: having tasted the experience of a community of work, they were not about to lose it. In the months that followed, they joined forces with various movements throughout the country. A broad movement began to grow, part of which joined ranks with the 1988 electoral struggle, beating the state party at the polls in Mexico City and in many other areas. They were unable to get rid of the party-state, however: electoral fraud led to the imposition of the official candidate, Carlos Salinas, as the country's new president.

The immediate effect of the defeat was a renewed drive towards loneliness and fear. With the loss of its objectives (a loss which was to last six years), action lost its meaning and slid back into inertia. Once the horizon for external transformation was closed, action turned inwards. People began attending meetings out of a sense of obligation, and the meetings themselves began to revolve around the bureaucratic administration of things. In-fighting got worse and started to blow up into all kinds of opportunism. The robes were quickly getting old and tattered. People's fear extended to include erstwhile compañeros. Loneliness came to be seen as a refuge. It was the same old sickness.

But some ground had been gained, as we found out when the need for urgent action returned. Only this time it was inspired, not by the concrete shaking under our feet, but by a declaration from the jungle and the wildfire cry which heralded it: Enough!

The Declaration of the Jungle speaks clearly. Things – precious wood, dams, oil, coffee plantations, 'free trade' agreements, courts, languages – had brought all their weight to bear on the indigenous communities, displacing them further and further down the *cañadas* (glens or valleys), excluding them from all that was materialised in their eleven demands: work, land, housing, food, health, education, independence, democracy, justice, liberty and peace. They had nothing left to lose but the lives of their children. The communities were under threat, the only strength they could count on was the force inseparable from their own existence: the lives of their members, their community and their work, and 'little' things – like their own bodies, reduced by centuries of hunger and sickness. They needed to draw on the power of things in order to resist, but the same power had robbed them of nearly all they had. They were left with the strength of their arms, their eyes, their words and the inhospitable jungle. Out of this, they had to recover everything in reverse, from the bottom up, with nothing to help them but the common unity of their work, and the power of the things within their grasp.

'They are rich in one thing only ... their people'[7]

The declaration of war, rather than being an instrumental step, was simply the only way in which they could live as human beings; that it was also a tool was of secondary importance. Life was being made impossible for them, and the day came when the only impossible thing was to accept the impossibility of living. They were surrounded. They could neither live nor not live. The only option left was to create a new life. The 'Enough!' was born: insubordination, rebellion and war, the Zapatista community, the specialists in breaking through boundaries.

The tremors were felt at once throughout the country. Meetings were called again (the break from loneliness) and people began to mobilise (the break from fear). The uprising opened a crack in the information blockade, enough to produce an effervescence of meetings. It was less easy to re-*unite*. Those first meetings, built on the remains of earlier ones in the hope of resurrecting them, fell victim to the weight of their own inertia: in their desire to understand the armed uprising, they found themselves trapped in memories of *foquismo* (the small-cell theory of guerrilla warfare); the EZLN initials reminded them too much of the FLMN and FSLN;[8] the participation of the indigenous population was a reminder of *Sendero*. It seemed that these meetings could not progress beyond their own memories. The absence of an open-ended future made action and common unity impossible. So the meetings became repetitive, and were unable to break new ground.

Nevertheless, it was clear from the start that the rebellion owed its existence to the people of the region. This was not just a commando group but various detachments which simultaneously occupied four towns and maintained an attack on the army headquarters for several days. Many women took part, and many of the rebels were armed only with sticks. Both the attack and the retreat were highly organised, and a fair number of combatants wore uniform. There was a plan, a command structure, discipline and equipment in a body of people whose number surpassed that of the population of an average-sized town of the region. And they had taken the country by surprise. The only possible explanation, although it left some questions unanswered, was that the uprising must have been worked on for a long time and in close collaboration with the great majority of the local population. For groups meeting in the city, the uncertainty continued, but from the very beginning they had a sense that they were witnessing a genuinely revolutionary and popular struggle. Hope began to stir within the collectivity of loneliness.

Just as there is a time for doubts, so too there are moments when you have to act with the certainties and hopes you have available. The military machinery of capitalism was advancing on the rebel communities. Action in the cities was imperative to counter government savagery. It was a question of now or never. Large-scale mobilisation was needed immediately. We city dwellers could set the march of our bodies on the streets to oppose the advance of the tanks on the country roads, just as we had used our backs in 1985 to shift the weight of fallen roofbeams. Small meetings of former compañeros were no longer enough. Isolated meetings were just as impotent as isolated individuals. So messengers were sent from one meeting to another, and coordinations sprang to life, 'meetings of meetings' where those who called the meeting were the same as those who were called to it.[9] These thousands of meetings began to come together around three different coalitions, each with a previous history: the NGOs (non-governmental organisations), the political Left, and organisations linked with economic demands. Increasing the size of meetings meant that there was more inertia to be overcome, and things got more institutionalised; but a coordination did emerge and succeeded in pulling together the mobilisation which was needed. On the basis of the accumulated work of these three poles, the new meetings forged ahead to culminate in the great demonstration of 12 January, which stopped the government genocide.

The city did not take sides with the Zapatista cause; it simply insisted on their right to exist and be heard. We were still unaware that this was precisely what the Zapatista cause was all about. The EZLN had broken through the first blockade, and the collectivity of loneliness had taken its first step towards community.

The battle over separate negotiations

The government halted its military offensive, while simultaneously taking a series of measures (summarised in the replacement of several important government functionaries), which involved massive mobilisation of material resources at both federal and local state level. Budget lines, the intelligence services, the electoral system, business activities were all affected. In politics, people are clusters of interconnected commitments. Within the state party, the ties connecting them add up to a poisonous network ruled by complicity, a mafia of mafias. As in every state, these commitments involve business, the extraction of surplus value and a share in its distribution, which requires things to be organised in a particular way. The government reshuffle meant that a good number of these commitments were renegotiated (though not exactly with the Zapatistas).

It was not a matter of the president deciding to act in a Machiavellian way. Machiavelli's Prince is today's State (or perhaps, in our case, Godfather would be a better name for it). In reality, the network of commitments was already collapsing under pressures, of which the EZLN was only the tip of the iceberg. The State was trying to neutralise the leading popular sectors, which were in the process of unifying with the Zapatista rebellion. Its first targets included the indigenous and peasant organisations in Chiapas, the urban coordinations and the political Left. Each, separately, was offered the chance to bring its demands to the negotiating table. If they agreed, and the strategy was successful, the State believed it could easily crush those who continued in opposition.

The strategy rested on the premise that the popular organisations would mobilise as usual through the inertia of the vote and the petition. In fact, starting on 1 January 1994, this inertia began to be overturned by the rank and file. But it was hard for people who had spent years in the struggle for winning delegates' posts to start following the idea of 'command obeying'. Likewise, people who were expert at managing the particular demands of their members did not easily adjust to a fight whose slogan was 'everything for everyone, nothing for ourselves'. The government move was timed to stop organisations being engulfed by the wave of popular excitement, and entering into community confrontation with the state party. It was not so much about negotiating with the Zapatistas, as about isolating them. The government hoped to seal them off behind a new barrier, the worst of all – that which is built with the backs of their own brothers.

The political Left and several organisations with economic demands, agreed to separate negotiations. The Zapatistas were in a tight corner: they could hardly reject a cease-fire imposed on the government by civil society, when they were trying to build links with civil society; but neither could they accept negotiations whose primary purpose was to isolate them from the rest of civil society. It looked like checkmate. The Zapatistas responded by saying 'We will dialogue, but not negotiate.' Time after time, they insisted 'We will go to the dialogue, but with reservations.' They made a dramatic call to other organisations: 'our demands are national demands, the dialogue must be national'; '... don't leave us alone'. Included was a challenge: 'Dignity'.

However, the Zapatistas' search to build community with the rest of the country's workers led them to put in the centre of their strategy the continuation of the other dialogue, the dialogue without reservations which was just beginning with civil society. As their weapons fell silent, their voices took over. The barricade thrown around them was soon demolished by the enormous quantity of videos and interviews which began to circulate. It was the government, and the organisations holding separate negotiations, which ended up isolated. The Zapatistas' success in communication reflected the authenticity of their message, rather than good technique: the sense of identification felt by those 'at the bottom' when they heard and saw the Zapatistas' talk proved decisive.

These voices began to reveal to us something that was just the opposite of the small guerrilla cell (*foco*); we were really seeing whole communities rising up in arms. But it was not an uprising which could have been organised overnight. It had been ripening for a long time, in the heart of the communities. The choice of Zapata as their figurehead was not an attempt to give Central American experience a Mexican face – Zapata was simply the figure most suited to personify their movement. They were confirming that the EZLN was not something we had begun to suspect was impossible anyway, and they were showing us just what it was: a real community of revolutionary work, involving whole towns and villages, and firmly rooted in history. It was a practical, immediate invitation to us to avoid the fate awaiting us in the kingdom of things, and to create a human future for ourselves.

On 4 March people's doubts were further allayed, when the Zapatista delegates returned to their communities and told the assemblies which had elected them what the government had offered at the end of the 'dialogue-with-reservations'. The assemblies discussed the offer and voted on it point by point. The consultation was an example of direct democracy in action, which bore out what Marcos had told us weeks before, about how the decision was made to take up arms:

> There's a discussion of the pros and cons until the community itself decides that it's time to vote. They record the results, showing how many were in favour, how many against, how many said they didn't know, with no distinction between men, women or children. Then ... the local representatives pass the results to the regional representatives, from there they go to the area coordination, from there to the Committees, and finally to the High Command.[10]

Actions like these, and the natural way in which the Zapatistas took up, and respected, the simple words of their members, were decisive in convincing people in the city that we did not have to keep our distance from them. It was no longer a question of judging them from the outside, from above, or from past experience. We could recognise ourselves in their action. The 'we' started to establish itself. The Zapatistas began to conquer the city, using the skill most characteristic of them: they used their weapons to speak with the simple and sincere voice of the community in arms. The words of the indigenous people opened gaping holes in the walls which had been thrown up around them, leaving exposed the lords of money and power on the other side.

In several areas, new coordinations came into being and began to mature. The 10 April anniversary of Zapata's murder by the founders of today's state party, was an opportunity for everyone to work together. During February and the first half of March, it was becoming clearer and clearer that the EZLN was winning the battle, at least in the central and southern parts of the country. Everything seemed to indicate that 10 April would be the day when the people would pass judgement, during a huge, popular, and Zapatista, demonstration in Mexico City's great main square. It would not bring down the government, but it could be the start of a massive anti-government movement, which would be almost impossible to stop.

The Godfather

The State had to resort to a switch in policy, which was even more abrupt than their about-face on 12 January. This time, they feared that the plebs who were planning to occupy the metropolitan main square might be the ones to mobilise huge material resources and begin a global restructuring. The State had to seize the initiative. They had to come up with something more decisive, with more impact, than anything they had done before – and they had to do it before 10 April. Within the mafia of mafias each *capo* responded to the emergency which threatened all of them.[11] Although there was only one crisis, there were several potential solutions. Anything was possible, from a Czechoslovakia-style transition, to a Pinochet-style *coup d'état*. The Godfather controls many people, and some seem to know what he is thinking without being told. The Godfather lives in rooms connected by a maze of secret corridors. We know very little about what actually happened: on 23 March, a bullet to the head killed the official party's presidential candidate, Luis Donaldo Colosio. Whatever lay behind it, it was just what was needed and came at precisely the right moment to deal with the crisis. It was not for nothing that the public gaze turned to the then president, Carlos Salinas, and his chief political advisor, José Córdoba Montoya.

Whoever was responsible for the killing, the whole state party became an immediate accomplice, together with their usual international allies. International reserves fell by 36 per cent in a few weeks,[12] but the United States authorised a $6 billion emergency loan and the Bank of Mexico expanded the monetary base in order to achieve more than 4.5 per cent growth in the economy during the second and third quarter of that year, around six times more than the growth rate during the previous five quarters. State terrorism was thus able to contain and reduce the wave of popular excitement.[13] The renegotiation of all the accords and deals between the different mafias was accompanied by a drastic revision of social beliefs and assumptions. Put simply, there was a general feeling that society had become a dangerous place overrun by wolves. The EZLN declared an emergency alert, fearing a new military offensive, while the political

Left was content with a political stand-off, pending a redefinition of the electoral contest. There was nobody capable of challenging the Godfather and of calling him to account for the killing and the massive monetary fraud. The power of things took over once again, and brutally reimposed the collectivity of loneliness and fear on the country, to such effect that in the August elections, the counterfeit currency was converted into votes for the Godfather.

The electoral battle for power was immediately decided in favour of the mafias, and reduced to an internal struggle between them. The political Left had simply retired to the sidelines. So it was the state party which emerged triumphant from the crisis, amid flying bullets and banknotes. Those on top monopolised politics, just as they did the money supply. The Zapatistas had to continue acting in the short term, but with their gaze fixed on the fruits that would be harvested in times set by the understanding of those at the bottom.

'No' to the Government, and the call for a national convention

The Zapatistas took until 10 June to formulate their reply, which appeared as the Second Declaration of the Jungle. Its message was basically a reaffirmation of their original cry of 'Enough!': a No! to the government offer, and a recommitment to open dialogue, without reservations, with civil society. With this last in mind, the Zapatistas began the construction of a new town on the edge of rebel territory, called Aguascalientes, built around an auditorium with space for 10,000 people.

The new thrust to break the blockade came in the form of a proposal for dialogue, which tied together the immediate electoral struggle with the future of the popular struggle. Far from suggesting that civil society should opt out of an electoral battle which seemed lost from the outset, the Zapatistas undertook to join in community with the many people who had decided to work for the electoral defeat of the state party. It was not an opportunist decision, but one based on the very principles of community building: 'It is necessary that the hope that walks in the large-scale mobilisations should return to the leading place where, by right and reason, it belongs.'[14]

Within the electoral battle, the Zapatistas were fighting to have the general interests of the movement take priority, arguing that the electoral struggle for power should come second to the development of popular power. They called for

... a National Democratic Convention (CND), both sovereign and revolutionary, to formulate proposals for a government of transition, and for a new national law ... The basic goal of the CND is to organise the voice of civil society and defend the will of the people.

It was understood that the CND would not resemble a parliamentary assembly: 'The CND will be formed through local, regional and state-level committees, in *ejidos*, neighbourhoods, schools and factories.'

The EZLN went further:

The problem of poverty in Mexico is not just to do with a lack of resources ... any response, whatever direction it takes, can only succeed in putting the problem off, so long as it ignores the need for a new set of political relations, at national, regional and local level; that is, for a framework of democracy, liberty and justice ...

We are not proposing a new world, but something much more provisional: just the anteroom for a new Mexico. This revolution will not end in a new class, or fraction of a class, or power group, but rather in a free and democratic 'space' for political struggle ... A new set of political relations will be born.[15]

Months later, Marcos was to call it 'a revolution to build the revolution'. The essential contribution of the Zapatistas was to demonstrate democracy to those on the Left who preached revolution, and demonstrate revolution to those advocating democracy. The Zapatistas are fighting for democratic revolution and an uninterrupted transition to the revolution, which will end the problem of poverty in Mexico and project a 'new world'.

We might question the sharp separation they make between politics and economics, the definition of democratic revolution solely in terms of changes in political relations and the non-inclusion of organisations with economic demands in 'the hope that walks in the large-scale mobilisations'. It is just at the point where political and economic factors interact, that the state community manipulates the power of things to bring down other communities and reduce them to collectivities of loneliness. (It can do so even though it may not control government posts, or may be scattered across different countries.) But it would be unfair to judge the Zapatista movement by this weakness of its Second Declaration in this respect. Their passage from jungle to city, over and against the attempts to encircle them; their 11 demands and the 34 claims in their talks with the government; the three watch-words at the end of each of their communiqués, and the two slogans which capture the content and character of their campaign: all of this goes beyond the frontiers of politics, economics and culture, to take its stand on the terrain of a unified transformation of social relations. In any case, covering the weak flank of their argument is implicit in the process of overcoming the barriers, which nobody has done as much as the Zapatistas to break: the barriers which divide the workers from one another.

Aguascalientes

The new Aguascalientes was declared open on 8 August 1994. It was the first session of the CND and nearly all of the Left were represented there. It did not signify the breach of the barricade erected on 23 March, because those represented there were trapped behind it. But it did finally demolish the previous barricades, and did much to free the Left from its rigid conceptual framework. It was a fitting homage by the Left to the community of people in arms. As Zapatista supporters, militia and combatants marched past the six thousand delegates, the auditorium on the edge of the jungle fell silent. The only sound was the synchronised tramp of hundreds of Zapatistas, each one freely keeping step with the rest. Those watching felt in the presence of the heart of the revolution, as if seeing the blood and muscle whose pulse brings oxygen to the work which moves the heavy wheel of history.

The CND did not reach any agreement for unity of action. Some felt too bound by a commitment to subordinate the struggle for Power to the struggle between powers. For others any commitment to support the electoral struggle was unacceptable. If the unification of the Left had been an immediate possibility, there would have been no need for Aguascalientes: it would have happened on its own in the time after April or after January.

Aguascalientes must be evaluated at the proper time, when those at the bottom reach agreement on common action to break down barriers and make revolutions that prepare revolutions. Marcos referred repeatedly to Aguascalientes as a ship, as a ship caught in the middle of a storm. It is a good image which captures the event precisely. We are all on board that ship, and we all run the same risks. We are all beaten and threatened by that huge force of things which rises from the sea and falls from the heavens. We are all easy prey to that inertia which, coming from the waves, from the timbers, from our own bodies, plays with us as if we were drops of water. We experience the collectivity of loneliness and fear, as each of us battles to stop being swept away by the waves beating on the deck, and clings to the protection of the walls collapsing around us, running from side to side in search of a secure resting place. The collectivity of fear and loneliness is itself our storm: the storm of things turned into a human storm and it is that which most threatens us with shipwreck.

Communities of work and struggle begin to arise. It does not matter where they come from: they can come from the machine room, or the sail locker, or from various places at the same time, thrown together at random by the forces unleashed around them. They will be powerless to start with, but even at the start they hold the seeds of the problem's solution and represent a project in common. All that is needed is a recognition that each person's search for survival requires the salvation of all and that there can be no common salvation without each person making a contribution. It is not hard to recognise, once you find the possibility of community within your reach. That is when the rudder begins to answer to the pull of 'everything for everyone, nothing for ourselves'; and the helmsman responds to the order of 'command obeying'. From then on, it is a matter of overcoming, little by little, the momentum of the two storms; and of picking your way through the debris they have left, to open up spaces, bring communities together, and give everyone the chance to join the community of work and struggle.

We shall discover in the process that the other storm, that which rises from the seas and falls from the skies, is just a storm in a teacup, which in reality was no more than the effect – real and material but no more than the effect – of the lack of unity between those who produce everything, whether in the city or in the country or in the jungle. We have still to reach port, but now we find ourselves sailing in other seas, the seas of freedom, at the dawn of a history which is truly human.

Aguascalientes is the Zapatista movement, the symbolic summary of their voyage, the graphic image of their project and their proposal, their metaphor for revolution and the course of history. If they prove to be right, then they will carry all of us with them, whether we like it or not. Country people and town people, from submodernist capitals or from modernist and postmodernist metropolitan cities, 'all of us are sailors, sailors on the sea'.[16] In fact, the Zapatistas are right twice over: we are indeed all in this together, and the only helm that can guide us to freedom is that which obeys just one order, the only order that can be given and obeyed in complete freedom: everything for everyone, nothing for ourselves.

Notes

1. Marcos, 'Durito V', 11 June 1995.
2. Jean-Paul Sartre, *Critique of Dialectical Reason* (London: Verso, 1982).

3. The second slogan is a particular case of the first: command and obedience are also to be shared by everyone.
4. The masses can be united both in the collectivity of loneliness, and in the revolutionary community. But in the first case, they are joined by an external, massifying force (most developed in corporativism); and in the second, they come together through their own, de-massified, self-determination.
5. Zapatista democracy is based on direct democracy, rather than reduced to it, as shown by the presence of delegates at all levels.
6. This is not only true of the economy.
7. Marcos, 'The long voyage from suffering to hope', 22 September 1994. *La Palabra de los Armados de Verdad y Fuego* [The Word of Those Armed with Truth and Fire] (Mexico City: Editorial Fuenteovejuna, 1994–1995), Volume 3, p. 114.
8. *Frente Sandinista de Liberación Nacional*, the Sandinista National Revolutionary Front of Nicaragua; and the *Frente Farabundo Martí de Liberación Nacional*, the Farabundo Martí National Liberation Front of El Salvador.
9. This was followed by 'the caravan of all caravans' and 'the march of all marches'. The phrasing denotes a movement from the bottom up, although the dynamic of this formula also came to be used to include the actions of those at the bottom in top-led initiatives.
10. Interview with Marcos, 3 March 1994: *La Palabra*, Vol. 1, p. 275.
11. A letter from the current President Zedillo, was later leaked: it was dated 20 March 1994 and addressed to the party's then candidate, Mr Colosio, advising him to strengthen his alliance with President Salinas in order to contain the wave of popular excitement which, in Zedillo's view, was about to engulf them.
12. They fell by US$9,448,000. Before the assassination, reserves stood at US$26,135,000.
13. The growth rate was 0.8 per cent in 1993, and 0.7 per cent in the first quarter of 1994.
14. The Second Declaration of the Lacandon Jungle, *La Palabra*, Vol. 2, pp. 208–214.
15. The Second Declaration of the Lacandon Jungle, *La Palabra*, Vol. 2, pp. 208–214.
16. From a poem by Leon Felipe, quoted by Marcos.

6

Zapatismo: Recomposition of Labour, Radical Democracy and Revolutionary Project

Luis Lorenzano

> As is our custom, at the start of this new year we are announcing the plans of our Zapatista Army for National Liberation. Just as in 1993 when we were preparing for war, in 1992 when we decided to go to war, in 1984 when we completed our first year and in 1983 when hope began to awaken, the Zapatista plan today remains the same as always: to change the world to make it better, more just, more free, more democratic, that is, more human.
> — EZLN, 17 November 1994 from EZLN,
> *La Palabra de los armados de verdad y fuego*
> [The word of those armed with truth and fire], Vol. 3

> We have nothing to be ashamed of. We are the product of the encounter between indigenous wisdom and resistance and the rebelliousness and valour of the generation of dignity which lit the dark night of the Sixties, the Seventies and the Eighties with its blood.
> — EZLN, *La Jornada*, 25 August 1995

> We did not propose it. The only thing that we proposed to do was to change the world; everything else has been improvisation. Our square conception of the world and of revolution was badly dented in the confrontation with the indigenous realities of Chiapas. Out of those blows, something new (which does not necessarily mean 'good') emerged, that which today is known as 'neo-Zapatismo'.
> — Subcomandante Marcos, 22 October 1994 from 'Carta a Adolfo Gilly', *Viento del Sur*, No. 4 (Summer 1995) p. 25

The three quotations chosen here serve as evidence of a history both of continuity as well as of transformation. From the affirmation that 'the Zapatista plan remains the same' to the recognition that 'our

126

square conception of the world and of revolution was badly dented', it is possible to recognise a fabric woven of continuity and change. Its fibre is 'wisdom, resistance, rebellion, courage'.

That history begins with the establishment of the first encampment of the Emiliano Zapata Guerrilla Nucleus in the Lacandon Jungle on 17 November 1983, and extends to the community insurrection which erupted into the public arena on the first day of January 1994. It is a story still in progress, pursuing its task of extending mobilisation, organisation and rebellion to all the exploited and oppressed of Mexico.

Without a doubt, and it would be foolish to try to hide it, in its earliest days, this initial Guerrilla Nucleus had a strong Leninist/Maoist orientation. It understood itself to be the 'revolutionary vanguard' which was to initiate and lead the 'prolonged popular war'. And according to testimony from Marcos himself (*Proceso*, 8 August 1994), they understood their task in terms of the 'implantation' of an armed *foco* (nucleus of guerrilla fighters) using practices and tactics analogous to those promoted by Ernesto Che Guevara.

This mixture, apparently contrived, of Leninism, Maoism, Guevarism should come as no surprise. In its various modalities, it was characteristic of almost all the Latin American radical Left in the years between the Cuban Revolution and the Sandinista triumph in Nicaragua. It was to be found, with its own particular characteristics, in the Ejército Revolucionario del Pueblo (Argentina), the Movimiento de la Izquierda Revolucionaria (Chile), the Fuerzas de Liberación Nacional (Venezuela), the Ejército de Liberación Nacional (Colombia) and the MLN-Tupamaros (Uruguay). And, of course, it was already present within the tendencies and organisations which constituted the Frente Sandinista de Liberación Nacional (Nicaragua), the Frente Farabundo Martí of El Salvador, and the Unión Nacional Revolucionaria Guatemalteca of Guatemala.

In spite of the differences which undoubtedly existed among these groups and experiences, they all shared one implicit – and many times explicit – assumption. Each considered itself to be the military-political organisation which was to lead the masses to take power and establish 'socialism'. Workers, peasants, students and other sectors of the population were expected to become militants in these organisations and follow their leadership. They all shared certain basic theoretical-political principles: the immediately socialist nature of the revolution, the need for an armed vanguard party, and armed struggle as a central and even sole strategy, leading, in practice, to a disdain for political confrontation. This concordance apparently arose not only from a similar analysis of the realities of Latin American countries but from the very experience of world revolution from October 1917 on.

From such ideological (and practical) parameters arose one of the currents which gave origin to today's EZLN. This is what is referred to in our second quotation. Marcos spoke of this when he alluded to the experiences of the original group, and also in an interview in February 1994 in which he recognised, with irony, that the ranks of the insurgents included the 'immense total of three ladinos' (ladinos refer to non-indigenous). But the primary factor which has made Zapatismo so noteworthy has been that the insurrection of 1 January 1994 and the series of political initiatives developed from then until now demonstrate practically no relationship to those antecedents. Any attempt to understand – or satanise – the EZLN as a mere extension of the guerrilla movements of the 1960s and 1970s would be not only useless but sterile and ill-intentioned or even reactionary. That was the position taken by the Mexican state when the insurrection began and when it sent out warrants for the arrest of those accused of being the 'non-indigenous, non-Chiapan' leaders of the movement. And it is also the attitude assumed by intellectuals close to neo-liberalism (such as Octavio Paz and Hector Aguilar Camin) and by certain would-be ex-radicals who regret their past.

On the contrary, from the time of the attempted implanting of the guerrilla *foco* in 1983 to the present, the original group experienced (and continues to experience) a profound metamorphosis: 'Our square conception ... was badly dented ... something new emerged.' That 'something new' is the redefinition, the rethinking not only of the project but of the very practice of revolution. Upon coming into contact with peasant-indigenous communities, this initial nucleus profoundly changed its conceptions. Its members assimilated not only the rich tradition of regional uprisings but also the community-based democratic culture and their conscious construction of communal alternatives. From that moment they began to shed their former, vanguardist criteria (*focos*, mobile columns, etc.), and to become the 'community in arms' that we know today. Thus, the problem faced by the state is not so much the EZLN's supposed 'hard core', but rather the abysmal problem (which the state has not yet managed to grasp) that the communities themselves have decided to enter into insurrection.

But likewise, it is important to underline that the Zapatista insurrection does not represent simply the latest phase in the region's cycle of indigenous and peasant rebellions. First of all, it does not bear the mantle of a millenarian, religious or mythical perspective (although it could appeal to such elements). More importantly, in contrast to uprisings which have sought to restore past conditions, the EZLN has been developing a clear programme of transformation for the future, through the radicalisation of democracy. This is the deeper meaning of the triple cry 'Democracy, freedom, justice'.

Thus we find ourselves before a double metamorphosis: that of the original group and that of the communities. The former broke with Leninist, Maoist and Guevarist conceptions to learn the indigenous cultural concept of 'command obeying'. The communities in turn broke with their centuries-old isolation, to comprehend the function of the state under neoliberalism, and to see themselves as part of the world of labour.

All of this leads to the necessity to re-examine all the assumptions of the revolutionary tradition, and not just in Latin America. And many valuable hypotheses can already be drawn from the EZLN experience. Perhaps those commentarists are right who have spoken of it as 'the first revolution of the twenty-first century', even though some of its conditions are specifically Mexican.

But these hypotheses (or lessons, as some would say) can best be understood through attempting to respond to some of the multiple questions posed by Zapatismo. Above all: How did the EZLN emerge and evolve? What is the meaning of their expressions such as 'command obeying', 'for everyone, everything; for ourselves, nothing', 'a revolution which makes the revolution possible', and others? What kind of nationalism are they insisting upon, and how is it connected with their demands for autonomy? In what ways are Zapatista communities part of the recomposition of the world of labour? And lastly: What theoretical-political value could this experience have for those who, in other countries and continents, continue demanding a world which is 'more just, more free, more democratic, that is, more human'?

As much as we can do in this chapter, we shall try to suggest certain answers to these questions. We shall do so by looking at certain thematic aspects, following as closely as possible the words and actions of the very communities which form part of the EZLN, since we believe that they speak with 'truth in the heart and the truthful word'.

In the beginning is 'command obeying'

'Command obeying' is probably the central concept of the Zapatista proposal. The concept comes from the indigenous peasant communities and refers to practices which in Western political tradition would be associated with direct democracy and the revocability of those in command. It can broadly be understood to be analogous to the Commune, the councils, the soviets.

The objection could be made that all of this is very outmoded, has been seen before and (as a Leninist, Trotskyist or 'orthodox Marxist' – of those that remain – might add) that it refers to the past of workers' struggles. But this sort of disqualification overlooks that which is most important. First, the practice of 'commanding obeying' clearly demonstrates the central difference between the Zapatistas and all former Latin American revolutionary experiences: the Zapatistas are not a 'guerrilla force' nor an 'armed party' with a particular social base, but rather they are the social base itself – the communities – in insurrection and structured as an army; this runs counter to both reformist and Leninist practices. And second, therefore, both warfare and politics are decided by the community. The 'leadership' (the members of the various Indigenous Revolutionary Clandestine Committees, federated by ethnic group and by community) hold their positions as long as they faithfully and effectively implement the mandates of the community. From the perspective of Western political tradition, the traditional indigenous-peasant community has undergone a metamorphosis to become the 'polis', a community not just of land, language and culture, but a political community, with deliberative, legislative and executive capacities. In a letter of 28 May 1994 Marcos provides one example of many such community decisions:

> Antonio son of Antonio returned with the minutes of the agreement that said: 'Men and women and children met in the community school to look into their hearts to see whether or not it was time to initiate the war for liberty and they divided into the three groups – of women, of children and of men – to discuss this, and then we came back together again in the school and the thinking of the majority was that the war should begin ... This agreement was confirmed by 12 men and 23 women and 8 children who have clear thinking, and those who could sign did so and those who could not stamped their fingerprints.'

Third, this is what explains the profoundly political nature of the EZLN, the fact that they said 'Enough!' and rose up ... in order to be heard and to weave a network of 'speaking and listening' among all individuals and organisations interested in promoting radical political transformation. This explains too the absence of the 'party' as an organism separate from the communities. Finally, it explains why and how the EZLN itself is not a separate 'autonomous' military apparatus, but rather, we would insist, it is the political community expressing itself as a community in arms.

While this answers certain questions it raises others. For example: whence this principle, at once social, cultural, ethical and political, of 'commanding obeying'? What conditions might allow for such a principle to spread, or are we rather dealing with an experience particular to 'backward' indigenous-peasant communities? How could all this be related to probable forms of recomposition among the world of labour? Does this experience look towards the past or the future? How did it develop?

In relation to the first question, this principle involves a socio-cultural dynamic which is expressed in clear, ethical-political values. Thus, in their pronouncements, the Zapatistas give great import to experiences (and concepts) which capitalism and its postmodern apologists believed to have buried forever: 'truth', 'dignity', 'sincerity', 'integrity'. This is the essence of the enormous contribution which the traditional agrarian community is making through the Zapatistas. But, as we have said, we are dealing with communities transformed into 'polis', and it is on the basis of this experience that the EZLN proposes its generalisation through the promotion of horizontal social solidarities (this seems to be the best interpretation of the constant affirmation of 'for everyone, everything; nothing for ourselves'). This is to occur through a strategy which leads to a 'revolution which makes the revolution possible', in Gramscian terms, a revolution which – as a first step – consists in overcoming the separation between 'political society' and 'civil society', by dissolving the former into the latter.

Out of all of this emerges the characteristic which initially surprised everyone: the EZLN's insistence that they are not proposing to take power. Rather they are seeking to contribute to a vast movement which would return power to society, understood as a dense and complex network of horizontal forms of solidarity. On 20 January 1994, the Zapatistas maintained:

We feel that revolutionary change in Mexico will not be the product of only one kind of action. That is, it will not be, in the strict sense, either an armed or a pacific revolution. It will primarily be a revolution resulting from struggle on various fronts, using many methods, under various social forms, with various degrees of commitment and participation. And its result will not be the victory of a party, an organisation or an alliance of triumphant organisations with their own specific social proposal, but rather a democratic space for resolving the confrontation of various political proposals. This democratic space will be based upon three fundamental, historically inseparable premises: democracy to define the dominant social proposal; the freedom to endorse one proposal or another; and justice as a principle which must be respected by all proposals.

The entire political trajectory of the EZLN can be understood as a patient and obstinate process of proposing and consulting on ways of moving in that direction: from the National Democratic Convention (August 1994), to the National Consultation (August 1995), to the call for a National Forum for an Independent Dialogue (29 September 1995). The Zapatistas feel that their experience represents a feasible alternative which could be generalised. The conditions which would make this possible depend, it can be argued, upon the way that the Zapatista experience is connected with – and actually forms part of – processes of recomposition taking place in the world of labour.

Obviously these last issues cannot be discussed in isolation. Their exploration requires that the Zapatista experience be understood not only within its national context, but in its world-wide context, that is, in the globalisation which is the recomposition of capital–labour relationships on a planetary scale. But in order to grasp the possible universality of the significance of Zapatismo, we must deepen our understanding of its particular characteristics. Thus we must return to the Chiapan communities in rebellion, to the aspects which justify and give form to the double affirmation we previously presented, this double connection: Zapatismo as political community/community in arms.

Traditional community and armed political commune

Thus we are faced with an immense repositioning, redefinition or rethinking of the project of transformation, in relation to how it was formerly proposed by vanguard or reformist organisations – from 'the party', 'the guerrilla forces', or the 'electoral struggle', to the commune; from the confrontation between military apparatuses to political confrontation based on a social stratum involved in prolonged insurrection; from 'taking power' to overcoming the separation between 'political society and civil society'; from the 'dictatorship of the proletariat' to 'democracy, liberty, justice', understood as the true 'revolution which makes the revolution possible'.

Zapatismo cannot be understood except as an experience of communal/popular power. The EZLN is not only the 'community in arms', but it is also an army which submits itself to the mandates of the community. Only thus can one explain issues such as its anti-vanguard nature, the absence of any 'party' formation in any of its modalities, its rapid reorientation towards political struggle (without renouncing either arms or insurrection), its persistent search for links with what it refers to (sometimes too broadly) as 'civil society', etc.

Over the course of ten years, both the original group which installed itself in the Lacandon Jungle and the communities of the region entered into a countless series of mutual learning experiences, in relation both to the revolution to which they aspired and the ways to promote it. Out of those lessons, evaluations and re-evaluations, they redefined their projects; that 'something new' emerged, of which Zapatismo is the bearer and promotor. This process must have been influenced by what could be called the 'negative yields' of the Central American revolutions, the fall of the Berlin Wall and the disintegration of the USSR.

But this rethinking of the programme, practice and ethic of revolution was not simply a process of 'intellectual' learning, but rather it had a material/cultural base: the community nature of the insurrection. This leads us to more questions still. The most important is: what 'commune' is being referred to here? This is key to understanding how and why the Zapatista experience is not a marginal or isolated event, but rather an indivisible part of the global recomposition of labour. This process involves the destruction of traditional forms of 'class' and 'class strata', accompanied by the emergence and construction of new forms.

The question, 'Which "commune" is being referred to here?', leads us to explore a variety of factors which are interwoven like the warp and woof on a loom, producing a fabric with a design which none of the fibres contained on their own.

A closer look at the fibres of this weave reveals the first to be an immense river which springs from the surviving traditional ways of the indigenous agrarian community. Central to this heritage are the ancestral practices of community democracy, dialogue and discussion of common problems (which the indigenous people call 'allowing your true word to meet my true word') and the principle of commanding obeying which structures what might be called 'public life'. It was from being nourished by these practices that the EZLN as such was truly born. But here we must be doubly careful, for, in spite of what dogmatic liberals and Marxists might believe, we are not referring here to a simple 'survival' and much less to 'archaic' characteristics, but rather to a fundamental mode by which 'new' communities were built – 'new' both in time and in their way of being. To understand these elements merely as continuity or as 'survivals' is to understand only one of the fibres, but such a vision is insufficient and could even represent a dangerous oversimplification. These practices and 'traditional' community formations in general have been deeply transformed both by the historical evolution of the communes and by the conscious action by those who were first members of the commune and then Zapatista combatants.

It is not possible here even briefly to describe the history of these communes' efforts to achieve conditions necessary for their social reproduction (struggles for land, production, marketing, health), a history marked by constant, massive and often bloody conflicts with the *caciques* and the state. Those who maintain that agrarian communes are an example of stagnation or backwardness are mistaken. Even in conditions of extreme poverty, the communities which comprise Zapatismo are highly dynamic, and, in peculiar form, possess advanced cultural and political characteristics.

On the contrary, this history demonstrates that in no way are we dealing with stagnant communities which live by routine, but rather with the conscious, organised and collective work of building 'new communities', founded no more than three or four decades ago. These communities were displaced and marginalised, it is true, but capable of confronting the challenges and hardships of opening a new agricultural frontier, and with a culture of opening breaches and paths, of cutting down the forest to plant fields, which, paradoxically, would later be turned to opening politico-social breaches.

Since this occurred in a context of permanent contradiction with the state and the *caciques*, we can suppose that throughout this process community bonds were strengthened and collective initiatives valued (including forms of struggle against the state, for self-defence and to achieve community demands). Here again are the roots of the 'for everyone, everything'. I speak of these aspects as a 'conscious work of building' since they are not automatically present within the traditional commune. They imply a series of transformations, evaluations, reorientations. Discussion of projects, implementation, evaluation of achievements and shortcomings: this is conscious work, which lays the very foundations for social life.

Moreover, a significant number of members of these communities have been temporarily employed by capitalist haciendas or in the cities (as labourers in the lumber industry, in building work, in the construction of highways or hydroelectric dams, etc). They have helped their communities understand their own social composition, and have served to counteract the tendency towards isolation that all borders inevitably generate. Thus temporary workers facilitate the flow of information, making it possible for them and their communities to identify with other strata of workers, and contributing their knowledge of the language of the dominant classes (Spanish), which their need for wage labour obliges them to acquire. Some of these features can be detected or inferred in various members of the General Command of the EZLN (such as Tacho), or of its military officers (such as Majors Moisés and Andrea), while others demonstrate cultures which are almost completely peasant-indigenous (the most obvious and well-known examples are the Comandantes Ramona and Trini). Here we can do no more than mention the importance in relation to all this of the work of the Christian catechists inspired by the theology of liberation.

Nevertheless, the dynamic nature and social composition of the communes provokes more questions than answers, as does the Zapatista experience in general. Indeed, it could even be argued that the Zapatistas are a permanent interrogation, not only of twentieth-century socialist thought, but of social life as a whole, which they address and question as to its capacity for self-organisation and self-transformation. Traditional community culture, its social composition and dynamism are necessary but not sufficient, elements to explain the metamorphosis through which the traditional commune became the political commune in arms and in insurrection.

In this reflection on the particularities of the Zapatistas (and before returning to the possible universality of the significations which they tie and untie), we need to examine the processes of change taking place within the communes which brought them together to form the EZLN, that is, which led them to form – and this is the decisive element – a communal army.

Political community: poor workers and the communal army

The questions that arise are simply a different way of approaching the question of what is 'new' about the Zapatistas, which has been present as a preoccupation since the quotations at the beginning of this chapter.

It would seem that the core of what is new about the Zapatistas is that in the course of these metamorphoses they have been generating a particular synthesis through which the 'archaic' (the indigenous-peasant agrarian community) is transformed into the 'advanced' (the social formation which we have compared to the 'commune' or the 'polis'): a political community which is a community of deliberations, decisions and responsibilities. This implies conditions, structures and meanings which differ from the traditional.

As far as the conditions which gave rise to this experience are concerned, there is an issue which, though obvious, has nevertheless hardly been touched upon by those who have written about the Zapatistas. This issue is: what was happening within the communities while they were becoming Zapatista and organising themselves as the EZLN?

We know, for example, that women have won a new place and new functions – including political-military ones, serving as officers and as members of the militia – and that they occupy positions of 'political' leadership. Ever present examples of this are Comandantes Ramona, Trini, Leticia, Hortensia and María Alicia. This is enormously important and marks a profound transformation in relation to the traditional commune (and not just in that respect: how many Leninist or reformist organisations could boast of having so many women among their leadership?). But what else has changed? Although public information is scarce indeed, indirect data and testimony exist to guide our inquiry.

Apparently, the great wave of EZLN affiliations occurred in 1992–93, following the reforms to Article 27 of the Constitution and the agrarian legislation, and on the eve of the implementation of the North American Free Trade Agreement (NAFTA). The former peasant organisations unravelled (especially the Asociación Regional Independiente Campesina (ARIC) – Unión de Uniones) and the Zapatistas gained an overwhelming majority in the regions of Las Cañadas, Los Altos and La Selva. The 'other transformations' mentioned earlier began to occur on a massive level during this period, although the phenomenon had begun to develop even earlier (probably around 1988).

According to a Zapatista mural displayed at the National Democratic Convention in August 1994 (and reaffirmed by statements by Tacho and Marcos), in those early days: 'The road was a long one. The burden was heavy. We received little support from the people. Survival was difficult.' However, it would be erroneous to think that before the period of massive affiliations in 1992, the EZLN was just a nucleus of combatants surviving in the heart of the mountains. On the contrary, evidence indicates that Zapatista communities (not just armed groups) existed long before 1992. At first, these communities provided cover, food, information and arms transport; they later became part of the emerging army, as 'officers', 'members of the militia', 'bases of support'. The decisive point is that this entire process, which began with individuals and families, came to include the entire community.

Information drawn from interviews confirms this. For example, we have the interview with Marcos published in *Proceso* on 8 August 1994: 'There is a town where the men are Zapatistas, the women are Zapatistas, the children are Zapatistas, the chickens are Zapatistas, the stones are Zapatistas, everything is Zapatista, and has been for a long time.' From this perspective, the question of 'the best-kept secret in the history of Mexico' (Tacho's speech at the inauguration of the National Democratic Convention) refers not only to combatants but to the question of how the secret was kept of the existence of communities, collectives of women, men and children who had decided to 'move beyond' state-political control, to organise their lives in new ways and prepare for insurrection.

Such a secret clearly had to be kept both from the outside world as well as from certain people within the community. For those who are only familiar with 'legal' and 'public' struggles, and for whom it is difficult to imagine the conditions of preparing for a prolonged insurrection, this may seem strange, but that is the way things are.

In relation to the outside world, the community had to develop new and different relationships with their suppliers, buyers, the Church, political parties and governmental representatives. Internally, the community had to distance itself from, expel or overwhelm with social, ethical and political pressure the corrupt or authoritarian individuals or groups that exist in every community and who, in this case, included those who had links (sinecures, concessions, privileges etc.) with the state apparatus and the dominant classes of the region (*caciques*, hacienda owners, merchants, transport companies). Though the favours they received were often meagre, these individuals or groups acted as 'mini-*caciques*' or 'proto-*caciques*', serving as the nexus through which subordination to the state operated.

'Keeping the secret' within the communities thus must have implied a tenacious commitment to the overwhelming task of persuasion and assimilation, or, in many cases, of 'purging'. The former was possible because of the strength of community ties, family relations and common cultural tradition. The latter involved forms of dissimulated marginalisation and boycott. The prohibition of alcohol in the communities assuredly played a role in facilitating such 'purging'. Thus those who might endanger the secret were either assimilated or subordinated (or isolated). These strategies were used on those close to the dominant party (the PRI), which represents not simply an ideological-political problem but a social one as well.

These processes of pressure, persuasion and assimilation as well as those of isolation and purification converged in one sense: they led to an increasing degree of cultural/political, and even more importantly, social homogeneity (which is not the same as forced unanimity). When corrupt, authoritarian elements, those who had served as 'mini-' or 'proto'-*caciques* were filtered out, the composition of the basis of community life became enormously relevant. In all probability, this process of homogenisation centred on the poorest farmworkers (poor peasants and temporary farm labourers). Thus a 'sociologically' decisive metamorphosis occurred: in the course of the prolonged and conflictive processes occurring within their midst, these (traditional but dynamic) communities were transformed into communities of workers 'without masters', and apparently without *caciques* (the principal and most prevalent form of bourgeois domination in the region).

The social composition of the EZLN described here is indirectly corroborated in the speech by Marcos to the CCRI (Comité Clandestino Revolucionario Indígena) General Command on 17 November 1994. This text is particularly important, since it is an example of the Zapatistas' political custom of evaluating each year the former year's work on the anniversary of the establishment of the first insurgent encampment (17 November 1983).

In his speech, Marcos refers to the errors committed:

> ... in terms of good government, the revolutionary laws of 1993 have not been upheld as we would have wished. In some cases, small property owners have been affected, people whose lands do not exceed the maximum recognised by our revolutionary agricultural laws. The CCRI-CG of the EZLN is in the midst of a process of adjustment to guarantee ... that genuine small property owners will not be affected.

From this it can clearly be inferred, first, that in the territory which the Zapatistas controlled from 12 January 1994 (the date of the military truce) until 9 February 1995 (the date of the Mexican government's unilateral breaking of that truce), the revolutionary laws promulgated on 1 January shaped the form of self-government among the communities in insurrection. This demonstrates that the concept of 'base of support', which at first seems to allude to the population committed to the uprising, actually has a much wider meaning: 'liberated territory'/self-organised population/regulation of daily life/organs for 'people's power'/the militias and the army. On this basis it can be seen that the principal laws relating to problems experienced by the population are 'The Rights and Obligations of the Peoples in Struggle', 'The Rights and Obligations of the Revolutionary Armed Forces', 'The Women's Revolutionary Law' and 'The Revolutionary Agrarian Law'. It is this last law that Marcos is referring to, noting errors of a 'Leftist' type: 'genuinely small agrarian landholdings' had not been respected. This is perfectly compatible with the process of social homogenisation centred on the poorest peasants; the latter tend, in most cases, to reject the validity of 'small property'.

To understand the significance of the admission of errors identified in the annual evaluation, it is important to bear in mind the contents of this Revolutionary Agrarian Law. The Law, even if it recognises, in Article 3, small agrarian property (100 hectares for poor-quality land, 50 hectares for good-quality land), is basically a collectivist law, although it leaves open the possibility of a broad spectrum of modes of organisation. Thus, Article 5 establishes that 'for all other lands', there will be collective ownership and the obligation to work them collectively (that is, without sub-dividing them). Article 7 gives priority for the possession of the 'means of production' (defined as machinery, fertilisers, etc.) to 'groups organised in cooperatives, collectives and associations' (which can be understood to be composed of poor peasants). After these dispositions, Article 12 says concisely: 'The individual monopolisation of land and the means of production will not be allowed.' The Law is made for poor peasants and farm labourers, particularly those who have maintained (or recovered) strong community traditions. Thus we can infer that the 'error' criticised by Marcos and the CCRI-CG in relation to the Agrarian Law meant that the dispositions of that Law were carried to an extreme, that its collectivist, communal character was developed in excess.

The agrarian community transforms itself into a workers' commune. This is the final explanation of why the EZLN is not an army 'separate' from the social body. It explains the nature of the EZLN as a communal army or 'community in arms'. It answers the question: 'What commune are we speaking of?', and thus it is key to tying together our former affirmations about the 'commune', the 'polis'. Communes of workers are the material basis of the armed political commune; their federation (in Indigenous Revolutionary Clandestine Committees) under a unified, collective and military-political command (the General Command) is the Zapatista Army of National Liberation (EZLN).

This helps us to understand the first cluster of meanings to be drawn from the rebellion initiated by the EZLN. If these communal transformations possess the above-mentioned characteristics, then clearly we are not dealing with an 'indigenous uprising' but rather an insurrection of communities of workers. The Zapatista revolution is not ethnic (although it is ethnically rooted), and it expresses itself as an undeniable part of class struggle at a national level. For the same reasons, the Zapatista community is not the traditional agrarian community (although its roots are to be found there).

Likewise, the internal changes profoundly alter the circulation of 'command' in the communities. First, because the opening of the agricultural frontier and then preparations for war, are, almost by definition, tasks of the young. What we know about the Zapatistas confirms this: older people (such as Comandantes Ramona and Trini) are the minority, whereas, to a great degree, 'command' is traditionally almost invariably associated with age. At the same time, we find women in leadership positions, which also does not usually occur in ancestral culture. All this signifies equally profound modifications in established values. Cautiously speaking, we could say that this new 'command' has developed a double component: it is both 'traditional' and 'Zapatista', and in many cases this double component is deposited in the same people. Thus, through the process of social and political homogenisation, the communities have also transformed their own internal structures.

Finally, the very meaning of community organisation has been substantially modified. Whereas the 'archaic' agrarian commune has been reduced to functions of mere self-subsistence, clearly the Zapatista commune signifies the recovery of the social conditions necessary for reproduction. This goes hand in hand with military and political objectives, namely, warfare, the unleashing of a whole series of political (and social) confrontations for the radical democratisation of all spaces of national life.

The formation of a communal army

This analysis clarifies certain basic questions and opens new ways to deepen the relationship between the recomposition of the Zapatista commune and more general processes of recomposition within the world of labour. However, it is still necessary to delve more deeply into the particular characteristics of the EZLN and of the political-social proposal which they are taking the lead in promoting. If the Zapatistas are heard, it is precisely in their condition as insurgents, a communal army. How did the military structure of the EZLN develop? This question not only exemplifies the differences which separate the EZLN from former Latin American guerrilla experiences, but it represents the other side of the development of these communities as communes of workers 'without masters'.

Let us begin with a declaration by Marcos:

> It is true that we are an armed movement which does not want to take power, as in the old revolutionary schemes, and that we call upon civil society to join us in peaceful action, to prevent war. That is the paradox of the EZLN. But we are confronted with a contradiction. I am referring to the EZLN of eleven years ago, which was established to take power through armed force. We were a military organisation in the classic sense of the word. For that reason, the primary contribution of what is known today as neo-Zapatismo came from the clash between that rigid conception and the reality of the indigenous communities. The insertion of a democratic structure into an authoritarian one; decision-making in indigenous communities versus decision-making in a completely vertical political-military organisation. [*Proceso*, December 5, 1994]

What a contradiction! In it lies the substance, the core of this entire history of continuous metamorphoses. The structure invented by the EZLN summarises the transformations both of the agrarian commune as well as those of the original core group. Various sources allow us to reconstruct, in general terms, the essential chapters of that history.

Here, of course, we are dealing with 'best-kept secrets', about which it will not be necessary to have all the details. With this caveat, however, there emerges from the enormous amount of available journalistic material and the profusion of interviews and declarations by the Zapatistas themselves, a true and coherent story. The first element of this narrative can be found in the political and cultural defeat suffered by the initial group of six combatants who arrived at the Lacandon Jungle in 1983, a resounding 'defeat' which eventually became the key to later success. While training themselves to survive in the mountains, this core group, which included Marcos, allowed the indigenous-peasant reality to call into question their manuals, their preconceived ideas and even all the experience accumulated in 70 years of 'revolutionary struggle' of Leninist, Maoist, Guevarist coinage. They subordinated their primarily militaristic concept of revolution to the essentially political concept of the communities. But this process took a long and circuitous route.

The initial column of six combatants was of mixed composition. Three of them were from the city, they were 'ladinos'. The other three were indigenous, and it was through them that the first contacts with the communities were made. The group waited two years before they began to approach the tiny rural communities. Upon doing so, they committed errors which compromised their clandestinity and exposed them to being denounced. Thus, for security reasons, they decided to make contact by approaching the family members of the three indigenous combatants: no one would denounce their own brother or cousin. Thus the mutual cultural ... and political influence began. This process was a slow one, but little by little, people began to arrive – family members from the communities: cousins, brothers' friends, brothers-in-law. This obliged the 'ladinos' to learn the indigenous languages (and thus their traditions) and to learn the work of the peasants: opening paths, cutting and carrying firewood, hunting and cooking wild animals ... and thus the fusion began. The Emiliano Zapata Guerrilla Nucleus rejected the possibility of including more combatants of urban origin: it grew out of the very communities themselves. By 1986 (three years later), their numbers had grown to 40 and they affirmed: 'Now our brothers from the communities are going to take us seriously; we almost look like a real army.' But the essential mutation was barely beginning to take place: they were just beginning to submit their vision of the project of transformation to the criteria of those who, in an organised fashion, had joined the nascent army. Through them, the feelings and thoughts of the communities could be heard and attended. Marcos remembers:

> That is how we began to confront our concept of change with the aspirations of the indigenous communities ... But we were still operating on the level of self-defence. People in the communities still had not developed a consciousness of taking the offensive. That was when we proposed that our training for warfare take place not only in the mountains but that we begin to prepare the towns to fight.

Here we see the importance of the convergence of the 'conscious work' of building community life and the dynamism of the opening of agricultural frontiers. The EZLN combatants learnt that they had not come to convince anyone of the need for armed struggle. The communities themselves gave the insurgents the task of training them militarily. Moreover, in line with their own tradition, it was also the communities who decided that the EZLN should initiate military campaigns only when they were prepared to participate actively.

When Zapatismo subordinated itself to communal structures, the communities transformed the project, and it grew explosively as thousands joined.

However, this process was not a linear one. They had to navigate the tortuous process of redefining their political (and social) project as well as the regionalisation of the military structure. In terms of the former, an apparently inviolable concept ('socialism') was metamorphosed into a set of meanings which were both broader and more fitting to the Mexican situation: 'Enough!', 'For everyone, everything; nothing for us', 'Democracy, liberty, justice'. Zapatista discourse was formed as a discourse which radically renewed the revolutionary project. The other aspect of this turn is still in progress and uncertain. For the discursive redefinition (which implies new ethical-political conceptions) has led the Zapatistas to develop a series of initiatives towards, with and from 'civil society', practices with which they are beginning to redefine the characteristics of the possible revolutionary subject.

The process of regionalising the military structure clearly demonstrated the character of the EZLN as a federation of political/ armed communes.

By 1987 a network of villages, settlements and *ejidos* took charge of the insurgency. The movement spread to other communities, which began to transform themselves into Zapatista political (and embryonically military) communes. The experiences of metamorphosis discussed above began to spread to various regions of La Selva, Las Cañadas and Los Altos.

Such processes extended the political organisation and expanded the military force in gestation. Later, a number of villages coordinated to establish a regional militia with its own military command elected by community assemblies. As a political-military vanguard, the founding cadre of the EZLN (the column of 40 men and women which had existed just one year before) integrated themselves into the social, cultural, political and military fabric of the communities. Every initiative they took had to be authorised by the regional command after deliberations in assembly. Thus, early in 1988, this process vanquished the 'square conceptions' mentioned at the beginning of this text. The EZLN left behind its thesis of vertical (militaristic) control of the movement. It ceded to the organised communities, or rather, the communities made the EZLN cede to them. As Marcos put it: 'I think that we were absolutely on target when we surrendered, when we said that it would be better to do what they say. That is when the EZLN spread and grew explosively.'

Paradoxically, this set of transformations of the initial project both ensured its success and put at risk its possible military effectiveness. When the regional command and the community-elected representatives took over political and organisational leadership, military leadership suffered a process of dispersion. Once militia units were established in each region, the command of these local forces remained in the hands of the communities in that zone. By 1990, the EZLN numbered several thousands of combatants, but their extremely decentralised federation faced difficulties in coordination which reduced their effectiveness. Once again, it was their ability to generate community organisation that led to the resolution of the problem. Their (geographic and military, although not political) decentralisation gave rise to greater horizontal relationships. Interregional commands began to develop as well as the structures which were later to become the Indigenous Revolutionary Clandestine Committee, the federated organisation which provides collective and unified political and military leadership. The military command, whose visible head is Subcomandante Insurgente Marcos, but which includes Major Moisés, Major Andrea, Captain Irma and many more, is politically and organisationally subordinated to a committee with regional, community and ethnic representation. Thus Marcos can maintain:

> The EZLN and the civil population are so intermixed that it is difficult to draw a line marking the interests or territory of one or the other. In order to eliminate the Zapatista Army, this territory itself must be wiped from the face of the planet: not only must it be destroyed, it must be completely erased, because there is constant danger present in the dead who lie below it.

Thus the EZLN completed its metamorphosis and, in the context of the deepening of the neoliberal attack on agrarian life and on society in general, they unleashed first the insurrection and the war, then the truce to achieve peace with profound changes in the Mexican state, and finally, the initiatives for a constant dialogue with social organisations, promoting 'the revolution which makes the revolution possible'. All of these processes represent transformations in the world of labour as well as a deep and broad rethinking of the revolutionary project and of the strategy for transformation, with meanings which are probably of universal value. These three aspects (Zapatismo, the recomposition of labour and rethinking) are indivisible. Any distinctions to be made among them could only be circumstantial or a matter of degree, and any separation can only be for strictly analytical purposes.

Neoliberalism, Zapatismo and the recomposition of labour

Just as the Zapatistas have been able – up to now – to avoid the risks and quagmires of vanguardism and reformism, here we wish to clarify two false conceptions which arise from certain problems of the Marxist tradition. The Zapatista movement is not a movement of 'peasants defending their archaic ways of living and producing', nor can labour be reduced only to that work which directly produces surplus value, as certain narrow-minded exegists of Marx's *Capital* tend to believe. We will summarise the major points related to the first aspect, which has been discussed at length above. The second will make it possible to come to new, broader understandings of issues related to social struggle, and thus, the alternatives which the Zapatistas (and others) are proposing.

In summary, Chiapan Zapatismo is composed primarily of a federation of workers' communes (of peasants and indigenous peoples); these are communes of land and culture, political and armed. These communes have built a permanent army (the EZLN) which nevertheless is 'the community in arms'. The communes are united through a federation, with a collective, unified political and military command which is the General Command of the Indigenous Revolutionary Clandestine Committees. As such, they propose to society as a whole, not a programme of purely peasant-indigenous demands, but alternatives within which the indigenous is an integral part of the radical democratic transformation of social life and of the state. The processes which led to the formation of the EZLN (and to its national and world resonance after 1 January 1994) are the result of a series of transformational syntheses between that which is 'traditional' and that which is 'advanced'. This results from a convergence and fusion between 'spontaneity' and 'consciousness', or more broadly, between 'social energy' and 'projects' which are continuously formulated and reformulated in the course of their implementation.

This recapitulation (particularly the last two points) brings us to what can be called 'labour in general', which has become labour which is concretised in the generation of community life and 'culture' (we are using the broadest meaning of the concept here, to encompass the labour of creating the material, social and intellectual foundations of the armed political commune). The work of self-transformation in the Zapatista communes ('praxis', to put it in Gramscian terms) produces that which did not exist before. It produces 'that which is new': a new social relationship, a new understanding, a new project.

Parallel processes of self-transformation are taking place in almost every stratum of labour, although in most cases it is not yet conscious (or not fully conscious). Too much has been said about the disintegrating effects of neoliberalism, and the impotence and weakening of the organisations built over decades (unions, political parties, social security networks, etc.). All this is true, not only on a global level, but also within the communities which were becoming Zapatista communities, and in their case even more so, since their very survival was at risk. Let us remember that their dynamism was intensified and diversified as a result of being thrown aside, displaced, expelled towards enormously difficult agricultural frontiers. But what the received categories of thought do not allow us to see is that amidst the ruins of the old welfare state and the almost chronic (and at times acute) crisis of 'neoliberalism', new figures of labour are being constructed, with other experiences and other social subjectivities, which constitute the current expressions of the conflict between labour and capital. In summary, what is not yet understood – not simply because of theoretical blindness, but because we are dealing here with still-unfolding social processes – is the potential of the new worker, the potential of the world-wide spread and diversification of wage labour, the antagonistic other face of the so-called 'globalisation'.

This is the recomposition of the world of labour of which Zapatismo is part. Its experience is not that of a relatively isolated and marginal social group, but belongs fully to these processes of recomposition and probably represents their highest form of expression to date.

Such is the broader significance of the development of Zapatismo as popular/communal power, within the conditions and context of the capitalist restructuring of agriculture, land tenure and land-based production. Within the Mexican national context, these processes of recomposition manifest themselves in profound changes in class structure (parallel to the changes taking place in world society) and in the emergence of the ever denser networks of groups formed around various needs. These networks, often referred to as 'civil society' or 'non-governmental organisations', are increasingly coming into conflict with the state form and are beginning to form part of class relations, contradictions and conflicts (even when the majority of their members identify themselves simply as 'citizens').

This complex web of problems requires that we develop a non-'sociological' approach to the determination of social classes and that we leave behind any 'ontological' consideration of which class or class fraction is to be the 'bearer of socialism'. Although the present essay on Zapatismo cannot treat this issue with the necessary care, we will nevertheless make a few observations in this regard. In the first place, our rejection of sociologisms means that a whole series of empirical considerations habitually employed (such as income level, education, status, etc.) must be subordinated to a double consideration: the buying-and-selling of labour power, which in capitalism is where the totality of social relations are brought together, and the positions taken within specific social (and state) formations, that is to say the positions (of lifestyle, consciousness and action) which are assumed in relation to the set of groups and sub-groups which constitute social life. Thus (potentially) revolutionary subjects are not such in and of themselves, but rather they are constructed through social experience. For this reason we reject ontologisms: the socialist project is just a potentiality of the conflict between capital and labour, a possible social alternative. Conflict is characterised by uncertainty and not by a historical necessity posited by who knows what development of the 'productive forces'.

Now let us return to our former affirmations. New questions arise, not just of a theoretical nature, but from the attempt to understand what is occurring. How can we understand Zapatismo as an expression of the potential of the new worker? What is the nature of the profound links which have been established between Zapatismo and non-governmental organisations in particular and a wide band of 'civil society' in general? To respond to these questions, we must take a roundabout road from the countryside to the city (with Mexico City as urban paradigm). From there, we will seek to generate certain conclusions in order to understand the implications of Zapatista proposals for the radical democratisation of social life, this 'revolution which makes the revolution possible', and we will explore their possible meanings.

Labour and the emergence of civil society

Broadly speaking, the whole of the Zapatista experience, which we have described and analysed using the concept of 'the work involved in the conscious construction of community life' (a form of productive work, though not productive of surplus value), can be understood clearly as a work of self-organisation and self-valorisation, developed at the margins of capital, and, in the specific case of Zapatismo, against capital, at the margin and against the capitalist institutionality of Mexican society. Communities of 'masterless' workers put into question all that concerns the current constitution of the world of labour. Thus we can safely maintain that Zapatismo currently represents the highest expression of profound processes of class recomposition, leading us from the weakness of labour (the breakdown of unions, solidarity networks, parties, etc.) to the potential of labour as the constructor of other social alternatives.

This is the strength of Zapatismo, the very heart of its radiation to Mexico and the world, the substance of the profound links that unite it with other strata of society. For another surprising aspect of the EZLN's three years of public existence (that is, of the communes in insurrection) is the government's persistent inability to politically or militarily isolate and crush the uprising. For this reason, we have described the process as a 'prolonged insurrection'. Every offensive on the part of the state (January 1994, February–March 1995, October 1995) has met with a wide mobilisation of a multitude of groups, organised and unorganised, intellectuals, artists, journalists, professionals of all sorts, housewives, employees, people from the poor neighbourhoods, the remnants of unionism which are growing at the margins of the already deceased welfare state (such as the groups which came together to form the 1 May Union Coordinating Committee), students, gang members, as well as militants and some of the cadres from opposition parties or parties outside the dominant political alliance which has promoted neoliberal restructuring. Such massive mobilisations, which peaked when more than 500,000 people participated in the May Day commemoration, represented the development of deep processes of political and social transformation.

The content of these mobilisations is politically important. In January 1994, soon after the outbreak of the insurrection and in response to the state's extremely repressive policy, the content of these mobilisations could be summarised in the two cries: 'Stop the massacre' and 'Dialogue between the two sides'. From February 1994 to February 1995, there was a call for initiatives for 'peace with profound transformation', which meant no to war, be it revolutionary or counter-revolutionary. Peaceful social mobilisation (including electoral participation) was expected to bring about political as well as economic and social change. In February–March 1995, in response to the state offensive, the theme of the mobilisations changed to: 'We are all Marcos', 'We are all Zapatistas', 'Zapata lives, the struggle continues.' This demonstrates an evolution from an initial, almost-neutral position to proposals for transformation and an increasing identification with the rebels. Such changes in social consciousness correspond to changes in the alignments and convergences of class. To see this last phenomenon it is necessary to lay aside the sociologistic and ontologistic errors of the past.

At the heart of these mobilisations have been dispersed groups with varying degrees of organisation, almost all of them founded around very specific common interests: human rights activists, feminists, people seeking housing, civil rights groups, members of the counter-culture (from the worlds of the theatre, rock music or folk protest music, the fledgling alternative youth press, video cooperatives), surrounded by secondary school and university-level students, families (especially women) from neighbourhoods where most people sell their labour power (wage workers or workers in the informal economy), those employed in 'services' of all kinds, especially the 'modern' services, such as press, advertising, computing. Mixed (and often lost) among this vast array of groups and individuals are handfuls of survivors from earlier Left experiences and a few cadres from the party apparatuses, who have nevertheless contributed (for better and for worse) their own organisational and propagandistic styles and habits.

With the notable exception of the old and new factory proletariat, whose absence, a result of the impact of massive unemployment on factory workers' rhythms of struggle in Mexico, constitutes a serious weakness in this embryonic social bloc, the conglomeration of strata, occupations and social situations which converge in these mobilisations is representative of the new forms of labour, the potential of the new worker. The new worker is distinguished by his or her capacity for self-organisation and 'self-valorisation' – not by being a 'class in-and-for-itself' in the *a priori* sense of some Marxist theory, and even less by the indicators of empirical sociology.

Globally, this new worker is established through the sale of their labour power and through the potential for autonomy, regardless of where they may be specifically located within the cycles of production and circulation of capital (as 'blue-collar worker', 'employee', 'professor', in the 'informal economy', etc.). In Mexico, the virtual closing-down of opportunities for upward social mobility and the backward nature of the state have meant that the most lucid and active strata of these 'new workers' have tended to identify with the Zapatistas ('We are all Marcos') and with the possibility of an alternative social project.

It was to these new workers that the Zapatistas addressed themselves through their calls for the National Democratic Convention, the National Consultation and the National Forum for Independent

Dialogue. Leaving aside the often confusing concepts and terms, this can be inferred from numerous communiqués of the CCRI and declarations by Marcos. One example is the following quote which points acutely to certain key issues:

> The problem is how to get the message across to everyone and to all organisations that, in addition to their own little project, they should open their horizon to a national project linked with what is happening ... how to call together all these groups, people, non-governmental agencies and organisations ... that space that we are trying to open so that we can make direct contact with these people ... But they too should be pushing to find the same wavelength in this other form of struggle for the same demands that we are making. [*Proceso*, 5 December 1994]

The continuing appeal of Zapatismo is due, to a great degree, to what might be called simple political and social 'intuition' or 'sensitivity' (with which the EZLN is certainly highly endowed); but this intuition and sensitivity is based on the fact that, even before the mobilisations, most of these 'groups, people, non-governmental organisations' were demonstrating a powerful capacity for self-organisation. And even if they were operating 'within' the limits of the state (none of them had proposed the gigantic task of organising and unleashing an insurrection), their activities in the social realm (human rights, civil rights, women's rights, youth rights, the right to culture, etc.) all demonstrated clear processes of self-valorisation. It is no coincidence that these were the strata or groups which responded first to the Declaration of War from the Lacandon Jungle.

Thus, we find that the two basic conditions proposed above for comprehending the new worker are present: the selling of labour power and the potential for autonomy. The strength of these massive demonstrations and the spontaneity with which they were organised demonstrate abilities that are part of the recomposition of the world of labour.

However, this potential cannot be understood in a linear fashion. It is beginning to unfold in the midst of deep processes of social disintegration marked by the reduction and segmentation of the labour market. The current phase of capitalism, the predominance and arrogance of money and the sharpening of conflicts between money capital and productive capital (of which the so-called 'tequila effect', the financial turmoil following the devaluation of the Mexican peso in December 1994, is but one example) is deepening the tendencies towards the breakdown of networks of solidarity, organisation and struggle. The recomposition of labour has been taking place within the very heart of these processes of decomposition, and on many occasions it is accelerated by the survival strategies developed by the labour force within the crisis itself (as in the case of those who work in the 'informal economy').

In summary, the processes of recomposition within the world of labour are intertwined in an extremely complex manner. The wage relationship (the purchase and sale of labour power) has become universal, having spread to practically all regions and countries; self-subsistence and pre-mercantile economies have disappeared or are on the brink of disappearing. Nevertheless, the generalisation of the wage relationship is giving rise to a tremendously heterogeneous labour force, which includes everything from professionals and state-of-the-art technical personnel, artists and communicators, to day labourers working at piece rate under appalling physical and cultural conditions (Ciudad Neza in Mexico, Manhattan or the Bronx in the US are but a few examples), passing through a whole range of worker situations in 'flexible' or still Taylorist industrial work. The tremendous social conflict of the last two decades, the struggle for the command over labour, of which neoliberalism represents only the theoretical-political formulation, has been leading to a situation in which the whole social structure has lost homogeneity; the recomposition of labour is not producing relatively homogeneous classes with a strong weight in society, as was the case with the former industrial proletariat which was concentrated in large industry; the new worker is emerging and wage labour is becoming universal in the midst of a process of fragmentation, characterised by the dispersion of experiences and interests. On top of all this, there are other aspects: capitalist restructuring under neoliberalism has tended to produce growing levels of unemployment and underemployment which, in a country like Mexico, has caused an increase in the phenomena of the so-called 'informal economy', particularly street vending. Neoliberal globalisation has demonstrated two antagonistic tendencies: on the one hand, it integrates productive processes, markets, finances, the circulation of information and mass messages; on the other, it tears societies apart, separating them into 'the included' (even if only to a minimal degree) and 'the excluded'. At the same time, most of these 'excluded' millions are men, women, young people and even children born of capitalism, bearers of the conflicts of the system. In most cases they were born into families and social strata which survived by selling their labour power, they have been raised to be 'future' sellers of labour power which, in this world, is often the best 'fate' they can expect.

Let us explore a little further the characteristics of these social figures (and subjectivities) which we conceptualise as 'the new worker', to see how certain possibilities and limitations come together in him or her.

In the first place, the fact that the restructuring of labour tends to break down wage strata which formerly were more or less homogeneous (attacks on workplace and industry-wide collective bargaining agreements are clear examples of this) is accompanied by the extension of the extraction of surplus value to practically every area of social life. The capitalist form of productive labour is to be found everywhere, not just nor even principally in the factory. The privatisation of forms of social security (retirement and pension plans, housing, medical services, education) is a key aspect of this process, as is the emergence of new productive sectors in which surplus value is condensed from labour with a high degree of intellectual content (laboratories and research centres, information services for companies and financial operations, agreements between industry and the universities, market analysts, strategy designers ... even stockbrokers and advertising specialists, to give just a few examples). Even among 'state-of-the-art' employees or professionals, wages are not high enough to permit capitalisation, although they do facilitate high levels of consumption.

Thus the new worker occupies every last corner of social space, through a multitude of differentiated localisations, forming a network whose points of union are of varying densities. The enormous socialisation of labour occurs, under present conditions, in the midst of the disassociation between the labour of individuals and groups (which we call fragmentation). At the same time, with the decline, obsolescence and discarding of former forms of organisation (primarily unions and parties) which served as the depositories of 'general interests' , the new worker is reorganising. This often involves articulating other aspects of social life, through groupings which are centred not on defending corporative interests (wages, jobs), but focus rather on particular questions (human rights, women, children, the disabled, minorities of all types, ecology, problems of urbanisation, the defence of education) which nevertheless involve alternative modes and strategies for dealing with the whole of social life. The new worker makes the leap from the 'immediate' (the singular) to the 'general', by taking the tortuous route of particularities.

This process is increasingly taking place through voluntary forms of association which do not depend on state or party tutelage: that is, through forms of self-organisation through which participants 'valorise themselves', often even at the margins of relationships of wage subordination. Through the course of these winding roads, they learn about the multiple talent for organising the social. They could even conclude that capitalism is just one of these many possibilities. We are now at the very core of our expectations related to the potential of the new worker. Would it be too bold to hope that these processes could lead from self-valorisation 'at the margins' of wage dependency to forms which would oppose it? There lies the uncertainty of the conflict, the road which can only be made by walking it, as the Zapatista communes demonstrate.

All of these factors are present within Mexican society and influence the course (and strategies) of the phase of social conflict connected with the prolonged insurrection of the Zapatista communes. They explain why and how almost all that has been loosely termed 'civil society' essentially forms part of the world of labour. They also reveal the class character not only of the massive mobilisations in response to critical moments in Chiapas but also of the social realignments and regroupings, the strength or weakness of which plays a vital role in the construction of potentially revolutionary subjects.

However, this potential cannot be understood in a linear fashion. The crisis has resulted in increasing degrees of social disintegration, but that is not the only thing that limits the new worker. Perhaps the most serious problem is the fragmentation of the new worker's own social body, that heterogeneity of formations, experiences and interests which prevents the worker from 'seeing' him or herself.

Within the realm of 'social culture' or social consciousness, where we find a tremendous degree of depoliticisation, the predominance of countless individualistic practices, and obsolete (if not completely useless) inherited concepts for thinking about society, one of the greatest limitations on the new worker is the fact that he or she still lacks identity. Largely as a result of the crisis of former social identities ('industrial proletariat', 'petit bourgeoisie', 'new middle classes', etc.) which corresponds to the crisis in the Keynesian state form of capitalism, the new worker does not recognise him or herself, just as he or she is not recognised by 'social scientists'. In the best of cases, the 'new workers' identify themselves as simple 'citizens' with general democratic expectations and specific interests in their particular field of action (human rights, feminism, etc.). This also explains Marcos's call to those: 'who in addition to their own little project should open their horizon to a national project'.

Labour, 'radical democracy', socialism

It is on this whole situation that the Zapatistas seek to make an impact, permanently and coherently. In this, they demonstrate an enormous capacity for congruency and perseverance, although this has gone unheeded by most political analysts, whether of the 'right' or the 'left', since both suffer from preconceived ideas. The former maintain that the EZLN's expressions in favour of democracy represent a sudden, opportunistic manoeuvre to conceal their terrible miasmas of archaism, dogmatism and totalitarianism. The latter are either concerned that the EZLN has 'dropped the banner of proletarian socialism', or they reproach them for having taken up arms instead of joining the ranks of the reformist or electoral parties (depending on whether the concern or reproach comes from vanguardists or from reformists 'à la Mexicana').

Such concepts, rooted in either fear or prejudice, ignore the popular/communal power of Zapatismo, its links with the recomposition of the world of labour and, consequently, the need for democracy demanded by the social movement.

Clearly, many of the Zapatistas' proposals (such as the dismantling of the state party system) arise in response to the particular characteristics of Mexico's political system or social formation which no longer exist in other regions or countries. However, by oscillating our focus from the particular to the general, we can draw inferences which help us understand the Zapatista experience as part of a project which in a very broad sense places before us that 'incompletion of modernity' of which Habermas speaks, being a theoretical and practical re-elaboration of a whole series of transformations which reopen breaches towards socialism as possibility and as present reality.

When we speak of 'the need for democracy', what kind of democracy are we referring to? Does, for example, the cry 'Democracy, Liberty, Justice' represent a profound opposition to capitalism? What possible links does it maintain with the world of labour and with socialism as a possible outcome of the conflict? Does that cry represent even a radical critique?

Let us begin with this last question. The radical nature of a programme of struggle, of the needs and demands which stem from social life, does not depend upon the use of extreme rhetoric and less still on the use of certain consecrated but empty words. Prefabricated phrases and verbiage aside, the radical nature of any particular need or demand cannot be defined in the abstract, but only as a critique of a critical situation. In Mexico today the needs and demands represented in cries for 'all rights for all', democracy, liberty, justice, dignity, are radical, because they imply a profound opposition to the very essence of the social and political system. This is what is referred to by the EZLN when they speak of 'a revolution to make the revolution possible'.

This represents the very heart of the Zapatista proposal, but it is open to multiple determinations, of which one is of decisive importance. In the face of people's boredom and disillusionment with state interventionism, which was channelled both in the 'East' and in the 'West' in favour of the restructuring of capital, the EZLN proposes a deepening of democracy through 'all kinds of participation': not the negation or overcoming of (bourgeois) democracy in order to establish some supposed 'dictatorship of the proletariat' or an 'anti-imperialist' dictatorship, but the opening of democratic participation to all, which, pursued coherently, implies opening (direct) power to society. And that can be understood as the logical extension of their demand of 'everything for everyone' (even power!), which emanates from their practices of communal power, of 'commanding obeying'.

Just as the Zapatista commune expresses a synthesis between the 'archaic' and the 'advanced', their global political proposal maintains and extends the body of democratic rights already won, while subordinating the state to permanent control by the population. Thus, in various communiqués and letters, the Zapatistas speak in favour of

> ... the right to democracy, so that everyone's opinions should have value, so that the popular will be respected and enforced, by electing or revoking, as needed, a form of government and governmental public servants. We demand that those who govern command obeying. [Communiqué of the CCRI, *La Jornada*, 8 October 1994]

This idea, that the government and government officials are revokable, signifies a profound radicalisation of democracy, and forms part of the libertarian experiences of socialism. And this is the orientation of the political reflections of Zapatismo. But its combat strategies to achieve this transformation are not rectilinear: 'It is necessary that all social relations in Mexico today undergo a profound, radical change. There must be a revolution, a new revolution. This revolution will only be possible from outside the system of the party state.'

While their analyses and proposals are necessarily located within the particular context of Mexico, they nevertheless contain strategic reformulations of potentially general application. This is truer still when they are analysed in light of the fragmentary nature of the new worker and of the movement's need for democracy. The problem of the party state constitutes but a first level of this issue; its content extends far beyond that. From the EZLN's various initiatives in the last few years (the call for the National Democratic Convention, the National Consultation, and the National Forum for Independent Dialogue), it can clearly be seen that Zapatismo is promoting ever greater levels of dialogue with 'civil society' and among the components of civil society. When this concept is combined with that of revocability, it is clear that they are promoting another kind of democracy, one which we have termed 'radical democracy'. The EZLN has been calling for dialogue among those who 'are equal' in their opposition to the party state, among 'everyone who sees this revolution as necessary and possible, and for the realisation of which all of us are important'.

No one says this better than the Zapatistas themselves:

> The great lesson, the most important teaching of this Consultation is that we can organise ourselves to speak and listen, that without anyone's sponsorship or permission we can develop the mechanisms for dialogue. The results of this Consultation tell us that we can, that there are tens of thousands of human beings willing to work and seek the way towards a world ... that we can build as we want it and not as Power wants it to be. We have made the Power of Money tremble ... dignity is starting to unite. The Power of Money is afraid because the uniting of dignities signifies its downfall.

The 'uniting of dignities' is the dialogue among equals, outside and against Power. It is the movement's need for democracy as the best way to overcome its fragmentation and to develop the social identities that the new worker requires to recognise him or herself as such; only in relation to 'the other' can they develop their own (personal and social) subjectivity. This means extending horizontally the processes of self-organisation and self-valorisation which today constitute the Zapatista communities as the highest expression of the recomposition of the world of labour.

The people referred to here are 'equals' in as much as they are sellers of their labour power and opponents of the dominant system, that is, because they are the insubordinate exploited. But at the same time they are heterogeneous and even distant from one another: in them is all the rich diversity of labour, as well as its fissures.

All of these divisions, these groupings, express particularised forms of social consciousness: together they compose what has come to be called 'civil society', which has been analysed in terms of its diversity and heterogeneity of experiences and subjectivities within the world of labour. In practically every case, no social spaces exist to facilitate processes of mutual recognition, processes which would make it possible to recognise identity in difference, unity in diversity – that which in other times and in other terms was conceptualised as 'class consciousness'.

The dialogues with 'civil society' and among its components serve as the space for these processes, starting from the recognition of diversity and the need to construct mutual identifications: space for the new worker to identify him or herself as such, to begin to structure a common programme embracing all their particular needs, and to advance through common action. It is through such a strategy, which constitutes an absolute novelty in relation to all earlier revolutionary experience, that the Zapatistas are contributing decisively to the construction of new class alignments, redefining the contours of the capital–labour conflict in ways that appear to match the characteristics of the new worker.

It can now be understood why the movement has insisted on the need for democracy: to construct the potentially revolutionary social subjectivities. It can be seen too how that democracy is radical: the dialogue between equals excludes capital and the state. It can be seen likewise the ways in which the EZLN opens ways of rethinking the emancipation of labour as the task of the workers themselves. Finally, it is clear that all this is not given *a priori*, nor guaranteed by any omniscient theory. The project of a more human world is simply an act of uncertain hope.

This experience of hope, together with the consciousness of uncertainty, is beautifully expressed in one of Marcos's letters: 'In sum, we are an army of dreamers, and therefore invincible. How can we fail to win, with this imagination overturning everything. Or rather, we do not deserve to lose ...'[1]

Note

1. The quotes and references to the communiqués of the EZLN refer to *La Jornada*, 3 January 1994, 8 October 1994, 18 November 1994, 1 October 1995; the text, 'Mexico: between the mirrors of the night and the crystal of the day', in *La Jornada* 9–11 June 1995; the Letter to Adolfo Gilly, in *Viento del Sur*, no. 4, Summer 1995; the quotations from interviews with Subcomandante Marcos from *Proceso*, nos 927 and 944 (8 August and 5 December 1994).

The information on which the section 'The Formation of a Communal Army' is based comes from an extensive report published in the form of a book, *EZLN: el ejército que salió de la selva* [EZLN: the army that came out of the jungle] (Mexico City: Editorial Planeta, 1994), written by two young journalists, Guido Camu Urzua and Dauno Totoro Taulis, who lived with the Zapatistas in the Lacandon Jungle for several months.

The most complete collection of the letters, interviews and communiqués of the EZLN in the first year of the uprising can be found in the three volumes of *La Palabra de los Armados de Verdad y Fuego* [The Word of Those Armed with Truth and Fire] (Mexico City: Editorial Fuenteovejuna, 1994–1995).

7

Dignity's Revolt

John Holloway

Dignity arose on the first day of January 1994

The 'Enough!' (*'¡Ya Basta!'*) proclaimed by the Zapatistas on the first day of 1994 was the cry of dignity. When they occupied San Cristóbal de las Casas and six other towns of Chiapas on that day, the wind they blew into the world, 'this wind from below, the wind of rebellion, the wind of dignity', carried 'a hope, the hope of the conversion of dignity and rebellion into freedom and dignity'.[1] When the wind dies down, 'when the storm abates, when the rain and the fire leave the earth in peace once again, the world will no longer be the world, but something better'.[2]

A letter from the ruling body of the Zapatistas, the Comité Clandestino Revolucionario Indígena (CCRI),[3] addressed just a month later to another indigenous organisation, the Consejo 500 Años de Resistencia Indígena,[4] emphasises the central importance of dignity:

> Then that suffering that united us made us speak, and we recognised that in our words there was truth, we knew that not only pain and suffering lived in our tongue, we recognised that there is hope still in our hearts. We spoke with ourselves, we looked inside ourselves and we looked at our history: we saw our most ancient fathers suffering and struggling, we saw our grandfathers struggling, we saw our fathers with fury in their hands, we saw that not everything had been taken away from us, that we had the most valuable, that which made us live, that which made our step rise above plants and animals, that which made the stone be beneath our feet, and we saw, brothers, that all that we had was DIGNITY, and we saw that great was the shame of having forgotten it, and we saw that DIGNITY was good for men to be men again, and dignity returned to live in our hearts, and we were new again, and the dead, our dead, saw that we were new again and they called us again, to dignity, to struggle.[5]

159

Dignity, the refusal to accept humiliation and dehumanisation, the refusal to conform: dignity is the core of the Zapatistas' revolution of revolution. The idea of dignity has not been invented by the Zapatistas, but they have given it a prominence that it has never before possessed in revolutionary thought. When the Zapatistas rose, they planted the flag of dignity not just in the centre of the uprising in Chiapas, but in the centre of oppositional thought. Dignity is not peculiar to the indigenous peoples of the southeast of Mexico: the struggle to convert 'dignity and rebellion into freedom and dignity' (an odd but important formulation) is the struggle of (and for) human existence in an oppressive society, as relevant to life in Edinburgh, Athens, Tokyo, Los Angeles or Johannesburg as it is to the struggles of the peoples of the Lacandon Jungle.

The aim of this chapter is to explore what it means to put dignity at the centre of oppositional thought. In the course of the argument it should become clear why 'Zapatismo' is not a movement restricted to Mexico but is central to the struggle of thousands of millions of people all over the world to live a human life against and in an increasingly inhuman society.

The essay aims not so much to give a historical account of the Zapatista movement as to provide a distillation of the most important themes, without at the same time concealing the ambiguities and contradictions of the movement. In order to distil a fragrant essence from roses, it is not necessary to conceal the existence of the thorns, but thorns do not enter into what one wants to extract. The purpose of trying to distil the theoretical themes of Zapatismo is similar to the purpose behind any distillation process: to separate those themes from the immediate historical development of the Zapatista movement, to extend the fragrance beyond the immediacy of the particular experience.

Dignity was wrought in the jungle

The uprising of January 1994 was more than ten years in the preparation. The EZLN[6] celebrates 17 November 1983 as the date of its foundation. On that date a small group of revolutionaries established themselves in the mountains of the Lacandon Jungle – 'a small group of men and women, three indigenous and three mestizos'.[7]

According to the police version, the revolutionaries were members of the Fuerzas de Liberación Nacional (FLN),[8] a guerrilla organisation founded in 1969 in the city of Monterrey, one of a number of such organisations which flourished in Mexico in the late 1960s and early 1970s. Many FLN members had been killed or arrested, but the organisation had survived. Its statutes of 1980 describe the organisation as 'a political-military organisation whose aim is the taking of political power by the workers of the countryside and of the cities of the Mexican Republic, in order to install a popular republic with a socialist system'. The organisation was guided, according to its statutes, by 'the science of history and society: Marxism-Leninism, which has demonstrated its validity in all the triumphant revolutions of this century'.[9]

The supposed origins of the EZLN[10] are used by the authorities to suggest an image of manipulation of the indigenous people by a group of hard-core professional urban revolutionaries. However, leaving aside the racist assumptions of such an argument, the supposed origins of the revolutionaries merely serve to underline the most important question: if, as is claimed, the small group of revolutionaries who set up the EZLN came from an orthodox Marxist-Leninist guerrilla group, how did they become transformed into what eventually emerged from the jungle in the early hours of 1994? What was the path that led from the first encampment of 17 November 1983 to the proclamation of dignity in the town hall of San Cristóbal? For it is precisely the fact that they are not an orthodox guerrilla group that has confounded the state time and time again in its dealings with them. It is precisely the fact that they are not an orthodox group of revolutionaries that makes them theoretically and practically the most exciting development in oppositional politics in the world for many a long year.

What, then, was it that the original founders of the EZLN learned in the jungle? A letter written by Marcos speaks of the change in these terms:

We did not propose it. The only thing that we proposed to do was to change the world; everything else has been improvisation. Our square conception of the world and of revolution was badly dented in the confrontation with the indigenous realities of Chiapas. Out of those blows, something new (which does not necessarily mean 'good') emerged, that which today is known as 'neo-Zapatismo'.[11]

The confrontation with the indigenous realities took place as the Zapatistas became immersed in the communities of the Lacandon Jungle. At first the group of revolutionaries kept themselves to themselves, training in the mountains, slowly expanding in numbers. Then gradually they made contact with the local communities, initially through family contacts, then, from about 1985 onwards, on a more open and organised basis. [12] Gradually, more and more of the communities sought out the Zapatistas to help them defend themselves from the police or the farmers' armed 'white guards'.[13] More and more became Zapatista communities, some of their members going to join the EZLN on a full-time basis, some forming part of the part-time militia, the rest of the community giving material support to the insurgents. Gradually, the EZLN was transformed from being a guerrilla group to being a community in arms (see Chapter 6).

The community in question is in some respects a special community. The communities of the Lacandon Jungle are of recent formation, most of them dating from the 1950s and 1960s, when the government encouraged colonisation of the jungle by landless peasants, most of whom moved from other areas of Chiapas, in many cases simply transplanting whole villages. There is a long tradition of struggle, both from before the formation of the communities in the jungle and then, very intensely, throughout the 1970s and 1980s, as the people fought to get enough land to ensure their own survival, as they tried to secure the legal basis of their landholdings, and as they fought to maintain their existence against the expansion of the cattle ranches. They resisted the threat to their survival posed by two government measures in particular: the Decree of the Lacandon Community,[14] a government decree which threatened to expropriate a large part of the Lacandon Jungle, and the 1992 reform of Article 27 of the Constitution, which, by opening the countryside up to private investment, threatened to undermine the system of collective landholding. The communities of the Lacandon Jungle are special in many respects, but arguably the rethinking of revolutionary theory and practice could have resulted from immersion in any community (see Chapter 5). What was important was probably not the specific characteristics of the Lacandon Jungle, so much as the transformation from being a group of dedicated young men and women into being an armed community of women, men, children, young, old, ill – all with their everyday struggles not just for survival but for humanity.

The Zapatistas learnt the pain of the community: the poverty, the hunger, the constant threat of harassment by the authorities or the 'white guards', the unnecessary deaths from curable diseases. When asked in an interview which death had affected him most, Marcos told how a girl of three or four years old, Paticha (her way of saying Patricia), had died in his arms in a village. She had started a fever at six o'clock in the evening, and by ten o'clock she was dead. There was no medicine in the village that could help to lower her fever:

> And that happened many times, it was so everyday, so everyday that those births are not even taken into account. For example, Paticha never had a birth certificate, which means that for the country she never existed, for the statistical office [INEGI], therefore her death never existed either. And like her, there were thousands, thousands and thousands, and as we grew in the communities, as we had more villages, more comrades died. Just because death was natural, now it started to be ours. [15]

From such experiences arose the conviction that revolution was something that the Zapatistas owed to their children: 'we, their fathers, their mothers, their brothers and sisters, did not want to bear any more the guilt of doing nothing for our children'.[16]

They learnt the struggles of the people, both the struggles of the present and the struggles of the past, the continuing struggle of past and present. The culture of the people is a culture of struggle. Marcos tells of the story-telling by the campfire at night in the mountains:

> ... stories of apparitions, of the dead, of earlier struggles, of things that have happened, all mixed together. It seems that they are talking of the revolution (of the Mexican revolution, the past one, not the one that is happening now) and at moments now, it seems that is mixed up with the colonial period and sometimes it seems that it is the pre-hispanic period.[17]

The culture of struggle permeates the Zapatista communiqués, often in the form of stories and myths: Marcos's stories of Old Antonio (*el viejo Antonio*) are a favourite way of passing on a culture impregnated with the wisdom of struggle.

And they learnt to listen:

> That is the great lesson that the indigenous communities teach to the original EZLN. The original EZLN, the one that is formed in 1983, is a political organisation in the sense that it speaks and what it says has to be done. The indigenous communities teach it to listen, and that is what we learn. The principal lesson that we learn from the indigenous people is that we have to learn to hear, to listen.[18]

Learning to listen meant incorporating new perspectives and new concepts into their theory. Learning to listen meant learning to talk as well, not just explaining things in a different way but thinking them in a different way.

Above all, learning to listen meant turning everything upside down. The revolutionary tradition of talking is not just a bad habit. It has a long-established theoretical basis in the concepts of Marxism-Leninism. The tradition of talking derives, on the one hand, from the idea that theory ('class consciousness') must be brought to the masses by the party and, on the other, from the idea that capitalism must be analysed from above, from the movement of capital rather than from the movement of anti-capitalist struggle. When the emphasis shifts to listening, both of these theoretical suppositions are undermined. The whole relation between theory and practice is thrown into question: theory can no longer be seen as being brought from outside, but is obviously the product of everyday practice. And dignity takes the place of imperialism as the starting point of theoretical reflection.

Dignity was presumably not part of the conceptual baggage of the revolutionaries who went into the jungle. It is not a word that appears very much in the literature of the Marxist tradition.[19] It could only emerge as a revolutionary concept in the course of a revolution by a people steeped in the dignity of struggle.[20] But once it appears (consciously or unconsciously) as a central concept, then it implies a rethinking of the whole revolutionary project, both theoretically and in terms of organisation. The whole conception of revolution becomes turned outwards: revolution becomes a question rather than an answer. '*Preguntando caminamos* – asking we walk' becomes a central principle of the revolutionary movement, the radically democratic concept at the centre of the Zapatista call for 'freedom, democracy and justice'. The revolution advances by asking, not by telling; or perhaps even, revolution *is* asking instead of telling, the dissolution of power relations.

Here too the Zapatistas learned from (and developed) the tradition of the indigenous communities. The idea and practice of their central organisational principle, '*mandar obedeciendo*' ('to command obeying'), derives from the practice of the communities, in which all important decisions are discussed by the whole community to the point where a consensus is reached, and in which all holders of positions of authority are assumed to be immediately recallable if they do not satisfy the community, if they do not command obeying the community. Thus the decision to go to war was not taken by some central committee and then handed down, but was discussed by all the communities in village assemblies.[21] The whole organisation is structured along the same principle: the ruling body, the CCRI, is composed of recallable delegates chosen by the different ethnic groups (Tzotzil, Tzeltal, Tojolabal and Chol), and each ethnic group and each region has its own committees chosen in assemblies on the same principle.

The changes wrought in those ten years of confrontation between the received ideas of revolution and the reality of the indigenous peoples of Chiapas were very deep. Marcos is quoted in one book as saying 'I think that our only virtue as theorists was to have the humility to recognise that our theoretical scheme did not work, that it was very limited, that we had to adapt ourselves to the reality that was being imposed on us.'[22] However, the result was not that reality imposed itself on theory, as some argue,[23] but that the confrontation with reality gave rise to a whole new and immensely rich theorisation of revolutionary practice.

The revolt of dignity is an undefined revolt

A revolution that listens, a revolution that takes as its starting point the dignity of those in revolt, is inevitably an undefined revolution, a revolution in which the distinction between rebellion and revolution loses meaning. The revolution is a moving outwards rather than a moving towards.

There is no transitional programme, no definite goal. There is, of course, an aim: the achievement of a society based on dignity, or, in the words of the Zapatista slogan, 'Democracy, Freedom, Justice'. But just what this means and what concrete steps need to be taken to achieve it are never spelt out. This has at times been criticised by those educated in the classical revolutionary traditions as a sign of the political immaturity of the Zapatistas or of their reformism, but it is the logical complement of putting dignity at the centre of the revolutionary project. If the revolution is built on the dignity of those in struggle, if a central principle is the idea of *'preguntando caminamos* – asking we walk', then it follows that it must be self-creative, a revolution created in the process of struggle. If the revolution is not only to achieve democracy as an end, but is democratic in its struggle, then it is impossible to pre-define its path, or indeed to think of a defined point of arrival. Whereas the concept of revolution that has predominated in this century has been overwhelmingly instrumentalist,[24] a conception of a means designed to achieve an end, this conception breaks down as soon as the starting point becomes the dignity of those in struggle. The revolt of dignity forces us to think of revolution in a new way, as a rebellion that cannot be defined or confined, a rebellion that overflows, a revolution that is by its very nature ambiguous and contradictory.

The Zapatista uprising is in the first place a revolt of the indigenous peoples of the Lacandon Jungle, of the Tzeltals, Tzotzils, Chols and Tojolabals who live in that part of the state of Chiapas. For them, the conditions of living were (and are) such that the only choice, as they see it, is between dying an undignified death, the slow unsung death of misery suffered, and dying with dignity, the death of those fighting for their dignity and the dignity of those around them. The government has consistently tried to define and confine the uprising in those terms, as a matter limited to the state of Chiapas, but the Zapatistas have always refused to accept this. This was, indeed, the main point over which the first dialogue, the dialogue of San Cristóbal, broke down.[25]

The Zapatista uprising is the assertion of indigenous dignity. The opening words of the Declaration of the Lacandon Jungle, read from the balcony of the town hall of San Cristóbal on the morning of the first of January 1994, were 'We are the product of 500 years of struggles.'[26] The uprising came just over a year after the demonstrations throughout America that marked the 500th anniversary of Columbus's 'discovery'. On that occasion, 12 October 1992, the Zapatistas had already marched through San Cristóbal, when about 10,000 indigenous people, most of them Zapatistas but under another guise,[27] had taken the streets of the city. After the first of January 1994, the Zapatistas at once became the focus of the increasingly active indigenous movement in Mexico. When the EZLN began its dialogue with the government in April 1995, the dialogue of San Andrés Larrainzar, the first theme for discussion was indigenous rights and culture. The Zapatistas used the dialogue to give cohesion to the indigenous struggle, asking representatives of all the main indigenous organisations of the country to join them as consultants or guests in the workshops which were part of the dialogue and concluding that phase of the dialogue with an Indigenous Forum, held in San Cristóbal in January 1996. The Indigenous Forum led in turn to the setting up of the Congreso Nacional Indígena (National Indigenous Congress) which gives a national focus to previously dispersed indigenous struggles. The first phase of the dialogue of San Andrés also led to the signing of an agreement with the government designed to lead to changes in the constitution which would radically improve the legal position of indigenous peoples within the country, granting them important areas of autonomy. (At the time of writing, the agreement still has not been implemented by the government.)

The Zapatista movement, however, has never claimed to be just an indigenous movement.[28] Overwhelmingly indigenous in composition, the EZLN has always made clear that it is fighting for a broader cause. Its struggle is for all those 'without voice, without face, without tomorrow', a category that stretches far beyond the indigenous peoples. Their demands – work, land, housing, food, health, education, independence, freedom, democracy, justice and peace – are not demands limited to the indigenous: they are demands for all. The Zapatista movement is a movement for *national* liberation, a movement not just for the liberation of the indigenous but of all.

The fact that the EZLN is an Army of National Liberation seems to give a clear definition to the movement. There have been many other movements (and wars) of national liberation in different parts of the world: Vietnam, Angola, Mozambique, Cambodia, Nicaragua, etc. Here we have what appears to be a clearly defined and well-established framework: national liberation movements typically aim to liberate a national territory from foreign influence (the control of a colonial or neo-colonial power), to establish a government of national liberation designed to introduce radical social changes and establish national economic autonomy. If the Zapatista movement were a national liberation movement in that sense, then, if the history of such movements is anything to go by, there would be little to get excited about: it might be worthy of support and solidarity, but there would be nothing radically new about it. This indeed has been the position of some critics on the left.[29]

Looked at more closely, however, the apparent definition of 'Army of National Liberation' begins to dissolve. In the context of the uprising, the term 'national liberation' has more a sense of moving outwards than of moving inwards: 'national' in the sense of 'not just Chiapanecan' or 'not just indigenous', rather than 'national' in the sense of 'not foreign'.[30] 'Nation' is also used in the Zapatista communiqués in the less clearly defined sense of 'homeland' (*patria*): the place where we happen to live, a space to be defended not just against imperialists but also (and more directly) against the state. 'Nation' is counterposed to the state, so that national liberation can even be understood as the liberation of Mexico from the Mexican state, or the defence of Mexico (or indeed whatever territory) against the state. 'Nation' in this sense refers to the idea of struggling wherever one happens to live, fighting against oppression, fighting for dignity. That the Zapatista movement is a movement of national liberation does not, then, confine or restrict the movement to Mexico:

it can be understood rather as meaning a movement of liberation, wherever you happen to be (and whatever you happen to do). The fight for dignity cannot be restricted to national frontiers: 'dignity', in the wonderful expression used by Marcos in the invitation to the Intercontinental Gathering held in the Lacandon Jungle in July 1996, 'is that homeland without nationality, that rainbow that is also a bridge, that murmur of the heart no matter what blood lives in it, that rebel irreverence that mocks frontiers, customs officials and wars'.[31] It is consistent with this interpretation of 'national liberation' that one of the principal slogans of the Zapatistas recently has been the theme chosen for the Intercontinental Gathering, 'for humanity and against neoliberalism'.[32]

The open-ended nature of the Zapatista movement is summed up in the idea that it is a revolution, not a Revolution – 'with small letters, to avoid polemics with the many vanguards and safeguards of THE REVOLUTION'.[33] It is a revolution, because the claim to dignity in a society built upon the negation of dignity can only be met through a radical transformation of society. But it is not a Revolution in the sense of having some grand plan, in the sense of a movement designed to bring about the Great Event which will change the world. Its claim to be revolutionary lies not in the preparation for the future Event but in the present inversion of perspective, in the consistent insistence on seeing the world in terms of that which is incompatible with the world as it is: human dignity. Revolution refers to present existence, not to future instrumentality.

The revolt of dignity is a revolt against definition

The undefined, open-ended character of the Zapatista movement sometimes rouses the frustrations of those schooled in a harder-edged revolutionary tradition. Behind the lack of definition there is, however, a much sharper point. The lack of definition does not result from theoretical slackness: on the contrary, revolution is essentially anti-definitional.

The traditional Leninist concept of revolution is crucially definitional. At its centre is the idea that the struggles of the working class are inevitably limited in character, that they cannot rise above reformist demands, unless there is the intervention of a revolutionary party. The working class is a 'they' who cannot go beyond certain limits without outside intervention. The self-emancipation of the proletariat is impossible.[34]

The emphasis on dignity puts the unlimited at the centre of picture, not just the undefined but the anti-definitional. Dignity, understood as a category of struggle, is a tension which points beyond itself. The assertion of dignity implies the present negation of dignity. Dignity, then, is the struggle against the denial of dignity, the struggle for the realisation of dignity. Dignity is and is not: it is the struggle against its own negation. If dignity were simply the assertion of something that already is, then it would be an absolutely flabby concept, an empty complacency. To simply assert human dignity as a principle (as in 'all humans have dignity', or 'all humans have a right to dignity') would be either so general as to be meaningless or, worse, so general as to obscure the fact that existing society is based on the negation of dignity.[35] Similarly, if dignity were simply the assertion of something that is not, then it would be an empty daydream or a religious wish. The concept of dignity only gains force if it is understood in its double dimension, as the struggle against its own denial. One is dignified, or true, only by struggling against present indignity, or untruth. Dignity implies a constant moving against the barriers of that which exists, a constant subversion and transcendence of definitions. Dignity, understood as a category of struggle, is a fundamentally anti-identitarian concept: not 'my dignity as a Mexican ...', but 'our dignity is our struggle against the negation of that dignity'.

Dignity is not a characteristic peculiar to the indigenous of south-east Mexico, nor to those overtly involved in revolutionary struggle. It is simply a characteristic of life in an oppressive society. It is the cry of 'Enough!' (*¡Ya Basta!*) that is inseparable from the experience of oppression. Oppression cannot be total; whatever its form, it is always a pressure which is confronted by a counter-pressure, dehumanisation confronted by humanity. Domination implies resistance, dignity.[36] Dignity is the other side, too often forgotten, too often stifled, of what Marx called alienation: it is the struggle of dis-alienation, of de-fetishisation. It is the struggle for recognition, but for the recognition of a self currently negated.

Dignity is the lived experience that the world is *not* so, that that is *not* the way things are. It is the lived rejection of positivism, of those forms of thought which start from the assumption that 'that's the way things are'. It is the cry of existence of that which has been silenced by 'the world that is', the refusal to be shut out by 'is'-ness, the scream against being forgotten in the fragmentation of the world into the disciplines of social science, those disciplines which break reality and, in breaking, exclude, suppressing the suppressed. Dignity is the cry of 'here we are!', the 'here we are!' of the indigenous peoples forgotten by neoliberal modernisation, the 'here we are!' of the growing numbers of poor who somehow do not show in the statistics of economic growth and the financial reports, the 'here we are!' of the gay whose sexuality was for so long not recognised, the 'here we are!' of the elderly shut away to die in the retirement homes of the richer countries, the 'here we are!' of the women trapped in the role of housewife, the 'here we are!' of the millions of illegal migrants who are not where, officially, they should be,[37] the 'here we are!' of all those pleasures of human life excluded by the growing subjection of humanity to the market. Dignity is the cry of those who are not heard, the voice of those without voice. Dignity is the truth of truth denied:[38]

> Us they forgot more and more, and history was no longer big enough for us to die just like that, forgotten and humiliated. Because dying does not hurt, what hurts is being forgotten. Then we discovered that we no longer existed, that those who govern had forgotten us in the euphoria of statistics and growth rates. A country which forgets itself is a sad country, a country which forgets its past cannot have a future. And then we seized our arms and went into the cities where we were animals. And we went and said to the powerful 'here we are!' and to all the country we shouted 'here we are!' and to all the world we shouted 'here we are!' And see how odd things are because, for them to see us, we covered our faces; for them to name us, we gave up our name; we gambled the present to have a future; and to live ... we died.[39]

This 'here we are!' is not the 'here we are!' of mere identity. It is a 'here we are!' which derives its meaning from the denial of that presence. It is not a static 'here we are!' but a movement, an assault on the barriers of exclusion. It is the breaking of barriers, the moving against separations, classifications, definitions, the assertion of unities that have been defined out of existence.

Dignity is an assault on the separation of morality and politics, and of the private and the public. Dignity cuts across those boundaries, asserts the unity of what has been sundered. The assertion of dignity is neither a moral nor a political claim: it is rather an attack on the separation of politics and morality that allows formally democratic regimes all over the world to coexist with growing levels of poverty and social marginalisation. It is the 'here we are!' not just of the marginalised, but of the horror felt by all of us in the face of mass impoverishment and starvation. It is the 'here we are!' not just of the growing numbers shut away in prisons, hospitals and homes, but also of the shame and disgust of all of us who, by living, participate in the bricking-up of people in those prisons, hospitals and homes. Dignity is an assault on the conventional definition of politics, but equally on the acceptance of that definition in the instrumental conception of revolutionary politics which has for so long subordinated the personal to the political, with such disastrous results. Probably nothing has done more to undermine the 'Left' in this century than this separation of the political and the personal, of the public and the private, and the dehumanisation that it entails.

Dignity encapsulates in one word the rejection of the separation of the personal and the political.[40] To a remarkable extent, this group of rebels in the jungle of the south-east of Mexico have crystallised and advanced the themes of oppositional thought and action that have been discussed throughout the world in recent years: the issues of gender, age, childhood, death and the dead. All flow from the understanding of politics as a politics of dignity, a politics which recognises the particular oppression of, and respects the struggles of, women, children, the old. Respect for the struggles of the old is a constant theme of Marcos's stories, particularly through the figure of Old Antonio, but was also forcefully underlined by the emergence of Comandante Trinidad as one of the leading figures in the dialogue of San Andrés. The way in which women have imposed recognition of their struggles on the Zapatista men is well known, and can be seen, for example, in the Revolutionary Law for Women, issued on the first day of the uprising, or in the fact that it was a woman, Ana María, who led the most important military action undertaken by the Zapatistas, the occupation of the town hall in San Cristóbal on 1 January 1994 (see Chapter 3). The question of childhood and the freedom to play is a constant theme in Marcos's letters. The stories, jokes and poetry of the communiqués and the dances that punctuate all that the Zapatistas do are not embellishments of a revolutionary process but central to it.

The struggle of dignity is the 'here we are!' of jokes, poetry, dancing, old age, childhood, games, death, love – of all those things excluded by serious bourgeois politics and serious revolutionary politics alike. As such, the struggle of dignity is opposed to the state. The Zapatista movement is an anti-state movement, not just in the obvious sense that the EZLN took up arms against the Mexican state, but in the much more profound sense that their forms of organisation, action and discourse are non-state, or, more precisely, anti-state forms.

The state defines and classifies and, by so doing, excludes. This is not by chance. The state, any state, embedded as it is in the global web of capitalist social relations, functions in such a way as to reproduce the capitalist status quo.[41] In its relation to us, and in our relation to it, there is a filtering out of anything that is not compatible with the reproduction of capitalist social relations. This may be a violent filtering, as in the repression of revolutionary or subversive activity, but it is also and above all a less perceptible filtering, a sidelining or suppression of passions, loves, hates, anger, laughter, dancing. Discontent is redefined as demands and demands are classified and defined, excluding all that is not reconcilable with the reproduction of capitalist social relations. The discontented are classified in the same way, the indigestible excluded with a greater or lesser degree of violence. The cry of dignity, the 'here we are!' of the unpalatable and indigestible, can only be a revolt against classification, against definition as such.

The state is pure Is-ness, pure Identity. Power says 'I am who am, the eternal repetition.'[42] The state is the great Classifier. Power says to the rebels: 'Be ye not awkward, refuse not to be classified. All that cannot be classified counts not, exists not, is not.'[43] The struggle of the state against the Zapatistas since the declaration of the cease-fire has been a struggle to define, to classify, to limit; the struggle of the Zapatistas against the state has been the struggle to break out, to break the barriers, to overflow, to refuse definition or to accept and transcend definition.

The dialogue between the government and the EZLN, first in San Cristóbal in March 1994, and then in San Andrés Larrainzar since April 1995, has been a constant double movement. The government has constantly sought to define and limit the Zapatista movement, to 'make it small', as one of the government representatives put it. It has constantly sought to define Zapatismo as a movement limited to Chiapas, with no right to discuss matters of wider importance. It did sign agreements on the question of indigenous rights and autonomy, but apparently without having at the time any intention of implementing them, still the state of affairs at the time of writing. In the section of the dialogue devoted to democracy and justice, however, the government representatives made no serious contribution and have apparently no intention of signing agreements in this area. The Zapatistas, on the other hand, have constantly used the dialogue to break out, to overcome their geographical isolation in the Lacandon Jungle. They have done this partly through their daily press conferences during the sessions of the dialogue, but also by negotiating the procedural right to invite advisers and guests and then inviting hundreds of them to participate in the sessions on indigenous rights and culture and on democracy and justice. These advisers come from a very wide range of indigenous and community organisations, complemented by a wide range of academics. Each of the two topics also provided the basis for organising a Forum in San Cristóbal, first on Indigenous Rights and Culture in January 1996 and then on the Reform of the State in July of the same year, both attended by a very large number of activists from all over the country.

On the one hand, the government's drive to limit, define, make small; on the other, the (generally very successful) Zapatista push to break the cordon. On the one hand, a politics of definition, on the other a politics of overflowing. This does not mean that the Zapatistas have not sought to define: on the contrary, the definition of constitutional reforms to define indigenous autonomy is seen by them as an important achievement. But it has been a definition that overflows, thematically and politically. The definition of indigenous rights is seen not as an end-point, but as a start, as a basis for moving on to other areas of change, but also as a basis for taking the movement forward, a basis for breaking out.

The difference in approach between the two sides of the dialogue has at times resulted in incidents which reflect not only the arrogance of the government negotiators but also the lack of understanding derived from their perspective as representatives of the state. This has even been expressed in the conception of time. Given the bad conditions of communication in the Lacandon Jungle, and the need to discuss everything thoroughly, the Zapatista principle of '*mandar obedeciendo*' ('to command obeying') means that decisions take time. When the government representatives insisted on rapid replies, the Zapatistas replied that they did not understand the indigenous clock. As recounted by Comandante David afterwards, the Zapatistas explained:

> We, as Indians, have rhythms, forms of understanding, of deciding, of reaching agreements. And when we told them that, they replied by making fun of us; well then, they said, we don't understand why you say that because we see that you have Japanese watches, so how do you say that you use the indigenous clock, that's from Japan.[44]

And Comandante Tacho commented: 'They haven't learned. They understand us backwards. We use time, not the clock.'[45]

Even more fundamentally, the state representatives have been unable to understand the concept of dignity. In one of the press conferences held during the dialogue of San Andrés, Comandante Tacho recounts that the government negotiators

... told us that they are studying what dignity means, that they are consulting and making studies on dignity. That what they understood was that dignity is service to others. And they asked us to tell them what we understand by dignity. We told them to continue with their research. It makes us laugh and we laughed in front of them. They asked us why and we told them that they have big research centres and big studies in schools of a high standard and that it would be a shame if they do not accept that. We told them that if we sign the peace, then we will tell them at the end what dignity means for us.[46]

The Zapatista sense of satire and their refusal to be defined is turned not only against the state, but also against the more traditional 'definitional' left. In a letter dated 20 February 1995, when the Zapatistas were retreating from the army after the military intervention of 9 February, Marcos imagines an interrogation by the state prosecutor, consisting of the prosecutor's accusations and his own responses:

The whites accuse you of being black: Guilty.
The blacks accuse you of being white: Guilty ...
The machos accuse you of being feminist: Guilty.
The feminists accuse you of being macho: Guilty.
The communists accuse you of being an anarchist: Guilty.
The anarchists accuse you of being orthodox: Guilty ...
The reformists accuse you of being an extremist: Guilty.
The 'historical vanguard' accuse you of appealing to civil society and not to the proletariat: Guilty.
Civil society accuse you of disturbing its tranquillity: Guilty.
The stock market accuses you of spoiling their lunch: Guilty ...
The serious people accuse you of being a joker: Guilty.
The jokers accuse you of being serious: Guilty.
The adults accuse you of being a child: Guilty.
The children accuse you of being an adult: Guilty.
The orthodox leftists accuse you for not condemning homosexuals and lesbians: Guilty.
The theorists accuse you for being practical: Guilty.
The practitioners accuse you for being theoretical: Guilty.
Everybody accuses you for everything bad that happens to them: Guilty.[47]

Dignity's revolt mocks classification. As it must. It must, because dignity makes sense only if understood as being-and-not-being, and therefore defying definition or classification. Dignity is that which pushes from itself towards itself, and cannot be reduced to a simple 'is'. The state, any state, on the other hand, is. The state, as its name suggests, imposes a state, an Is-ness, upon that which pushes beyond existing social relations. Dignity is a moving outwards, an overflowing, a fountain; the state is a moving inwards, a containment, a cistern.[48] The failure to understand dignity, then, is not peculiar to the Mexican state: it is simply that statehood and dignity are incompatible. There is no fit between them.

Dignity's revolt, therefore, cannot aim at winning state power. From the beginning, the Zapatistas made it clear that they did not want to win power, and they have repeated it ever since. Many on the more traditional 'definitional' left were scandalised when the repudiation of winning power gained more concrete expression in the Fourth Declaration of the Lacandon Jungle at the beginning of 1996, when the Zapatistas launched the formation of the Zapatista Front of National Liberation (FZLN) and made the rejection of all ambition to hold state office a condition of membership.[49] The repudiation of state power is, however, simply an extension of the idea of dignity. The state, any state, is so bound into the web of global capitalist social relations that it has no option, whatever the composition of the government, but to promote the reproduction of those relations, and that means defining and degrading. To assume state power would inevitably be to abandon dignity. The revolt of dignity can only aim at abolishing the state or, more immediately, at developing alternative forms of social organisation and strengthening anti-state power: 'It is not necessary to conquer the world. It is enough to make it anew.'[50]

The central principles on which the Zapatistas have insisted in developing alternative forms of social organisation are those of *'mandar obedeciendo'* ('to command obeying') and *'preguntando caminamos'* ('asking we walk'). They have emphasised time and time again the importance for them of taking all important decisions through a collective process of discussion, and that the way forward cannot be a question of their imposing their line, but only through opening up spaces for discussion and democratic decision, in which they would express their view, but their view should count only as one among many. In relation to the state (and assuming that the state still exists), they have said many times that they do not want to hold state office, and that it does not matter which party holds state office as long as those in authority 'command obeying'. The problem of revolutionary politics, then, is not to win power but to develop forms of political articulation that would force those in office to obey the people (so that, fully developed, the separation between state and society would be overcome and the state effectively abolished). Just what this would mean has not been spelt out by the EZLN,[51] apart from the obvious principle of instant recallability: that the president or any other office-holder should be instantly recallable if they fail to obey the people's wishes, as is the case with all the members of the EZLN's ruling body, the CCRI.[52]

Although the details are not clear, and cannot be, since they could only be developed in struggle, the central point is that the focus of revolutionary struggle is shifted from the *what* to the *how* of politics. All the initiatives of the Zapatistas (the Convención Nacional Democrática, the 'consultation' on the future of the EZLN, the invitation of advisers to the dialogue with the government, the organisation of the forum on indigenous rights and culture and on the reform of the state, the intercontinental meeting for humanity and against neoliberalism, amongst others) have been directed at promoting a different way of thinking about political activity. Similarly, all the contacts with the state and even the proposals for the 'reform' of the state have in fact been anti-state initiatives in the sense of trying to develop new political forms, forms of action which articulate dignity, forms which do not fit with the state. The principal problem for a revolutionary movement is not to elaborate a programme, to say *what* the revolutionary government will do (although the EZLN has its 16 demands as the basis for such a programme). The principal problem is rather *how* to articulate dignities, how to develop a form of struggle and a form of social organisation based upon the recognition of dignity. Only the articulation of dignities can provide the answer to what should be done: a self-determining society must determine itself.

Dignities unite

The Zapatistas rose up in order to change Mexico and to make the world anew. Their base in the Lacandon Jungle was far away from any important urban centre. They were not part of an effective international or even national organisation. (If indeed they are part of the FLN, as the state maintains, it has remained remarkably ineffective.) Since the declaration of the cease-fire on 12 January 1994, they have remained physically cordoned within the Lacandon Jungle.

Cut off in the jungle, how could the EZLN transform Mexico, or indeed change the world? Alone there was little that they could do, either to change the world, or even to defend themselves. 'Do not leave us alone' ('*No nos dejen solos*') was an oft-repeated call during the first months of the cease-fire. The effectiveness of the EZLN depended (and depends) inevitably on their ability to break the cordon and overcome their isolation. The revolt of dignity derives its strength from the uniting of dignities.

But how could this uniting of dignities come about when the EZLN itself was cornered in the jungle and there was no institutional structure to support them? Marcos suggests a powerful image in a radio interview in the early months of the uprising:

> Marcos, whoever Marcos is, who is in the mountains, had his twins, or comrades, or his accomplices (not in the organic sense, but accomplices in terms of how to see the world, the necessity of changing it or seeing it in a different way) in the media, for example, in the newspapers, in the radio, in the television, in the journals, but also in the trade unions, in the schools, among the teachers, among the students, in groups of workers, in peasant organisations and all that. There were many accomplices or, to use a radio term, there were many people tuned in to the same frequency, but nobody turned the radio on ... Suddenly they [the comrades of the EZLN] turn it on and we discover that there are others on the same radio frequency – I'm talking of radio *communication*, not *listening* to the radio – and we begin to talk and to communicate and to realise that there are things in common, that it seems there are more things in common than differences.[53]

The idea suggested by Marcos for thinking about the unity of struggles is one of frequencies, of being tuned in, of wavelengths, vibrations, echoes. Dignity resonates. As it vibrates, it sets off vibrations in other dignities, an unstructured, possibly discordant resonance.

There is no doubt of the extraordinary resonance of the Zapatista uprising throughout the world, as evidenced by the participation of over 3,000 people from 43 different countries in the Intercontinental Meeting organised by the EZLN in July 1996: 'What is happening in the mountains of the Mexican south-east that finds an echo and a mirror in the streets of Europe, the suburbs of Asia, the countryside of America, the towns of Africa and the houses of Oceania?'[54] And equally, of course, what is happening in the streets of Europe, the suburbs of Asia, the countryside of America, the towns of Africa and the houses of Oceania, that resonates so strongly with the Zapatista uprising?

The notion of resonance, or echo, or radio frequency may seem a very vague one. It is not so. The EZLN have engaged in a constant struggle over the past few years to break through the cordon, to overcome their isolation, to forge the unity of dignities on which their future depends. They have fought in many different ways. They have fought, with enormous success, by letters and communiqués, by jokes and stories, by the use of symbolism (see Chapter 1) and by the theatre of their events. They have fought by the construction of their 'Aguascalientes', the meeting place constructed for the National Democratic Convention (Convención Nacional Democrática) in July 1994, and by the construction of a series of new Aguascalientes in the jungle after the first one had been destroyed by the army in its intervention of February 1995. They have fought too by the creative organisation of a whole series of events which have been important catalysts for the opposition in Mexico and (increasingly) beyond Mexico. The first important event was the National Democratic Convention, organised immediately the EZLN had rejected the proposals made by the government in the Dialogue of San Cristóbal and held just weeks before the presidential elections of August 1994: an event which brought more than 6,000 activists into the heart of the jungle only months after the fighting had finished. The following year, the EZLN built on the popular reaction to the military intervention of February 1995 to organise a consultation throughout the country on what the future of the EZLN should be, an event in which over a million people took part. The new dialogue with the government, begun in April 1995, also became the basis for inviting hundreds of activists and specialists to take part as advisers in the dialogue, and for organising the forums on indigenous rights and culture (January 1996) and on the reform of the state (July 1996). The same year also saw the organisation of the Intercontinental Meeting for Humanity and against Neoliberalism, held within the Zapatista territory at the end of July. In each case, these were events which seemed impossible at the time of their announcement, and events which stirred up enormous enthusiasm in their realisation.

The communiqués and events have also been accompanied by more orthodox attempts to establish lasting organisational structures. The National Democratic Convention (CND) established a standing organisation of the same name, with the aim of coordinating the (non-military) Zapatista struggle for democracy, freedom and justice throughout the country. After internal conflicts had rendered the CND ineffective, the Third Declaration of the Lacandon Jungle in January 1995 proposed the creation of a Movement for National Liberation, an organisation which was stillborn. The Fourth Declaration of the Lacandon Jungle, a year later, launched the Frente Zapatista de Liberación Nacional (the Zapatista National Liberation Front – FZLN) to organise the civilian struggle thoughout the country. This, although it has provided an important point of organisational support for the Zapatistas, has stirred up none of the enthusiasm aroused by the EZLN itself.

The relative failure of the institutional attempts to extend the Zapatista struggle lends weight to the argument that the real force of the Zapatista uniting of dignities has to be understood in terms of the much less structured notion of resonance. The notion of resonance is indeed the counterpart of the idea of *'preguntando caminamos'* ('asking we walk'). We advance by asking, not by telling: by suggesting, arguing, proposing, inviting, looking for links with other struggles which are the same struggle, looking for responses, listening for echoes. If those echoes are not there, we can only propose again, argue again, probe again, ask again: we cannot create echoes where they do not exist.

All this does not mean that organisation is not important, that it is all just a matter of vibrations and spontaneous combustion. On the contrary, the whole Zapatista uprising shows the importance of profound and careful organisation. It does suggest, however, a different, less structured and more experimental way of thinking about organisation. The concept of organisation must be experimental in a double sense: experimental, simply because there is no pre-given model of revolutionary organisation, but also experimental in the sense that the notion of dignity and its corollary, 'asking we walk', mean that revolutionary organisation must be seen as a constant experiment, a constant asking. The notion of dignity does not imply an appeal to spontaneity, the idea that revolt will simply explode without prior organisation. It does imply thinking in terms of a multitude of different forms of organisation and, above all, thinking of organisation as a constant experiment, a constant probing, a constant asking, a constant searching: not just to see if together we can find some way out of here, but because the asking is in itself the antithesis of Power.[55]

Yet there is obviously a tension here implied in the very notion of the 'uniting of dignities'. The Zapatistas speak, not just of 'dignity', but of 'dignities'. Clearly, then, it is not a question of imposing one dignity or of finding what 'true dignity' really means. It is a question rather of recognising the validity of different forms of struggle and different opinions as to what the realisation of dignity means. This does not mean a complete relativism in which all opinions, even fascist ones, are granted equal validity. Conflicts between different dignities are inevitable: it is clear, for example, that the Zapatista women's understanding of the dignity of their struggle has brought them into conflict with the men's understanding of their dignity (see Chapter 3). What the concept of dignity points to is not the correctness of any particular solution to such conflicts, but rather a way of resolving such conflicts in which the particular dignities are recognised and articulated. Even here, the Zapatistas argue that there is not just one correct way of articulating dignities: while they themselves organise their discussions on the basis of village assemblies, they recognise that this may not be the best form of articulating dignities in all cases. What form the articulation of dignities might take in a big city, for example, is very much an open question, although there are obviously precedents[56] and, in some cases, deep-rooted traditions of forms of direct democracy. The struggle to unite dignities in a world that is based on the denial and fragmentation of dignities is not an easy one.

Dignity is the revolutionary subject

Dignity is a class concept, not a humanistic one.

The EZLN do not use the concept of 'class' or 'class struggle' in their discourse, in spite of the fact that Marxist theory has clearly played an important part in their formation. They have preferred, instead, to develop a new language, to speak of the struggle of truth and dignity: 'We saw that the old words had become so worn out that they had become harmful for those that used them.'[57] In looking for support, or in forming links with other struggles, they have appealed, not to the working class or the proletariat, but to 'civil society'. By 'civil society', they seem to mean 'society in struggle', in the broadest sense: all those groups and intitiatives engaged in latent or overt struggles to assert some sort of control over their future, without aspiring to hold governmental office.[58] In Mexico, the initial reference point is often taken as the forms of autonomous social organisation that arose in Mexico City in response to the earthquake of 1985 and the state's incapacity to deal with the emergency.

It is not difficult to see why the Zapatistas should have chosen to turn their back on the old words. That does not mean, however, that all the problems connected with these words are thereby erased. The Zapatistas have been criticised by some adherents of the traditional orthodox Marxist left for not using the concept of class. It is argued that, because they do not use the traditional triad of class struggle, revolution and socialism, preferring instead to speak of dignity, truth, freedom, democracy and justice, their struggle is a liberal one, an armed reformism which has little possibility of leading to radical change. An extreme form of this sort of application of a class analysis is the argument that the Zapatista uprising is just a peasant movement and, while it should be supported, the proletariat can have little confidence in it.

The orthodox Marxist tradition works with a definitional concept of class. The working class may be defined in various ways: most commonly as those who sell their labour power in order to survive; or as those who produce surplus value and are directly exploited. The important point here is that the working class is defined.

In this definitional approach, the working class, however defined, is defined on the basis of its subordination to capital: it is because it is subordinated to capital (as wage workers, or as producers of surplus value) that it is defined as working class. Capitalism, in this approach, is understood as a world of pre-defined social relations, a world in which the forms of social relations are constituted, firmly fixed or fetishised.[59] The fixity of the forms of social relations is taken as the starting point for the discussion of class. Thus, working-class struggle is understood as starting from the (pre-constituted) subordination of labour to capital. Any sort of struggle that does not fall within this definition is then seen as non-class struggle (which consequently raises problems as to how it should be defined).

The definitional approach to class raises two sorts of problems. First, it inevitably raises the question of who is and who is not part of the working class. Are intellectuals like Marx and Lenin part of the working class? Are those of us who work in the universities part of the working class? Are the rebels of Chiapas part of the working class? Are feminists part of the working class? Are those active in the gay movement part of the working class? In each case, there is a concept of a pre-defined working class to which these people do or do not belong.[60]

The second (and more serious) consequence of defining class is the definition of struggles that follows. From the classification of the people concerned there are derived certain conclusions about the struggles in which they are involved. Those who define the Zapatista rebels as being not part of the working class draw from that certain conclusions about the nature and limitations of the uprising. From the definition of the class position of the participants there follows a definition of their struggles: the definition of class defines the antagonism that the definer perceives or accepts as valid. This leads to a blinkering of the perception of social antagonism. In some cases, for example, the definition of the working class as the urban proletariat directly exploited in factories, combined with evidence of the decreasing proportion of the population who fall within this definition, has led people to the conclusion that class struggle is no longer relevant for understanding social change. In other cases, the definition of the working class and therefore of working-class struggle in a certain way has led to an incapacity to relate to the development of new forms of struggle (the student movement, feminism, ecologism and so on). The definitional understanding of class has done much in recent years to create the situation in which 'the old words had become so worn out that they had become harmful for those that used them'.

The notion of dignity detonates the *definition* of class, but does not thereby cease to be a class concept. It does so simply because the starting point is no longer a relation of subordination but a relation of struggle, a relation of insubordination/subordination. The starting point of dignity is the negation of humiliation, the struggle against subordination. From this perspective there does not exist a settled, fixed world of subordination upon which definitions can be constructed. Just the contrary: the notion of dignity points to the fact that we are not just subordinated or exploited, that our existence within capitalist society cannot be understood simply in terms of subordination. Dignity points to the fact that subordination cannot be conceived without its opposite, that is, the struggle against subordination – insubordination. A world of subordination is a world in which subordination is constantly at issue. The forms of social relations in capitalist society cannot be understood simply as fetishised, constituted forms, but only as forms which are always in question, which are imposed only thorugh the unceasing struggle of capital to reproduce itself. Once the starting point is dignity, once the starting point is the struggle to convert 'dignity and rebellion into freedom and dignity', then all that was fixed becomes shaky, all that appeared to be defined becomes blurred.

From the perspective of dignity, then, class cannot be understood as a defined group of people. This is quite consistent with Marx's approach. His understanding of capitalism was based not on the antagonism between two groups of people but on the antagonism in the way in which human social practice is organised. Existence in capitalist society is a conflictual existence, an antagonistic existence. Although this antagonism appears as a vast multiplicity of conflicts, it can be argued (and was argued by Marx) that the key to understanding this antagonism and its development is the fact that present society is built upon an antagonism in the way that the distinctive character of humanity, namely creative activity (work in its broadest sense), is organised. In capitalist society, work is turned against itself, alienated from itself; we lose control over our creative activity. This negation of human creativity takes place through the subjection of human activity to the market. This subjection to the market, in turn, takes place fully when the capacity to work creatively (labour power) becomes a commodity to be sold on the market to those with the capital to buy it. The antagonism between human creativity and its negation thus becomes focused in the antagonism between those who have to sell their creativity and those who appropriate that creativity and exploit it (and, in so doing, transform that creativity into labour). In shorthand, the antagonism between creativity and its negation can be referred to as the conflict between labour and capital, but this conflict (as Marx makes clear) is not a conflict between two external forces, but between work (human creativity) and work alienated.

The social antagonism is thus not in the first place a conflict between two groups of people: it is a conflict between creative social practice and its negation, or, in other words, between humanity and its negation, between the transcending of limits (creation) and the imposition of limits (definition). The conflict, in this interpretation, does not take place after subordination has been established, after the fetishised forms of social relations have been constituted: rather it is a conflict *about* the subordination of social practice, *about* the fetishisation of social relations.[61] The conflict is that between subordination and insubordination, and it is this which allows us to speak of insubordination (or dignity) as a central feature of capitalism. Class struggle does not take place within the constituted forms of capitalist social relations: rather the constitution of those forms is itself class struggle. This leads to a much richer concept of class struggle in which the whole of social practice is at issue. *All* social practice is an unceasing antagonism between the subjection of practice to the fetishised, perverted, defining forms of capitalism and the attempt to live against-and-beyond those forms. There can thus be no question of the existence of non-class forms of struggle.

Class struggle, in this view, is a conflict that permeates the whole of human existence. We all exist within that conflict, just as the conflict exists within all of us. It is a polar antagonism which we cannot escape. We do not 'belong' to one class or another: rather, the class antagonism exists in us, tearing us apart. The antagonism (the class divide) traverses all of us.[62] Nevertheless, it clearly does so in very different ways. Some, the very small minority, participate directly in and/or benefit directly from the appropriation and exploitation of the work of others. Others, the vast majority of us, are, directly or indirectly, the objects of that appropriation and exploitation. The polar nature of the antagonism is thus reflected in a polarisation of the two classes,[63] but the antagonism is prior to, not subsequent to, the classes: classes are constituted through the antagonism.

Since classes are constituted through the antagonism between work and its alienation, and since this antagonism is constantly changing, it follows that classes cannot be defined. The concept of class is essentially non-definitional. More than that, since definition imposes limits, closes openness, negates creativity, it is possible to say that the capitalist class, even if it cannot be defined, is the defining class, the class that defines, that identifies, that classifies. Labour (the working class, the class that exists in antagonism to capital) is not only incapable of definition but essentially anti-definitional. It is constituted by its repressed creativity: that is to say, by its resistance to the (ultimately impossible) attempt to define it. Not only is it mistaken to try to identify the working class ('are the Zapatistas working class?'), but class struggle itself is the struggle between definition and anti-definition. Capital says 'I am, you are'; labour says 'we are not, but we are becoming; you are, but you will not be': or 'We are/are not, we struggle to create ourselves.'

Class struggle, then, is the unceasing daily antagonism (whether it be perceived or not) between alienation and dis-alienation, between definition and anti-definition, between fetishisation and de-fetishisation. The trouble with all these terms is that *our* side of the struggle is presented negatively: as dis-alienation, anti-definition, de-fetishisation. The Zapatistas are right when they say that we need a new language, not just because the 'old words' are 'worn out' but because the Marxist tradition has been so focused on domination that it has not developed adequate words to talk about resistance.[64] Dignity is the term that turns this around, that expresses positively that which is supressed, that for which we are fighting. Dignity is that which knows no is-ness, no objective structures. Dignity is that which rises against humiliation, dehumanisation, marginali-sation, dignity is that which says 'we are here, we are human and we struggle for the humanity that is denied to us.' Dignity is the struggle against capital.

Dignity, then, is the revolutionary subject. Where it is repressed most fiercely, where the antagonism is most intense, and where there is a tradition of communal organisation, it will fight most strongly, as in the factory, as in the jungle. But class struggle, the struggle of dignity, the struggle for humanity against its destruction, is not the privilege of any defined group: we exist in it, just as it exists in us, inescapably. Dignity, then, does not exist in a pure form, any more than the working class exists in a pure form. It is that in us which resists, which rebels, which does not conform. Constantly undermined, smothered and suffocated by the myriad forms of alienation and fetishisation, constantly overlaid, distorted, repressed, fragmented and corrupted by money and the state, constantly in danger of being extinguished, snuffed out, dignity is the indestructable (or maybe just the not yet destroyed) NO that makes us human. That is why the resonance of the Zapatistas goes so deep: 'as more and more rebel communiqués were issued, we realised that in reality the revolt came from the depths of ourselves'.[65] The power of the Zapatistas is the power of the *¡Ya Basta!*, the negation of oppression, which exists in the depths of all of us, the only hope for humanity.

Dignity's revolution is uncertain, ambiguous and contradictory

Uncertainty permeates the whole Zapatista undertaking. There is none of the sense of the inevitability of history which has so often been a feature of revolutionary movements of the past. There is no certainty about the arrival at the promised land, nor any certainty about what this promised land might look like. It is a revolution that walks asking, not answering.

Revolution in the Zapatista sense is a moving outwards rather than a moving towards. But how can such a movement be revolutionary? How can such a movement bring about a radical social transformation? The very idea of social revolution is already greatly discredited at the end of the twentieth century: how does the Zapatista uprising help us to find a way forward?

There is a problem at the heart of any concept of revolution. How could it be possible for those who are currently alienated (or humiliated) to create a world of non-alienation (or dignity)? If we are all permeated by the conditions of social oppression in which we live, and if our perceptions are constrained by those conditions, shall we not always reproduce those conditions in everything we do? If our existence is traversed by relations of power, how can we possibly create a society that is not characterised by power relations?

The simplest way out of this problem is to solve it by bringing in a saviour, a *deus ex machina*. If there is some sort of figure who has broken free of alienation and come to a true understanding, then that figure can perhaps lead the masses out of the present alienated society. This is essentially the idea of the vanguard party proposed by Lenin: a group of people who by virtue of their theoretical and practical experience can see beyond the confines of existing society and who, for that reason, can lead the masses in a revolutionary break.[66] There are, however, two basic problems. How is it possible for anyone, no matter what their training, to so lift themselves above existing society that they do not reproduce in their own action the concepts and faults of that society? Even more fundamental: how is it possible to create a self-creative society other than through the self-emancipation of society itself? The experience of revolution in the twentieth century suggests that these are very grave problems indeed.

However, if the notion of a vanguard is discarded, and with it the notion of a revolutionary programme, which depends on the existence of such a vanguard, then what are we left with? The Leninist solution may have been wrong, but it was an attempt to solve a perceived problem: the problem of how you bring about a radical transformation of society in a society in which, apparently, the mass of people are so imbued with contemporary values that self-emancipation seems impossible. For many, the failure of the Leninist solution proves the impossibility of social revolution, the inevitability of conforming.

The Zapatista answer is focused on the notion of dignity. The notion of dignity points to the contradictory nature of existence. We are humiliated but have the dignity to struggle against the humiliation to realise our dignity. We are imbued with capitalist values, but also live a daily antagonism towards those values. We are alienated but still have sufficient humanity to struggle against alienation for a non-alienated world. Alienation is, but it is not, because dis-alienation is not but also is. Oppression exists, but it exists as struggle. It is the present existence of dignity (as struggle) that makes it possible to conceive of revolution without a vanguard party. The society based on dignity already exists in the form of the struggle against the negation of dignity.[67] Dignity implies self-emancipation.

The consistent pursuit of dignity in a society based on the denial of dignity is in itself revolutionary. But it implies a different concept of revolution from the 'storming the Winter Palace' concept that we have grown up with. There is no building of the revolutionary party, no strategy for world revolution, no transitional programme. Revolution is simply the constant, uncompromising struggle for that which cannot be achieved under capitalism: dignity, control over our own lives.

Revolution can only be thought of in this scheme as the cumulative uniting of dignities, the snowballing of struggles, the refusal of more and more people to subordinate their humanity to the degradations of capitalism. This implies a more open concept of revolution: the snowballing of struggles cannot be programmed or predicted.

Revolution is not just a future event, but the complete inversion of the relation between dignity and degradation in the present, the cumulative assertion of power over our own lives, the progressive construction of autonomy. As long as capitalism exists (and as long as money exists), the degradation of dignity, the exploitation of work, the dehumanisation and immiseration of existence will continue: the assertion of dignity clearly comes into immediate conflict with the reproduction of capitalism. This conflict could only be resolved by the complete destruction of capitalism. What form this might take, how the cumulative uniting of dignities could lead to the abolition of capitalism, is not clear. It cannot be clear if it is to be a self-creative process. What is clear is that the experience of the last hundred years suggests that social transformation cannot be brought about by the conquest (be it 'democratic' or 'undemocratic') of state power.

This notion is not reformist, if by reformism is meant the idea that social transformation can be achieved through the accretion of state-sponsored reforms. Anti-reformism is not a question of the clarity of future goals but of the strength with which those forms (especially the state) which reproduce capitalist social relations are rejected in the present. It is a question not of a future programme but of present organisation.

An uncertain revolution is, however, an ambiguous and contradictory revolution. Openness and uncertainty are built in to the Zapatista concept of revolution. And that openness means also contradictions and ambiguities. At times it looks as if the EZLN might accept a settlement that falls far short of their dreams, at times the presentation of their aims is more limited, apparently more containable. Certainly, both the direction and the appeal of the uprising would be strengthened if it were made explicit that exploitation is central to the systematic negation of dignity and that dignity's struggle is a struggle against exploitation in all its forms. The very nature of the Zapatista concept of revolution means that the movement is particularly open to the charge of ambiguity. Yet historical experience suggests that ambiguities and contradictions are deep-rooted in any revolutionary process, no matter how clearly defined the line of the leadership. Rather than deny the contradictions, it seems better to focus on the forms of articulation and political experiment that might resolve those contradictions. It is better to recognise, as Tacho does, that in undertaking revolution, the Zapatistas are 'going to classes in a school that does not exist'.[68]

But what does the EZLN want? What is their dream of the future? Clearly, there are many dreams of the future:

For one it can be that there should be land for everybody to work, which for the peasant is the central problem, no? In reality they are very clear that all the other problems turn on the question of land: housing, health, schools, services. Everything that makes them leave the land is bad and everything that lets them stay on it is good. To stay with dignity.[69]

That is a dream of the future, a simple dream perhaps, but its realisation would require enormous changes in the organisation of society.

Or again, in another interview, Marcos explains the Zapatista dream in these terms:

In our dream the children are children and their work is to be children. Here no, in reality, in the reality of Chiapas the work of the children is to be adults, from the time they are born and that is not right, we say that that is not right ... My dream is not of agricultural redistribution, the great mobilisations, the fall of the government and elections and a party of the left wins, whatever. In my dream, I dream of the children and I see them being children. If we achieve that, that the children in any part of Mexico are children and nothing else, we've won. Whatever it costs, that is worth it. It doesn't matter what social regime is in power, or what political party is in government, or what the exchange rate between the peso and the dollar is, or how the stock market is doing, or whatever. If a child of five years can be a child, as children of five years should be, with that we are on the other side ... We, the Zapatista children, think that our work as children is to play and learn. And the children here do not play, they work.[70]

Again a simple dream, possibly to some a reformist dream, but one that is totally incompatible with the current direction of the world, in which the exploitation of children (child labour, child prostitution, child pornography, for example) is growing at an alarming rate. This dream of children being children is a good example of the power of the notion of dignity: the consistent pursuit of the dream would require a complete transformation of society.

A society based on dignity would be an honest, mutually recognitive society, in which people 'do not have to use a mask ... in order to relate with other people'.[71] It would also be an absolutely self-creative society. In an interview for the Venice Film Festival, Marcos replied to the standard question, 'what is it that the EZLN wants?': 'We want life to be like a cinema poster from which we can choose a different film each day. Now we have risen in arms because, for more than 500 years, they have forced us to watch the same film every day.'[72]

There are no five-year plans here, no blueprint for the new society, no pre-defined utopia. There are no guarantees, no certainties. Openness and uncertainty are built into the Zapatista concept of revolution. And that openness means also contradictions and ambiguities. At times it looks as if the EZLN might accept a settlement that falls far short of their dreams, at times the presentation of their aims is more limited, apparently more containable. These contradictions and ambiguities are part and parcel of the Zapatista concept of revolution, of the idea of a revolution that walks asking. And what if they fail? By the time this is published, there is no guarantee that the EZLN will still exist. It may be that the Mexican government will have launched an open military assault (already tried on 9 February 1995 and an always present threat): it is even possible that the army could be successful, more successful than the last time they tried it. It is also possible that the EZLN will become exhausted: that they will be drawn by tiredness, by their own ambiguities or by the simple lack of response from civil society into limiting their demands and settling for definitions. All of these are possible. The important point, though, is that the Zapatistas are not 'they': they are 'we' – *we* are 'we'. When the huge crowds who demonstrated in Mexico City and elsewhere after the army intervention of 9 February 1995 chanted 'we are all Marcos', they were not announcing an intention to join the EZLN. They were saying that the struggle of the Zapatistas is the life-struggle of all of us, that we are all part of their struggle and their struggle is part of us, wherever we are. As Major Ana María put it in the opening speech of the Intercontinental Meeting:

Behind us are the we that are you.[73] Behind our balaclavas is the face of all the excluded women. Of all the forgotten indigenous people. Of all the persecuted homosexuals. Of all the despised youth. Of all the beaten migrants. Of all those imprisoned for their word and thought. Of all the humiliated workers. Of all those who have died from being forgotten. Of all the simple and ordinary men and women who do not count, who are not seen, who are not named, who have no tomorrow.[74]

We are all Zapatistas. The Zapatistas of Chiapas have lit a flame, but the struggle to convert 'dignity and rebellion into freedom and dignity' is ours.[75]

Notes

1. EZLN, *La Palabra de los Armados de Verdad y Fuego* (Mexico City: Editorial Fuenteovejuna, 1994/ 1995), Vol. 1, pp. 31–32. The three volumes of this series are a collection of the interviews, letters and communiqués of the EZLN during 1994, an invaluable source. All translations of Spanish quotations are by the author.
2. EZLN, *La Palabra*, Vol. I, p. 35.
3. Clandestine Revolutionary Indigenous Committee.
4. The Council of 500 Years of Indigenous Resistance.
5. EZLN, *La Palabra*, Vol. I, p. 122; emphasis in the original. The continuing importance of this passage was underlined when it was quoted by Comandante Ramona in her speech to a meeting in Mexico City on 16 February 1997 organised to protest against the government's failure to fulfil the Agreements of San Andrés.
6. Ejército Zapatista de Liberación Nacional: Zapatista Army of National Liberation.
7. Subcomandante Insurgente Marcos, 17 November 1994: EZLN, *La Palabra*, Vol. III, p. 224. Subcomandante Marcos is the spokesperson and military leader of the EZLN. He is, however, subordinate to the CCRI, a popularly elected body. 'Mestizos' are people of mixed indigenous and European origin – the vast majority of the Mexican population.
8. Forces of National Liberation.
9. Quoted in C. Tello Díaz, *La Rebelión de las Cañadas* (Mexico City: Cal y Arena, 1995) pp. 97, 99.
10. The EZLN's reply to the government's claim is contained in a communiqué of 9 February 1995: 'In relation to the connections of the EZLN with the organisation called "Forces of National Liberation", the EZLN has declared in interviews, letters and communiqués that members of different armed organisations of the country came together in its origin, that the EZLN was born from that and, gradually, was appropriated by the indigenous communities to the point where they took the political and military leadership of the EZLN. To the name of the "Forces of National Liberation", the government should add as the antecedents of the EZLN those of all the guerrilla organisations of the 70s and 80s, Arturo Gámiz, Lucio Cabañas, Genaro Vázquez Rojas, Emiliano Zapata, Francisco Villa, Vicente Guerrero, José María Morelos y Pavón, Miguel Hidalgo y Costilla, Benito Juárez and many others whom they have already erased

from the history books because a people with memory is a rebel people.' *La Jornada*, 13 February 1995.

11. Subcomandante Insurgente Marcos, 'Carta a Adolfo Gilly', *Viento del Sur*, No. 4 (Summer 1995) p. 25.

12. See the account given by Tello, *La Rebelión*, p. 105, of the meeting between some of the insurgent leaders and the community of the *ejido* of San Francisco on 23 September 1985.

13. See the account given by Marcos in an interview with Radio UNAM, 18 March 1994: EZLN, *La Palabra*, Vol. II, p. 69. The 'white guards' are paid paramilitary groups who, often in collusion with the authorities, suppress protest and dissent with violence.

14. Decree of the Lacandon Community. See Tello, *La Rebelión*, pp. 59ff.

15. Radio UNAM interview with Marcos, 18 March 1994: EZLN, *La Palabra*, Vol. II, p. 69–70.

16. Marcos, Letter to children of a boarding school in Guadalajara, 8 February 1994: EZLN, La Palabra, Vol. I, p. 179.

17. Radio UNAM interview with Marcos, 18 March 1994, EZLN, *La Palabra*, Vol. II, p. 62.

18. Marcos interview with Cristián Calónico Lucio, 11 November 1995, ms. p. 47. The interview is unpublished in written form, but formed the basis of a video.

19. Ernst Bloch's *Naturrecht und Menschliche Würde* (Frankfurt: Suhrkamp, 1961) is a notable exception. Although theoretically very relevant, it probably did not exercise any influence on the Zapatistas.

20. In a recent interview, Marcos confirms that it was as a result of the integration of the revolutionaries with the indigenous communities that they started using the concept of dignity. 'More than the redistribution of wealth or the expropriation of the means of production, revolution starts to be the possibility that human beings can have a space of dignity. Dignity begins to be a very strong word. It is not our contribution, it is not a contribution of the urban element, it is the communities who contribute it. Such that revolution should be the assurance that dignity be realised, be respected.' Yvon Le Bot, *El Sueño Zapatista* [The Zapatista Dream] (Mexico City: Plaza & Janés, 1997) p. 146.

21. See for example the interview of Marcos with correspondents of the *Proceso*, *El Financiero* and *The New York Times*, February 1994: EZLN, *La Palabra*, Vol. I, p. 216.

22. G. Camú Urzúa and D. Tótoro Taulis, *EZLN: el ejército que salió de la selva* (Mexico City: Editorial Planeta, 1994) p. 83

23. Camú and Tótoro, *EZLN*.
24. The supreme example of the instrumentalist theory of revolution is, of course, Lenin's *What is to be Done?*
25. See the CCRI communiqué of 10 June 1994: EZLN, *La Palabra*, Vol. II, p. 201.
26. EZLN, *La Palabra*, Vol. I, p. 5.
27. See the account given by Tello, *La Rebelión*, p. 151; see also Le Bot, *El Sueño*, p. 191.
28. On the refusal of the Zapatistas to define their movement as an indigenous movement, see Le Bot, *El Sueño*, p. 206, where Marcos says in interview: 'The principal preoccupation of the Committee [CCRI] and of the delegates was that the movement should not be reduced to the indigenous question. On the contrary, if it had been up to them, at least to that part of the committee [those who come from the areas with the strongest traditions] our discourse would have abandoned completely any reference to the indigenous.'
29. The Zapatista use of national symbols, such as the Mexican flag and the national anthem, disconcerted some, especially of the European participants in the recent Intercontinental Gathering in Chiapas. For a critique of the alleged 'nationalism' of the EZLN, see, for example, Sylvie Deneuve, Charles Reeve and Marc Geoffroy, *Au-delà des passe-montagnes du Sud-Est mexicain* [Beyond the balaclavas of south-east Mexico] (Paris: Ab irato, 1996); and Katerina, 'Mexico is not only Chiapas nor is the rebellion in Chiapas merely a Mexican affair', *Common Sense*, No. 22 (Winter 1997).
30. In this sense, for example, see the Third Declaration of the Lacandon Jungle (1 January, 1995): 'The indigenous question will not be solved unless there is a RADICAL transformation of the national pact. The only way to incorporate, with justice and dignity, the indigenous peoples into the nation is by recognising the peculiar characteristics of their social, cultural and political organisation. The autonomies are not a separation but rather the integration of the most humiliated and forgotten minorities into contemporary Mexico. That is how the EZLN has understood it since its formation and tha is how the indigenous bases which form the leadership of our oranisation have directed. Today we repeat it: OUR STRUGGLE IS NATIONAL' (*La Jornada*, 2 January 1995, p. 5).
31. *La Jornada*, 30 January 1996, p. 12
32. This is, of course, not the only interpretation possible. See, for example, S. Deneuve et al., *Au-delà des passe-montagnes*. Although

it seems incorrect to interpret the Zapatista use of national liberation in the narrow, statist sense, there is no doubt that the term 'national liberation' opens up an enormous, and dangerous, area of ambiguity, simply because the notion of 'nation' and 'state' have been so interwoven that it is difficult to disentangle them completely. It is argued below that the undoubted contradictions and tensions in the discourse of the Zapatistas are not the result of eclecticism, but are the outcome of the consistent pursuit of the principle of dignity. They are not necessarily less serious for that. For a further discussion of Zapatista nationalism, see REDakation (Hrsg), *Chiapas und die Internationale der Hoffnung* (Cologne: Neuer ISP-Verlag, 1997), pp. 178–84.

33. Subcomandante Insurgente Marcos, 'México: La Luna entre los espejos de la noche y el cristal del día' [Mexico: Moon between the mirror of night and the crystal of day], *La Jornada*, 9/10/11 June 1995, p. 17 (11 June).

34. This is most clearly elaborated in Lenin's *What is to be Done?* For example: 'We said that there could not yet be Social-Democratic consciousness among the workers. This consciousness could only be brought to them from without. The history of all countries shows that the working class, exclusively by its own effort, is able to develop only trade union consciousness ... The theory of socialism, however, grew out of the philosophical, historical and economic theories that were elaborated by the educated representatives of the propertied classes, the intellectuals': V.I. Lenin, 'What is to be Done' in *Essential Works of Lenin* (New York: Bantam Books, 1966), p. 74.

35. The notion of dignity is little used by mainstream political theory. Where it is used, it is often connected with notions of self-ownership (for example, Robert Nozick, *Anarchy, State and Utopia* (New York: Basic Books, 1981), p. 334) or self-possession (for example, Michael Walzer, *Spheres of Justice* (Oxford: Blackwell, 1983), p. 279). The use of the term in mainstream political theory and philosophy differs crucially from the Zapatista concept in two respects: firstly, its primary point of reference is the individual; and, secondly, it refers to an abstract, indeterminate and idealised present in which it is assumed that people already have the 'right' to dignity. At best, this is a sort of flabby wishful thinking which has little to do with the Zapatista concept of dignity as struggle against the denial of dignity, and is far removed indeed from seeing 'our fathers with fury in their hands'.

36. See, for example, James C. Scott, *Domination and the Arts of Resistance* (New Haven: Yale University Press, 1990).
37. It is not surprising that the *¡Ya Basta!* of the Zapatistas has been strongly echoed by the *'sans papiers'*, the movement of illegal immigrants in France.
38. The Zapatistas use truth and dignity as basically interchangeable concepts. The Zapatistas speak of what they say as the 'word of those who are armed with truth and fire' (*'la palabra de los armados de verdad y fuego'*). The fire is there, but the truth comes first, not just as a moral attribute, but as a weapon: they are *armed* with truth, and this is a more important weapon than the firepower of their guns. Although they are organised as an army, they aim to win by truth, not by fire. Their truth is not just that they speak the truth about their situation or about the country, but that they are true to themselves, that they speak the truth of truth denied.
39. ELZN communiqué of 17 March 1995 in *La Jornada*, 22 March 1995.
40. The separation of personal and political, of private and public, is at the same time their mutual constitution. The point is not to conflate the personal and the political, the public and the private, but to abolish them (to abolish the separation which constitutes both). On this, see Karl Marx, *On the Jewish Question*, Marx–Engels Collected Works, Vol. III (Moscow: Progress Publishers, 1975). To that extent, the phrase 'the personal is political' is misleading.
41. It is as a form of the capital relation that the state defines and classifies. The defining action of the state is one moment of the definition inherent in the alienation of labour, the containment of human creativity. For a development of the general argument, see John Holloway, 'Global Capital and the National State' in W. Bonefeld and J. Holloway (eds), *Global Capital, National State and the Politics of Money* (London: Macmillan, 1995) pp. 116–40.
42. Communiqué of May 1996, *La Jornada*, 10 June 1996.
43. Communiqué of May 1996, *La Jornada*, 10 June 1996.
44. *La Jornada* 17 May 1995.
45. *La Jornada*, 18 May 1995.
46. *La Jornada*, 10 June 1995.
47. *La Jornada*, 5 March 1995
48. 'The cistern contains; the fountain overflows': William Blake, 'The Proverbs of Heaven and Hell': in, for example, *William Blake* (Harmondsworth: Penguin, 1958) p. 97.

49. 'A political force whose members do not hold or aspire to hold popularly elected offices nor governmental posts at any level. A political force which does not aspire to take power. A force which is not a political party' (*La Jornada*, 2 January 1996).

50. First Declaration of La Realidad, January 1996, *La Jornada*, 30 January 1996.

51. They have often mentioned the idea of plebiscites or referendums as a necessary part of a new political system. It is clear, however, from the experience of other states that plebiscites and referendums are quite inadequate as a form of articulating popular decision making, and are in no sense comparable to the communal discussions which are central to the Zapatistas' own practice.

52. 'And we demand that the authorities should be able to be removed just as soon as the communities decide it and come to an agreement. It could be through a referendum, or some other similar mechanism. And we want to transmit this experience to every level: when the President of the Republic is no use any more he should be automatically removed. As simple as that.' Press Conference given by Subcomandante Marcos, 26 February 1994 in EZLN, *La Palabra*, Vol. I, p. 244.

53. Radio UNAM interview with Marcos, 18 March 1994, EZLN, *La Palabra*, Vol. II, p. 97.

54. Closing speech by Marcos to the Intercontinental Meeting in La Realidad: *Chiapas*, no. 3, p. 107.

55. The question of what sort of organisation should develop out of the Intercontinental Meeting of the summer of 1996 was addressed by Marcos in his closing speech: 'What follows? A new number in the useless enumeration of numerous internationals? A new scheme that will give tranquillity and relief to those anguished by the lack of recipes? A world programme for world revolution? A theorisation of utopia which will allow us to maintain a prudent distance from the reality that torments us? An organigram that will secure us all a post, a responsibility, a name and no work? What follows is the echo, the reflected image of the possible and the forgotten: the possibility and necessity of talking and listening ... The echo of this rebel voice transforming itself and renewing itself in other voices. An echo that converts itself into many voices, into a network of voices that, in the face of the deafness of Power, chooses to speak to itself, knowing itself to be one and many, knowing itself to be equal in its aspiration to listen and make itself heard, recognising itself to be different in the tonalities and levels of the voices which

form it ... A network that covers the five continents and helps to resist the death promised to us by Power. There follows a great bag of voices, sounds that seek their place fitting with others ... There follows the reproduction of resistances, the I do not conform, the I rebel. There follows the world with many worlds which the world needs. There follows humanity recognising itself to be plural, different, inclusive, tolerant of itself, with hope. There follows the human and rebel voice consulted in the five continents to make itself a network of voices and resistances.' (Closing speech by Marcos to the Intercontinental Meeting in La Realidad: *Chiapas*, no. 3, p. 112.)

56. Obvious precedents are, for example, Marx's discussion of the Paris Commune in the *Civil War in France* (Marx–Engels Collected Works, London: Lawrence and Wishart, 1979), or Pannekoek's discussion of workers' councils in the early years of this century. See, for example, S. Bricianer, *Pannekoek and the Workers' Councils* (Saint Louis: Telos Press, 1978).

57. *La Jornada*, 27 August 1995.

58. 'Civil society, those people without party who do not aspire to be in a political party in the senes that they do not aspire to be the government, what they want is that the government should keep its word, should do its work': Marcos interview with Cristián Calónico Lucio, 11 November 1995, ms. p. 39.

59. On the dialectic of constituting and constituted, see the article by Werner Bonefeld, 'Capital as Subject and the Existence of Labour', in W. Bonefeld, R. Gunn, J. Holloway and K. Psychopedis (eds), *Open Marxism*, Vol. III (London: Pluto Press, 1995), pp. 182–212; see also J. Holloway, 'The State and Everyday Struggle', in S. Clarke (ed.), *The State Debate* (Basingstoke: Macmillan, 1991).

60. The understanding of the working class as a defined group has been extended *ad infinitum* to discussions about the class definition of those who do not fall inside this group – as new petty bourgeoisis, salariat, etc.

61. What Marx calls primitive accumulation is thus a permanent and central feature of capitalism, not a historical phase. On this, see Werner Bonefeld, 'Class Struggle and the Permanence of Primitive Accumulation', *Common Sense*, No. 6 (1988).

62. For a development of this point, see Richard Gunn's article, 'Notes on Class', *Common Sense*, no. 2 (1987); and also Werner Bonefeld, 'Capital, Labour and Primitive Accumulation: Notes on Class and Constitution', unpublished ms (1997).

63. Thus, for Marx, capitalists are the personification of capital, as he repeatedly points out in *Capital*. The proletariat too first makes its appearance in his work not as a definable group but as the pole of an antagonistic relation: 'a class ... which ... is the *complete loss* of man and hence can win itself only through the *complete rewinning of man*': K. Marx, 'Contribution to the Critique of Hegel's Philosophy of Law: Introduction', in *Marx–Engels Collected Works*, Volume III (London: Lawrence & Wishart, 1979), p. 186.

64. The autonomist concept of self-valorisation is perhaps the closest that the Marxist tradition comes to a concept that expresses positively the struggle against-and-beyond capital, but the term is clumsy and obscure. On self-valorisation, see, for example Harry Cleaver, 'The Inversion of Class Perspective in Marxian Theory: From Valorisation to Self-Valorisation', in W. Bonefeld, R. Gunn and K. Psychopedis (eds), *Open Marxism*, Volume II (London: Pluto Press, 1992) pp. 106–145.

65. Antonio García de León in his prologue to an edition of the Zapatista communiqués: EZLN, *Documentos y Comunicados: 1º de enero / 8 de agosto de 1994* (Mexico City: Ediciones Era, 1994), p. 14.

66. The *deus ex machina* idea stretches far beyond Leninism, of course. It can be seen also in those theories which privilege the revolutionary role of the intellectuals. On a quite different plane, the same notions are reflected in the state's understanding of the Zapatista movement and its (racist) assumption that the real protagonists of the movement are urban white or mestizo intellectuals, such as Marcos.

67. 'Alienation could not even be seen, and condemned of robbing people of their freedom and depriving the world of its soul, if there did not exist some measure of its opposite, of that possible coming-to-oneself, being-with-oneself, against which alienation can be measured': Ernst Bloch, *Tübinger Einleitung in die Philosophie* (Frankfurt: Suhrkamp, 1963), Vol. II, p. 113. Dignity, in other words.

68. Le Bot, *El Sueño*, p. 191.

69. Radio UNAM interview with Marcos, 18 March 1994, EZLN, *La Palabra*, Vol. II, p. 89.

70. Radio UNAM interview with Marcos, 18 March 1994, EZLN, *La Palabra*, Vol. II, p. 89.

71. Marcos interview with Cristián Calónico Lucio, 11 November 1995, ms. p. 61. This would of course mean a society without power relations.

72. *La Jornada*, 25 August 1996.
73. This is clumsy, but the best translation I could find for the more elegant 'Detrás de nosotros estamos ustedes'.
74. 'Discurso inaugural de la mayor Ana María', *Chiapas*, No. 3, p. 103.
75. Many people have commented on various drafts of this chapter: Eloína Peláez, Werner Bonefeld, Mary Buckley, John Wilson, Enrique Rajchenberg, Ana Esther Ceceña, Massimo de Angelis, Monty Neill, Steve Wright, the discussion group at the Instituto de Ciencias Sociales y Humanidades in Puebla, the Common Sense group in Edinburgh, the Wildcat group in Germany. To them all, very many thanks.

Index